ECO-SANITY

ECO-SANITY

A Common-Sense Guide to Environmentalism

By

Joseph L. Bast

Peter J. Hill

Richard C. Rue

Madison Books

Published by Madison Books
4720 Boston Way
Lanham, Maryland 20706

3 Henrietta Street
London WC2E 8LU England

Distributed by National Book Network

The paper used in this publication is recycled and meets the minimum requirements of American National Standard for Information Sciences—Permanence of Paper for Printed Library Materials, ANSI Z39.48–1984. ∞™
Manufactured in the United States of America.

Library of Congress Cataloging-in-Publication Data

Bast, Joseph L. (Joseph Lee).
Eco-sanity : a common sense guide to environmentalism / Joseph L. Bast, Peter J. Hill, Richard C. Rue.
p. cm.
Includes bibliographical references.
1. Environmentalism. 2. Social ecology. I. Hill, Peter Jensen. II. Rue, Richard. III. Title.
GE195.B37 1994
363.7—dc20 94–10687 CIP

ISBN 1–56833–028–6 (cloth : alk. paper)

Drawings by Sandra L. Bast (Smits)

Contents

Preface vii
Acknowledgments xi
Authors' Note xiii

1. A fable for today 1

2. Our world is getting cleaner 7

Messengers of doom, 7
Air quality, 11
Water quality, 15
Food supply, 19
Forests, 22
Solid waste, 24
Energy supplies, 28
Conclusion, 32

3. What about cancer? 35

The cancer scare, 35
What is cancer? 36
Is the rate of cancer increasing? 37
Cancer and pollution, 40
Animal testing and false alarms, 43
Epidemiology and false alarms, 47
Conclusion, 49

4. The "crisis of the month" club 51

January: Global Warming, 53
February: Ozone Depletion, 62
March: Acid Rain, 74
April: Deforestation, 82
May: Pesticides, 90

June: Nuclear Power, 102
July: Automobiles, 110
August: Resource Depletion, 121
September: Plastic, 132
October: Electromagnetic Fields, 141
November: Oil Spills, 148
December: Toxic Chemicals, 154
Which problems are real? 177

5. Prosperity and the environment 181

Markets and pollution, 188
Why markets protect the environment, 192
Conclusion, 198

6. Why can't the government protect the environment? 201

Government's record, 202
The environment and "market failure," 215
Conclusion, 222

7. Rules for eco-sanity 225

Facts to remember, 229
Rules of critical thinking, 231
Lessons from science, 234
Principles of political economy, 238
Lessons from false alarms, 240

8. A common-sense agenda 243

Cleaner air, 247
Cleaner water, 252
Managing toxic chemicals, 255
Protecting public lands and wildlife, 257
Solid waste solutions, 260
What concerned environmentalists should do, 264

9. The end of the road 267

The eco-sanity exit, 268

Notes 271
Bibliography 301
Index 307
Authors 315
The Heartland Institute 317

Preface

IF THE MODERN environmental movement in the United States was born in 1962 with the publication of Rachel Carson's *Silent Spring*, then the movement is 32 years old as this book goes to print. Much has happened during those 32 years, both to the environment and to the people who participated in the movement. This book examines the movement's accomplishments, as measured by the actual condition of the environment: the air, water, forests, natural resources, and ecosystems. The authors then ask whether the tactics used during the movement's adolescence are still appropriate for its fast-approaching middle-age.

The environment, by most but not all measures, suffers less from man-made harms today than it did in 1962. As the title of Chapter Two states, our world is getting cleaner. This is due in part to the efforts of environmentalists who called the public's attention to pollution and the destruction of wildlife habitat worldwide. At this very general but most important level, the environmental movement must be judged a success.

The tactics and strategies used by the youthful environmental movement — while often successful — bore a strong resemblance to the problem-solving approaches of adolescents and young adults. Emotional appeals, for example, often overruled more reasoned approaches. The environmental movement could be counted on to prefer immediate action over further research, and the fast and easy "fix" over the slower and more difficult institutional changes that might be more effective and longer lasting.

The environmental movement often confused scientific and economic issues with moral issues. Pollution, for example, was considered evil, while unspoiled nature was good. Polluters — usually faceless corporations — were portrayed as villains, while popular reformers were treated as selfless crusaders. Compromise was usually seen as surrendering principles, rather than as a necessary step toward achieving goals.

Looking back on those early years of organized "environmentalism," a number of economists have suggested that the same (or an even greater) level of environmental protection could have been attained during the 1960s and 1970s *without* the enormous government bureaucracy and heavy regulatory compliance costs created in response to the environmental movement's demands. But this observation misses an important fact: The young environmental movement's uncompromising and often uneconomic demands mobilized broad public support for the movement's agenda. It is unlikely that calls for more research or cost-benefit analysis would have captured the attention of the nation's policy makers or the imagination of its younger generation. The environment probably would not have been as high on anyone's agenda during those years if environmental activists had remained rigidly true to science, called for less-ambitious reforms, or carefully applied cost-benefit analysis to every new proposal.

The tactics of the young environmental movement worked for a second reason: The causes of environmental destruction during the 1960s and 1970s were fairly easy to identify. They were belching smokestacks, municipal sewers, and open-air dumps. Simplistic responses — mandating technological solutions and banning certain activities — produced immediate and discernible improvements in environmental quality. The costs of such improvements were much less visible than the benefits, hidden in higher consumer prices and jobs lost when factories were forced to close. Thanks to inflation and rising prosperity, the general public tolerated the unnecessary costs associated with protecting the environment.

By the mid-1980s, the conditions that made the early tactics of the environmental movement successful were changing. The moral tone that helped transform environmentalism into a popular cause became suspect in the more cynical 1980s. With movie actors, journalists, politicians, and even major corporations all striving to position themselves as "green," the usual casting of the environment debate into good guys versus bad guys became more difficult and less persuasive.

Slower economic growth, a lower rate of price inflation, and intensifying international competition all contributed to growing public awareness of and skepticism about the costs of environmental regulation. "Green at any price" became an unacceptable slogan after the public learned its real effects on employment, consumer prices, and tax rates. Finally, the nature of environmental hazards changed, too, during the 1980s. Regulations and technology controlled the most visible sources of pollution, leaving less visible and more-difficult-to-regulate sources to be addressed. Careful science and reforms aimed at changing underlying incentives — dismissed in the past by the impatient young environmental movement — emerged as the only effective remedy to these remaining problems.

A large part of the environmental movement, we contend, has been slow to change its tactics in response to these changing realities. Like young adults refusing to accept the responsibilities of adulthood, these environmentalists continue to issue demands without acknowledging their real costs and effects on others. They cling to the obsolete notions of villains and crusaders, blinding them to the contributions of science and economics and making them easy prey for alarmists and media hype.

This commitment to the older tactics can be readily seen in campaigns to ban the use of chlorine and to eliminate all traces of dioxin in air and water emissions, despite overwhelming scientific evidence that such actions are unnecessary (from both human health and ecological perspectives) and would be hugely expensive. It can also be seen in what we call "the crisis of the month" fundraising strategy of many mainstream environmental organizations, where "crises" are manufactured out of flimsy evidence to scare people into making contributions.

The authors of this book call on the environmental movement to adopt tactics and strategies more appropriate to the movement's age and to the realities it now faces. A more mature environmental movement would consistently rely on reason and deliberation, not emotion and fear. It would be considerate of the rights and expectations of those affected by its proposals. It would accept the necessity of compromise and, sometimes, the need to move slowly until necessary information is collected. At other times, it would move more quickly than it now does to focus attention and resources on serious environmental problems.

We anticipate that some readers will try to pigeonhole the authors and this book as being part of what one news magazine called "an anti-environment backlash." *This characterization of our effort would be wrong*. We do not question either the sincerity or the effectiveness of the environmental movement. We do not call for an end to efforts to protect the environment, or even for their moderation. Instead, we advance a detailed agenda for carrying the effort forward in ways that could improve dramatically the quality of air and water and extend protection of wildlife. Our concern is principally with the tactics and methods used by the environmental movement to attain its ends — ends that we generally support.

The authors are themselves environmentalists and part of the movement they criticize. We place a high value on protecting and preserving nature, and we have demonstrated our commitment to the environmental movement in many ways. We have belonged to many of the organizations whose tactics we now question, and we remain dues-paying members of some of them. We have donated time to mainstream environmental groups and have participated in volunteer efforts to clean up the debris of civilization that has found its way to beaches, roadsides, and remote wilderness areas. We are, all three of us, avid outdoorsmen who have hiked trails and canoed rivers from Maine to California and a dozen states in between.

With over 70 percent of the American people now calling themselves environmentalists, it may seem unnecessary for the authors to "present credentials" to write a book such as this. But another mark of the environmental movement's immaturity is its reliance on the *ad hominem* attack — attacking people's characters or motives instead of their ideas or reasoning. Consequently, we fully expect that some of the persons we challenge will devote more attention to *who we are* than to *what we say*.

The main purpose of this book, in conclusion, is less to "rebut the myths" of modern-day environmentalism than it is to begin a discussion about how the environmental movement can become more effective at achieving its ends. We believe environmentalists should adopt new methods of thinking about and reacting to environmental hazards; we call these new methods "the rules for eco-sanity" and set them forth in Chapter Seven. We sincerely hope that the reader and the environmental movement as a whole will benefit from our efforts.

Acknowledgments

The research of others figures prominently in the chapters that follow. We recognize and thank the following persons: Bruce N. Ames, Frances Cairncross, Sir Richard Doll, Al Gore, Jay Lehr, Richard Peto, Paul Portney, William Rathje, Lynn Scarlett, and Elizabeth Whelan.

We also thank the following people who reviewed early drafts of the manuscript; their insightful comments and rigorous criticisms made for a far better book than would have been possible without them:

Dean Baim
Bernard Baltic
Cecil Bohanon
Dennis Brennen
Richard Buchli
George Clowes
Tracie Eaton
Michael Finch
Harold Henderson
Thomas Hetland, FSC
William Irvine
Kent Jeffreys
Jim Johnston
Douglas Kinney
Ross Korves
David Littmann
Everett Moffat
Stephen Moshier
David Padden
Cheryl Parker
Frank Resnik
Allan Rosewarn
Pamela Schick
Jane Shaw
Thomas Shull
Richard Stroup
Thomas Ulen
Karen Ver Voort

Any remaining errors, of course, are the authors'.

Finally, we express our thanks to The Heartland Institute and its many supporters for bringing the authors together and giving us the time and logistical support to produce this book. Diane Bast, publications director of The Heartland Institute, helped edit and typeset the final product. Under her hand a rough manuscript became a polished book.

Authors' Note

We have avoided cluttering the text with footnotes by listing principal sources in the Notes and Bibliography sections at the back of the book. Readers who wish to review the original articles and books we relied on may do so by referring to the sources listed there.

1. A fable for today

There once was a town . . .

THERE ONCE WAS a town in America's heartland where people lived in fear of their environment. They were afraid to drink tap water, eat apples from the nearby orchards, or live near electric power lines. Fear of getting cancer from man-made pollutants was everywhere. Every day, new dangers seemed to comc to light.

Even though everything about this town seemed pleasant and healthy, fear of environmental hazards hung like a cloud over the town's residents. Some bought bottled water for drinking and cooking because they were afraid of chlorine and other trace chemicals in the town's water supply. Others paid extra for "organically grown" fruits and vegetables to avoid pesticide residues. A group of young town residents picketed the local fast food restaurant because it used polystyrene containers, which the young activists believed would damage the ozone layer and contribute to a waste-disposal crisis.

Fear of man-made chemicals affected everyone in this town, sometimes in major ways. The owner of the orchard, for example, saw his sales collapse when claims were made that a chemical he had used on his apple trees without incident for twenty years might cause cancer. He eventually had to sell the orchard to a developer, who bulldozed the apple trees to make way for duplexes.

Other people's lives were disrupted when government regulations aimed at reducing air pollution forced a local factory to close. The new law required the firm to buy expensive equipment to reduce smokestack emissions — even though the plant's managers had put forward a less-costly plan to reduce emissions to the level required by the law. Unable to pay for the new equipment, the owners closed the factory. Many of the laid-off workers couldn't find new jobs, and even those who did received lower pay and fewer benefits.

Because of the fear that gripped the town, many health problems were blamed on environmental hazards. A woman who had two healthy children lost a third child due to miscarriage. Her doctor was unable to explain why the miscarriage occurred, and through conversations with other women in town she learned that several of them had also experienced unexplained miscarriages. These women spent many months trying to prove a connection between their personal tragedies and man-made pollutants.

What could have caused the miscarriages? Perhaps fumes from the nearby factory? Or maybe the chemicals used by the apple grower? The search for the true cause of the miscarriages pitted family against family and neighbor against neighbor. Instead of organizing hikes in the nature preserve or cleanup days in the park, many of the town's environmentalists spent their time attending hearings, organizing protests, and writing letters to elected officials.

Doctors in the community were vague about what they believed was causing the miscarriages. Elected officials were slow to respond and seemed to talk out of both sides of their mouths. What were they covering up? Had they been bought off by the factory owners? A scientist at a nearby college said on television that pesticides were causing the miscarriages, but he was a botanist, not a toxicologist or human health expert. Whom should the residents believe?

The real tragedy

The suffering experienced by the residents of this town would be tragic in any case, but it was all the worse because *none of the fears that caused the suffering had any scientific basis.* The town's residents were not in danger of being poisoned or getting cancer from chemicals in their air, water, or food.* To say they were victims of a gigantic hoax is too strong a claim to make, since many of the people who spread the fears and misinformation were sincere. But it is certain the townspeople were misinformed and misled.

This is not to say that no *potential* environmental hazards threatened the town — unsanitary conditions in the school's cafeteria, automobile pollution controls that were disconnected or not functional, or workers in a factory who were not given protective clothing — but these weren't the threats on which the town folk and experts chose to focus.

Consider the case of chlorine in drinking water. According to Stig Regli, with the Office of Groundwater and Surface Water of the Environmental Protection Agency,

> The risk of *death* from known pathogens in untreated surface water appears to be at least 100 to 1,000 times greater than the risk of *cancer* from known DBPs [disinfectant byproducts] in chlorinated drinking water. It also appears that the risk of *illness* from pathogens in untreated surface water is at least 10,000 to 1 million times greater than the risk of cancer from DBPs in chlorinated drinking water.

Similarly, most scientists agree that pesticide residues pose a smaller threat to our health than do *naturally occuring* substances found even in organically grown food. The Food and Drug Administration estimates that pesticides account for just 0.01 percent of the cancer risk associated with food.

Let's continue to examine the fears of our town. Fully halogenated chloroflourocarbons (CFCs), the substances thought to cause damage to the ozone layer, are no longer used in the manufacture of polystyrene plastic. Many scientists now question whether man-made CFCs are

---

*This statement, like any universal statement, cannot be proven by scientific research. (This rule of science is discussed in Chapters 6 and 7.) Since the topic of this chapter is a hypothetical situation, we make the statement here with this qualification.

responsible for destruction of the ozone layer. Polystyrene plastic accounts for less than 1 percent of the volume of a typical municipal landfill, making it an unlikely cause of a waste-disposal "crisis."

What about the government regulations that forced the factory to close? The U.S. Environmental Protection Agency estimates that compliance with air pollution control regulations from 1981 to 1990 cost businesses $292 billion, or $360 per year for every household in America. Regulatory compliance, according to research conducted by many independent scholars, typically costs between four and six times as much as the least-costly pollution control options that would achieve the same level of emission reductions.

And the unexplained miscarriages? Unfortunately, miscarriages are more common than most of us realize, and most are not medically explainable. It is not difficult for one woman who has experienced an unexplained miscarriage to find others who have suffered the same fate, and then to believe that the events have a common cause — perhaps a chemical in the water, or fumes from a nearby factory. The victims of miscarriages and other poorly understood health maladies deserve our sympathy. But we should remember that victims are rarely *experts* on the causes of their afflictions.

Reporters and local doctors often become parties to the fruitless search for an environmental cause of what are, in fact, unrelated personal tragedies. *Bad news sells*, so the media will pay rapt attention to people who have bad news to share. Doctors may genuinely desire to help their patients understand a personal tragedy — but they seldom are experts in epidemiology (the study of how diseases spread) or toxicology (the study of poisons), so they often don't know when to attribute illnesses to a specific cause rather than to pure chance.

In summary, our town was stricken by fear and misinformation, not by real environmental threats. Considerable expense and emotional trauma could have been avoided if only better information had been made available to the town's residents.

Only a fable?

Communities like the one in our fable really do exist in America today: Love Canal, New York; Times Beach, Missouri; Harrisburg,

Pennsylvania; Newark, New Jersey; Midland, Michigan; Alsea, Oregon; Hartford, Tennessee; Fountain Valley, California; Montecito, California; and Guilford, Connecticut, among others. Real people have lost their homes, their livelihoods, and even their lives due to various environmental scares.

Americans continue to pay a heavy price for their irrational fear of chemicals. Billions of dollars are being wasted on attempts to reduce toxic and other emissions to levels far below those shown to have any negative effect on human health or wildlife. People have lost their jobs because environmental regulations were imposed without regard to costs or consequences. In 1989, when an environmental group and compliant national media frightened fruit buyers with the Alar scare, orchard owners across the country lost hundreds of millions of dollars in sales.

Thirty-two years ago, biologist Rachel Carson opened her influential book, *Silent Spring*, with a chapter titled "A Fable for Tomorrow." She too described a town, but in her community invisible chemicals were poisoning the birds, farm animals, and vegetation. Carson's chilling picture of the town's silent spring, caused by the death of its birds and wildlife, helped launch the modern environmental protection movement.

Carson was responding to instances where the improper use of pesticides and other chemicals resulted in the needless killing of birds and other wildlife. Writing many years before the scientific community had thoroughly studied the effects of man-made chemicals on nature and human health, she can be forgiven for overstating the scope of environmental hazards. But today, the journalists and environmental advocacy groups who continue to fuel popular fears with superficial reporting and sensational claims have no similar excuse.

Such conduct may attract donations to environmental organizations, and viewers and advertising dollars to television producers. But it is irresponsible in light of the abundant evidence now available regarding the true nature of environmental and health risks. The American people haven't been told the truth about environmental hazards or the effects of many chemicals on their health. Instead, they are being subjected to half-truths and allegations meant to evoke fear and even terror.

2. Our world is getting cleaner

Messengers of doom

IF YOU READ *Time* or *Newsweek*, or watch television programs such as *Phil Donahue* or the network evening news, you have been told repeatedly that our world is getting dirtier, not cleaner. For example,

- A widely reported study titled *Global 2000 Report to the President*, produced in 1980 by agencies of the federal government, concluded "if current trends continue, the world in 2000 will be more crowded, more polluted, less stable ecologically, and more vulnerable to disruption than the world we live in now."

- Popular books by activists such as Ralph Nader, Paul Ehrlich, and Paul Brodeur have carried such titles as *Laying Waste*, *America the*

Poisoned, *Currents of Death,* and *Who's Poisoning America?* These books, and the extensive publicity surrounding them, describe a "cancer epidemic" caused by industrial pollution and toxic waste.

- The Vice President of the United States, Al Gore, writes in *Earth in the Balance* that "the volume of garbage is now so high that we are running out of places to put it," and that automobiles are "posing a mortal threat to the security of every nation that is more deadly than that of any military enemy we are ever again likely to confront."

- British ecologist Norman Myers, writing in February 1994, warned that mankind is "set to eliminate between one-third and two-thirds of Earth's species," causing "a massive draining of the planetary gene pool." By the middle of the next century, he claimed, "we shall have lost virtually all our topsoil, and no substitute for soil exists."

If these accounts are true, then surely life today is less safe and less healthy than it was a generation ago. Widespread concern over air and water pollution, solid waste disposal, and depletion of natural resources would seem to be justified.

But there is a big problem with what these reporters and experts say: *They are wrong*. Dr. Elizabeth Whelan, executive director of the American Council on Science and Health, author of twelve books on health issues, and a graduate of the Harvard School of Public Health and the Yale School of Medicine, writes:

> I have reviewed literally thousands of popular and scientific articles on the topic of environmental factors and human health. . . . What I found in my literature review was an astounding gap between the consensus in the scientific and medical community on environmental issues, versus what is being presented in popular publications, on television and radio, and in books for the layman.

Dr. Whelan is not alone. Dr. Julian Simon, professor of economics at the University of Maryland, and Herman Kahn, director of the prestigious Hudson Institute prior to his death in 1983, wrote:

> The original *Global 2000* is totally wrong in its specific assertions and its general conclusion. . . . Many of its arguments are illogical or

misleading. It paints an overall picture of global trends that is fundamentally wrong, partly because it relies on non-facts and partly because it misinterprets the facts it does present.

At the 1992 Earth Summit in Rio de Janeiro, a group of 425 scientists and economists, including 27 Nobel laureates, decried the inaccuracy and exaggeration that has come to characterize the positions of leading environmental organizations. The group's statement, which now bears the signatures of more than 2,700 scientists and intellectual leaders, included these words:

> We are . . . worried, at the dawn of the 21st Century, at the emergence of an irrational ideology that is opposed to scientific and industrial progress and impedes economic and social development. . . . We intend to assert science's responsibility and duties toward society as a whole. We do, however, forewarn the authorities in charge of our planet's destiny against decisions which are supported by pseudoscientific arguments or false and irrelevant data. . . . The greatest evils which stalk our earth are ignorance and oppression, not science, technology, and industry.

The authors have conducted their own review of the evidence and have reached the same conclusion: The views of the alarmists have been proven to be wrong. Most trends — cancer rates, air and water quality, human health, acres of wooded lands, and a dozen other indicators of environmental quality in the U.S. — show improvement, not decline. Global trends also show improvement, though less dramatically than trends in the U.S. Although generalizations are difficult to make in the complex arena of environmental quality, available evidence supports the following statements:

Most Americans today live in an environment that is cleaner than it was at any time in the past half-century.

The environment in the U.S. today is safer than it has been at any time in recorded history.

On the following pages we document these claims. Before proceeding, however, it is necessary to clarify several points. First, when we say the environment in the U.S. is *cleaner* than at any time in the past half-century, we mean average human exposure to potentially harmful pollutants is as low as it was during the 1930s or 1940s. When we say the environment today is *safer* than at any time in recorded history, we mean the probability that a substance or natural process (such as global climate change) will cause human injury is the lowest it has ever been.

Next, the phrase *environmental quality* merits definition as well. We measure environmental quality in terms of "clean" and "safe," as well as in terms of the *preservation* of natural processes and life forms. The proposition that environmental quality today is better than it was fifty years ago is difficult to defend, because each person places a different value on the individual components of such a broad measure. Does safe drinking water, for example, offset the extinction of the passenger pigeon, ivory-billed woodpecker, and Carolina parakeet? Whereas *clean* and *safe* can be objectively measured and reported, *quality* (it seems to us) is subjective and hence controversial. The authors believe environmental quality in the U.S. has improved since the 1960s and possibly since earlier times, but we recognize that others may disagree even after reviewing the evidence presented on the following pages.

Third, the world is cleaner today partly because environmentalists called attention to the need to protect the environment. We say "partly" because other social and economic forces were leading to greater environmental protection in the U.S. even before the modern environmental movement emerged, and these forces would have continued to operate with or without an organized environmental movement. Nevertheless, government regulations and extensive private efforts to protect the environment arose in response to the prodding of the environmental movement, and it is not likely that as great an effort would have been made if environmentalists hadn't sounded the alarm.

Finally, our effort in the pages that follow to "set the record straight" is not meant as a criticism of the environmental movement as a whole or of its goals (as we understand them). Just the opposite is true: The environmental movement can take credit for the substantial reductions in pollution and the expanded protection of wildlife that we document. Our criticism is focused on the "messengers of doom" who never issue retractions when their warnings are found to be false; who continue to issue warnings even after problems have been solved; and who are increasingly inclined to issue warnings that are without scientific support. If the environmental movement is to be effective in the 1990s and beyond, it must abandon these tactics and adopt ones that are more responsible and effective.

Our first premise, which we will attempt to prove in this chapter, is that the *world is becoming cleaner, not dirtier, over time.*

Air quality

Let's start with the air we breathe. Is it cleaner today than it was ten years ago? Fifty years ago?

Measurements of air quality

Reliable measurements of air quality in the U.S. are available only for the years since 1975. All six of the pollutants tracked by the EPA show dramatic improvement between 1975 and 1991: Total suspended particle concentrations (dust and airborne ash) fell by 24 percent; sulfur dioxide by 50 percent; carbon monoxide by 53 percent; ozone by 25 percent; nitrogen dioxide by 24 percent; and lead by 94 percent. There can be little debate that air quality in the U.S. improved considerably during this period.

We can estimate air quality prior to 1975 by examining the levels of pollutant *emissions*, rather than the concentration of pollutants in the air. Estimates of air pollutant emissions in the U.S. are available for every year since 1940. As the table on the following page shows, emissions of most pollutants increased between 1940 and 1970, but then fell (except for nitrogen oxides) between 1970 and 1990.

The picture presented by these numbers is somewhat mixed, with emissions of three pollutants falling since 1940 (although we don't have the exact figures for lead) and three increasing. Significantly, though, *total emissions fell by 12.6 percent* between 1940 and 1990, and an even more impressive 33.8 percent between 1970 and 1990. Compliance with the Clean Air Act Amendments of 1990 is expected to significantly reduce sulfur oxide and nitrogen oxide emissions, two of the three pollutants whose emissions in 1990 were still above their 1940 levels.

In summary, air *quality* has improved dramatically since 1975, the first year for which reliable measurements are available. And while

The Air is Getting Cleaner
(in millions of metric tons, except lead in thousands of metric tons)

Emission	1940	1970	1990	% change 1940-1990	% change 1970-1990
Particulate matter	23.1	18.5	7.5	- 67.5	- 60.5
Sulfur oxides	17.6	28.3	21.2	20.4	- 25.1
Nitrogen oxides	6.9	18.5	19.6	184.0	5.9
VOCs	15.2	25.0	18.7	23.0	- 25.2
Carbon monoxide	82.6	101.4	60.1	- 27.2	- 40.7
Lead	n.a.	203.8	7.1	n.a.	- 96.5
Total emissions	145.4	191.9	127.1	- 12.6	- 33.8

Source: U.S. Environmental Protection Agency, *National Air Pollutant Emission Estimates*, 1940-1990, March 1992.

emissions of some air pollutants remain higher today than they were in 1940, overall emissions are lower and continue to fall.

Other developed countries have come close to the U.S. record for reducing air pollutant emissions. The table on the following page shows total air pollutant emissions for nine countries in 1970 and 1985. Significantly, every country reduced its total emissions. The U.S. ranked second only to the Netherlands, and it is likely that more current data would place the U.S. first among the nations in this list.

Why air quality is improving

Why has air quality improved so dramatically during the past twenty years? One reason is the enactment of local, state, and national laws setting air quality standards and requiring factories, utilities, and auto manufacturers to take steps to reduce air pollution. The most important of these laws was the Clean Air Act, passed by Congress in 1963 and amended in 1970 and 1990. Environmentalists played a major role in the passage of these and other laws.

Thanks largely to the efforts of automobile manufacturers to comply with the Clean Air Act, a car built in 1993 emits 97 percent less

Air Pollutant Emissions Are Falling Around the World
(total emissions in thousands of metric tons)

Country	1970	1985	1985 as percent of 1970
Netherlands	3,918	2,697	68.8
USA	190,300	133,000	69.9
Germany	24,047	17,020	70.8
UK	15,830	13,210	83.4
Italy	12,142	10,185	83.9
Sweden	3,394	2,942	86.7
France	13,340	11,712	87.8
Canada	22,146	19,600	88.5

Source: OECD figures analyzed in Mikhail S. Bernstam, *The Wealth of Nations and the Environment*, p. 17.

hydrocarbons and carbon monoxide and 90 percent less nitrogen oxide than a car built twenty years earlier. Between 1987 and 2000, the gradual retirement of older vehicles from the domestic auto and truck fleet will reduce hydrocarbon emissions by 50 percent, carbon monoxide emissions by 52 percent, and nitrogen oxide emissions by 34 percent. The combined effect of fleet turnover and use of reformulated gasoline in many American cities will mean that by the year 2000, new cars will emit a remarkable *99 percent* less hydrocarbons and carbon monoxide than they did in 1973.

Another reason air is getting cleaner is the greater use of electricity over time. Electricity is gradually replacing other sources of energy in manufacturing, services, and household appliances. This frequently results in greater energy efficiency and less pollution, because large electric generation plants operate at higher efficiency levels and under stricter emission controls than do smaller gas and oil burning engines. Electrification also makes possible the use of new devices — such as microwave ovens and fax machines — that are substitutes for more energy-intensive products. In 1991, for the first time, the industrial, commercial, and residential sectors of the U.S. economy consumed over half of their energy in the form of electricity.

A third reason for rising air quality is that industry is using raw materials more efficiently. New technologies allow businesses to capture and recycle gases and particles that once simply escaped into the air. Some examples of how technology is leading to cleaner air include "clean coal" burning processes — which eliminate up to 99 percent of potential sulfur dioxide emissions — and the use of infrared heat to dry ink in printing processes and paint in automobile finishing processes.

Effect of air pollution on human health

What effect, if any, does air pollution have on human health? Have reductions in air pollutant emissions led to less disease or a lower incidence of cancer?

It is common to hear environmentalists assert that air pollution is a leading cause of cancer, but there is in fact very little evidence to support such a claim. One of the most complete and authoritative studies ever done of the question, *what causes cancer?* was conducted in 1981 by Sir Richard Doll and Dr. Richard Peto, two leading epidemiologists. Their report was commissioned by the U.S. Office of Technology Assessment and has been endorsed by the National Cancer Institute.

Doll and Peto estimate that air pollution accounts for *just 1 percent* of all U.S. cancer each year. Even this is a "crude estimate," they say, since they found no sound evidence linking air pollution to cancer rates. Because their calculations were based on observed rates of cancer in urban versus rural populations over many years, their finding applies to a period of time when air pollution was much worse than it is today. It is reasonable, then, to assume that the risk, if it exists at all, is even smaller today.

The relationship between pollution and human health will be revisited many times in later chapters of this book. It is not our purpose to give the final word on this complex issue, nor are we qualified to do so. It is possible that air pollution has a greater effect on human health than Doll, Peto, and other experts suspect. But we *can* report to the reader that we have not found reliable scientific evidence in support of this possibility, and our view appears to be supported by the largest part of the scientific community.

Conclusion

Air quality in the U.S. today is indisputably better than it was twenty years ago. In some important ways, it is better than even fifty years ago, though in other ways it may not be as good. Other developed countries seem to be following the same path as the U.S., reducing their total air pollutant emissions since 1970.

The sources of improving air quality include compliance with federal regulations, for which the environmental movement can take partial credit. In later chapters we will comment further on the character of these laws and whether they were cost-effective solutions to the air pollution problem; here it is sufficient to note that they played a very important role in improving air quality during the 1970s and 1980s.

New research is constantly being conducted, but at the time of this writing, the leading experts in the field have found no link between air pollution and cancer. It would appear that current levels of air pollution are too low to pose a threat to human health.

Regarding the air we breathe, we can confidently say that our world is getting cleaner, not dirtier, over time.

Water quality

In 1969, the Cuyahoga River in Ohio caught fire and burned for several hours, a result of the river's heavy chemical contamination. Dangerously high levels of pollution were reported in the drinking water of New Orleans in 1974, and Duluth sometime later. Lake Erie was so heavily polluted during the 1960s that many environmentalists declared it "dead," predicting that Lake Michigan wasn't far behind.

But water quality in the U.S. was already beginning to improve in the 1960s. The first National Water Quality Inventory, conducted in 1973, found that water pollution levels had decreased considerably in most major waterways during the decade of the 1960s. According to Dr. A. Myrick Freeman III, a senior fellow at Resources for the Future, between 93 and 96 percent of the nation's waters were fishable in 1972.

The cleanup of America's rivers and lakes continued during the 1970s and 1980s. Federal law required factories to install specific pollution control technologies and gave municipalities federal grants equal to

75 percent of the cost of planning and building new sewage treatment facilities. During the 1980s, approximately $23 billion a year was spent by governments and private industry to comply with the Federal Water Pollution Control Act Amendments of 1972. More than $75 billion in tax funds have been spent since the early 1970s to build municipal waste treatment plants. Additional billions of dollars were spent on water pollution abatement efforts unrelated to the 1972 law.

Not all of this money was spent efficiently. The federal law's inflexible technology mandates often meant that less-expensive ways to abate water pollution were not pursued. The law's focus on factories and municipal sewage systems — called point sources — ignored the reality that between 57 and 98 percent of pollutants entering a river or lake come from nonpoint sources, such as run-off from fields, lawns, and construction sites. Generous federal subsidies led municipalities to design "gold-plated" treatment facilities that were often over-sized or unnecessarily complex. And because the federal government subsidized sewage *treatment* but not sewage *reduction*, relatively inexpensive ways to prevent sewage from being produced in the first place were disregarded.

Despite these public policy shortcomings, water quality continued to improve during the 1970s and 1980s. By the 1990s, three-quarters of the U.S. population was served by wastewater treatment facilities. Freeman notes that "some improvement in water quality [has occurred] since 1972. In terms of aggregate measures or national averages, it has not been dramatic. But there are local success stories of substantial cleanup in what had been seriously polluted water bodies."

The Cuyahoga River, for example, is now fishable. Swimming has resumed in the Hudson River north of New York City. Salmon spawn in Maine's once-polluted Androscoggin River, and the Great Lakes support a growing sport fishing industry. The presence of toxins in rivers and lakes has consistently trended downward since the 1960s. For example, the Michigan Department of Natural Resources recently reported that in the Great Lakes, "levels of PCB, DDT, mirex and mercury in lake trout and herring gull eggs decreased dramatically in the mid- to late-1970s after extensive controls and restrictions on the use of these chemicals were implemented." According to the Council on Environmental Quality, concentration levels continued to fall during the 1980s and early 1990s. In its August 1993 report to the International Joint Commission, the Virtual Elimination Task Force noted that "considerable progress has been made to reduce inputs of persistent toxic substances to the Great Lakes Basin Ecosystem. As a result, ecosystem health today is improved from conditions 20 years ago."

The table on the following page shows that water quality in the Mississippi River dramatically exceeds that of rivers in other industrialized nations. The Rhine River in Germany, for example, has 3.4 times the concentration of nitrates as does the Mississippi; 7.5 times as much ammonium; and nearly twice the level of biological oxygen demand (indicative of higher amounts of organic pollution).

The quality of water in the world's oceans also appears to be good, although long-standing pollution problems exist in coastal waters. Fish, shellfish, and other marine life suffer from the effects of coastal sewage treatment and industrial discharges, as well as run-off from farms, construction sites, and other land uses. The Council on Environmental Quality reported in 1993 that "in contrast to coastal regions, the open sea remains relatively clean. . . . The oil slicks and litter common along sea lanes remain, for the most part, of minor consequence to communities of organisms living in the open-ocean areas." (The problem of oil spills is discussed in greater detail in Chapter Four.) Following the enactment of federal legislation in 1990, 29 of the 35 U.S. coastal states and territories produced plans to protect coastal waters from pollution. Together, these states and territories encompass 94 percent of the U.S. coastline.

Finally, the safety of drinking water in the U.S. testifies to the high quality of water. "[T]he animal evidence provides no good reason to expect that chlorination of water or current levels of man-made pollution of water pose a significant carcinogenic hazard," according to Dr. Bruce N. Ames and his colleagues. Doll and Peto agree, saying "we know of no established human carcinogen that is ever present in sufficient quantities in large U.S. public water supplies to account for any material percentage of the total risk of cancer. . . . [I]t is again not plausible that any material percentage of the total number of cancers in the whole United States derives from this source." We will have more to add on this point in the next chapter.

There is plenty of room for further improvements to water quality in the U.S. and other countries. Public policy changes could encourage municipalities to reduce the volume of sewage that is produced, rather than merely treat it. Problems with nonpoint sources of water pollution can often be addressed by community education programs, land use compacts, and small investments in used-oil drop-off programs and similar initiatives.

An even-handed assessment finds that water quality has consistently improved since the 1950s and 1960s. Thanks to the spread of modern water and sewage treatment technologies, water today is cleaner and safer than it has been since before reliable measures of water quality were available. While some problems remain to be solved, there can be little debate that water quality in the U.S. is getting better, not worse.

U.S. Rivers Are Cleaner

In the table below, water quality in the Mississippi River is compared to water quality in the largest rivers in France, Germany, and Britain. The concentration of each kind of pollution in the Mississippi has been set equal to 1 and levels in other river systems are expressed as multiples of the Mississippi figures. The Seine River in France, for example, has about twice the level of biological oxygen demand, five times the level of nitrates, and 3.6 times the level of phosphates as the Mississippi. (Higher levels of biological oxygen demand are an indication of higher amounts of organic pollutants.)

	Mississippi (U.S.)	Seine (France)	Rhine (Germany)	Thames (U.K.)
Biological Oxygen Demand	1.00	2.13	1.87	1.67
Nitrates	1.00	5.42	3.45	6.98
Phosphates	1.00	3.65	1.09	n.a
Ammonium	1.00	22.43	7.57	9.19
Lead	1.00	4.38	0.61	0.33

Source: Authors' calculations based on OECD data, typically mg/liter, average levels of 1980s; data reported in Global Climate Coalition, *The U.S. vs. European Community: Environmental Performance*, August 1993, p. 9.

Food supply

Two environmental concerns arise regarding food: The ability of the world's farmers to produce enough food to keep pace with a growing population, and the safety of the food we eat. Is the world "running out of food"? Are there dangerous chemicals in our food supply?

No one has done more to raise fears of worldwide hunger and famine than Dr. Paul Ehrlich, author of *The Population Bomb* (1968) and *The Population Explosion* (1990). Ehrlich began his first book with these frightening words:

> The battle to feed all of humanity is over. In the 1970s the world will undergo famines — hundreds of millions of people are going to starve to death in spite of any crash programs embarked upon now. At this late date nothing can prevent a substantial increase in the world death rate . . .

Ehrlich is a master of the scare tactic. In addition to repeated predictions of massive worldwide starvation, he has predicted that world population growth will be stopped only by wholesale death from starvation, that the U.S. will experience food riots and a dramatic fall in life expectancy, and that Lakes Erie and Michigan will experience ecological "death."

None of these predictions has come true or is ever likely to come true. On the matter of population growth, the world's annual population growth rate fell from 2.0 percent in the 1960s to 1.6 percent during the 1990s, and it is predicted to drop to 1.4 percent during the first decade of the twenty-first century. The United Nations now expects the world's population to stabilize sometime late in the next century at between ten and twelve billion.

Death by starvation is not the cause of this declining rate of population growth. "Only a tenth as many people died of starvation in the third quarter of the twentieth century as in the last quarter of the nineteenth, despite the fact that the world's population was vastly larger," says Ronald Bailey in his important new book, *Eco-Scam: The False Prophets of Ecological Apocalypse.* Developing countries more than doubled their food production between 1965 and 1988, an increase that easily outpaced their population growth. China and India, two countries where food shortages were a grim reality during the 1950s and 1960s, are now self-sufficient in grain.

According to Dr. D. Gale Johnson, a distinguished professor of agricultural economics at the University of Chicago, "Except where civil wars exist or despotic governments prevail, there has never been a time during the last two centuries when the people in the developing world were better fed or when their food supply was more secure. . . . The scourge of famine due to natural causes has been almost conquered and could be entirely eliminated by the end of the century."

Contrary to Ehrlich's prediction, there have been no food riots in the U.S. The average life expectancy in the U.S. has not decreased, but instead has lengthened from 70.8 years in 1970 to 75.4 years in 1990. Our average life expectancy is projected to reach 76.6 years by the year 2000. Lakes Erie and Michigan are fishable and swimmable. Hunger is primarily a problem caused by civil war and by totalitarian governments in Third World countries. Declining prices for food worldwide mean supply is increasing relative to demand. For many developed nations, managing food *surpluses* poses a much greater problem than do food shortages.

"The fact is that not one of Ehrlich's many frightful predictions has ever come true," writes Ronald Bailey. "He makes a prediction, and when refuted by scientific evidence or events, he simply makes another assertion incorporating the latest apocalyptic fads. Being proved wrong apparently never bothers him." Nevertheless, it should bother us.

What about the second question, concerning the *safety* of the food we eat? We are all rightly concerned about the presence of pesticides and other chemicals in our food supply. Some of these substances, in large amounts, have been demonstrated to cause cancer in laboratory animals.

We will examine the link between chemicals and cancer more closely in the next chapter. Here, it is sufficient to review the evidence specifically related to food and cancer. Do food additives contribute significantly to our cancer risk? What about pesticide residues?

Dr. Bruce Ames, professor of biochemistry and molecular biology at the University of California - Berkeley, calls the threat from pesticide residues "minuscule." He says "we are ingesting in our diet at least 10,000 times more by weight of natural pesticides than of man-made pesticide residues. These are natural 'toxic chemicals' that have an enormous variety of chemical structures. . . ." Many of these natural carcinogens, he notes, are extremely powerful and present in common foods at high levels. Some examples appear in the box below. "This analysis on the levels of synthetic pollutants in drinking water and of synthetic pesticide residues in foods suggests that this pollution is likely to be a minimal carcinogenic hazard relative to the background of natural carcinogens," concludes Ames.

Dr. Robert J. Scheuplein, director of the Office of Toxicological Sciences at the Food and Drug Administration, agrees with Ames, finding that *over 99 percent of the cancer risk associated with food comes*

Ranking Possible Cancer Hazards

How much do additives and pesticides add to our cancer risk? Dr. Bruce Ames used published results from animal tests to compare and rank the risks associated with various foods and drinks. The table below is based on his findings. Ames does *not* believe animal tests are reliable guides for determining risks; this table should not be interpreted literally, but only as an illustration of how very small would be the risk posed by pesticides and food additives *even if* animal studies were reliable.

Source and daily exposure	**Risk factor**	
Wine (one glass)	4,700.0	
Beer (12 ounces)	2,800.0	
Cola (one)	2,700.0	
Bread (two slices)	400.0	
Mushroom (one, raw)	100.0	
Basil (1 gram of dried leaf)	100.0	
Shrimp (100 grams)	90.0	
Brown mustard (5 grams)	70.0	
Saccharin (in 12 oz of diet soda)	60.0	
Peanut butter (one sandwich)	30.0	
Cooked bacon (100 grams)	9.0	
Water (one liter)	1.0	
Additives and pesticides in other food	0.5	←
Additives and pesticides in bread and grain products	0.4	←
Coffee (one cup)	0.3	

Bruce Ames et al., "Ranking Possible Carcinogenic Hazards," *Science* 236 (April 17, 1987), p. 271. See article for explanation of methodology and interpretation of results.

from naturally occurring substances in food. He estimates that food additives account for just 0.2 percent of food-related cancer risk; pesticides, 0.01 percent; and animal drugs, 0.01 percent.

Although these estimates of the safety of our food are endorsed by most of the scientific community, the popular media treats us to one story after another of how chemicals in our food *might be* "poisoning" us or our children. Some environmental groups take advantage of the cancer scare by featuring it in their newsletters and fundraising appeals. Faced with all this over-heated propaganda, it is not surprising that we should fear for the safety of our food supply. But if we can get past the hype and dishonesty, we can see that *real science shows our food is safe to eat.*

Forests

A recent fundraising letter from The Wilderness Society, signed by its president, Karin P. Sheldon, made the following claims:

> . . . [T]he Forest Service is selling off the vast natural inheritance that lies within our National Forests — and losing millions of dollars of taxpayer money in the process. . . . [T]he Forest Service continues to cut the forests much faster than they can recover. . . . Our National Forests, National Parks, our National Wildlife Refuges, the vast wilderness lands of Alaska, and the huge stretches of the American West that are managed by the Bureau of Land Management — these are all under attack from corporations who measure the value of the land only in dollars, in board-feet of lumber, in barrels of oil, in tons of minerals.

The truth in this statement is that the federal government does indeed subsidize lumbering in National Forests, sometimes in ecologically delicate areas that recover only slowly or not at all. Environmentalists are correct to oppose this activity. But other assertions in this passage hardly fit the facts as we know them.

"Less logging now occurs in the national forests than at any time since the early 1950s," writes Hal Salwasser of the National Forest Service. "For example, 29 percent less timber volume was harvested in 1991 than in 1988. The area harvested by clearcutting has declined by 34 percent during the same period, part of a transition to an estimated 70 percent reduction by mid-decade."

According to the U.S. Forest Service, annual timber growth in the U.S. now exceeds harvest by 37 percent. Annual growth has exceeded harvest *every year since 1952.* In 1992, just 384,000 acres — six-tenths of 1 percent of the National Forest land open to harvesting — were actually harvested.

As a result of growth steadily exceeding harvests, the number of wooded acres in the U.S. has grown by 20 percent in the past twenty years. The average annual wood growth in the U.S. today is an amazing *three times* what it was in 1920. In Vermont, for example, the area covered by forests has increased from 35 percent a hundred years ago to about 76 percent today.

Underlying these numbers is a remarkable transformation that has taken place in American forestry, and is gradually taking place around the world. "Forestry today is experiencing a transition similar to that experienced two or three millennia ago in agriculture," write Roger A. Sedjo and Marion Clawson, senior fellows with Resources for the Future. "Just as agriculture evolved from gathering and hunting to cropping and livestock raising, similarly *forestry is beginning to evolve from the gathering of natural inventories to the cropping of forest plantations."*

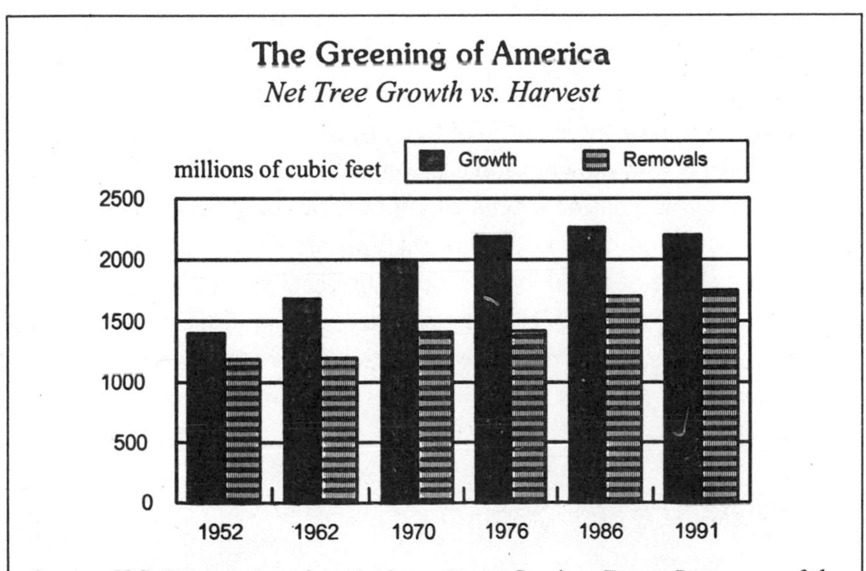

Source: U.S. Department of Agriculture, Forest Service, *Forest Resources of the United States 1992*, General Technical Report RM-234 (Washington, DC: Department of Agriculture, September 1993).

In all the developed countries in the world, including the U.S. and Canada, forestry is now conducted on a *sustainable yield* basis, whereby growth exceeds harvests. Not only does this ensure future supplies of wood and wood fiber products, but it also creates habitat for a wide array of wildlife and protection for many plant species. Research by the British Columbia Ministry of Forests has found that second-growth forests support populations and varieties of wildlife that are comparable to those in natural forests, and they contain a diversity of tree species as high or higher than existed prior to logging.

Even forests that have been clear-cut and replanted support diverse wildlife populations and contain trees of various ages, sizes, and species. Trees in commercial forests, which are harvested before disease and fire take their toll, tend to be younger, larger, and healthier than their natural forest counterparts. Though designed primarily to supply wood products, some "man-made" forests are nearly indistinguishable from "real" forests. The beautiful wilderness scenes in the popular movie *Last of the Mohicans*, for example, were filmed in a formerly clear-cut commercial forest, not a natural forest.

The advance of sustainable yield forestry does not mean that forests in America face no threats. The federal government does indeed sell the right to harvest wood on public lands at a loss of millions of dollars each year, in effect subsidizing logging in natural areas that otherwise would not be logged. Some 342,000 miles of government-built roads — eight times the mileage of the U.S. interstate highway system — run through our National Forests, causing soil erosion and encouraging development. There is an ongoing national debate over how best to balance the demand for nature conservation, wood products, and recreation. Environmentalists must be a part of this debate or their interests will be ignored.

These are forestry problems that can be readily addressed and solved. By most measures, the condition of forests in the U.S. is improving, not deteriorating.

Solid waste

Solid waste is another key concern of environmentalists. Americans seem to produce so much of it that some people wonder if there is enough room to dispose of it all safely. Over the years, not only has the amount of garbage we produce increased, but its contents have changed, too. Plastics, batteries, paint, used oil, and a wide range of disposable and single-use products (such as disposable diapers and paper cups) are part of the garbage we generate today.

We now know that traditional ways of handling solid waste — often by depositing it in open-air dumps located in swamps and old gravel pits — created potential health hazards and environmental dangers. Lead from discarded batteries and paint, for example, could leach through the soil beneath a dump and into groundwater, or run off into rivers or onto adjoining property during rainstorms. The rodents, insects, and birds attracted to an open-air dump could act as carriers of disease. The "good old days" of cheap garbage disposal, in short, were anything but good.

In response to pressure from the environmental community and many concerned citizens, sweeping changes have been made to the way solid waste is handled in the U.S. First, less solid waste is now routed to landfills. While 81 percent of solid waste went to landfills in 1980, just 67 percent went to landfills in 1990. The rest was recycled or composted (17 percent) or incinerated (16 percent). The U.S. Environmental Protection Agency (EPA) projects that the portion of solid waste going to landfills will continue to fall during the 1990s.

Landfill technology also has changed dramatically. "The distance the nation has traveled from the incredible ignorance that turned gravel quarries into garbage dumps to today's sophisticated landfills is equivalent, in astronomical terms, to light-years," says Dr. Jay H. Lehr, who for 25 years was executive director of the Association of Ground Water Scientists and Engineers. "No one today can say that the state-of-the-art landfill resembles the garbage dump of yesteryear in either appearance or impact. . . . The systems have to be designed, built and maintained in a manner that will enable water from a 24-hour, once-in-25-years-storm event to run off without any significant negative consequences to the landfill. Landfills can no longer cause a discharge of pollutants into waters covered under the Clean Water Act or other related surface water control programs."

Modern operational landfills are banned from floodplains and must exclude certain hazardous waste; each day's addition must be covered with dirt or some other material to control odors, scavengers, and run-off. Modern landfills have impermeable clay floors and heavy plastic membranes beneath them to prevent leaks, and when filled they are capped with thick layers of clay. Many landfills have sophisticated systems for collecting liquids that accumulate at the bottom of the landfill (called "leachate") and for venting and sometimes recycling methane gas. After a landfill has stopped receiving waste, it must be managed for a minimum of thirty years to ensure that no water is allowed to percolate through the landfill and cause leachate.

The New High-Tech Landfill

New landfills have very little in common with the old open-air dumps we grew up with. The table below shows the percentage of landfills in operation today having new landfill technologies.

Technology	Percent
Have liners	81
Collect leachate	68
Monitor groundwater	95
Control surface water	87
Monitor landfill gas	65
Have financial assurance for post-closure	81

Source: National Solid Wastes Management Association, *Landfill Tipping Fees, 1990 Review*, p. 2.

Improvements in the way landfills are sited, designed, and managed have paid off in greater public safety. The EPA estimates that the risk of injury to health posed by living near a landfill in the U.S. is in the range of one in a million, a risk so small it exists only hypothetically. Health risks arising from garbage incineration are in this same range, thanks to the compliance of waste-to-energy plants with 1991 EPA regulations that control air emissions and ensure that residue or ash from incineration can be safely handled in modern landfills.

The new safety requirements forced many older landfills and dumps to close, resulting in a temporary shortage of landfill space. This, in turn, has fueled speculation that we might be "running out of room" for our garbage. Adding to the problem is local opposition to landfills and incinerators, partly due to false concerns about safety, but also due to quite-understandable objections to truck traffic, odors, and the obstruction of views that sometimes accompany landfills.

In most parts of the country today, the landfill capacity shortage is over. New landfills are approximately four times the size of the ones they replace, and entrepreneurs now regularly offer to share with local governments some of the economic benefits from the landfill. Charles City County, in rural Virginia, for example, is paid $5.00 for each ton of garbage dumped in a landfill operated within its borders by a private company. The company also picks up local garbage for free.

There is virtually no danger that America will "run out of room" to store solid waste in the future. According to A. Clark Wiseman, an economist at Gonzaga University, "At the current rate, if all the nation's solid waste for the next 500 years were piled or buried in a single landfill to a depth of 100 yards — about half the eventual height of Staten Island's Fresh Kills landfill — this 'national landfill' would require a square site less than 20 miles on a side. With compaction, even this volume could be halved."

In addition to further improvements in landfill and incineration technology, the future will see continued growth in recycling programs. Markets for recycled paper, aluminum, steel, and glass are well established and growing. The country is beginning to see the rise of plastic recycling, with some 40 percent of polyethylene terephthalate (PET) plastic soft drink bottles recycled in 1992. The plastics industry is hoping a process called "thermal decomposition," which breaks down plastics into their original petrochemical components, will lead to a rapid increase in the rate at which other kinds of plastic are recycled.

Also helping to make solid waste disposal less difficult in the 1990s is a process called *light-weighting.* Light-weighting means using less material to make a container or package. For example, steel cans are about 60 percent lighter than they were in 1955, aluminum cans weigh only two-thirds as much as they did just ten years ago, and glass bottles are 30 percent lighter. Plastic bottles have declined in weight by 25 percent since 1980, and disposable diapers now use 50 percent less paper pulp due to absorbent gel technology.

A review of the evidence suggests that there is no impending garbage crisis facing America. The opposite is true: We have made great headway against the nation's solid waste. There is plenty of room to put it, and the means of disposal are vastly superior to what they were just a decade ago. While this problem can never be "completely solved," we nevertheless can take comfort in knowing that solid waste today is handled in a safer and more environmentally sound manner than ever before.

Energy supplies

Many environmentalists will find the preceding discussion somewhat reassuring, but they will wonder whether the progress we have reported can be sustained. Part of this concern rests on the fear that conventional energy sources will be depleted. The final question we address in this chapter, then, is an old and familiar one: *Are we in danger of running out of fossil fuels?* To answer this question, we must first understand several important facts about the world's energy supplies.

Proven reserves vs. total resources

The estimated proven reserves of oil in the world in 1992 totaled 991 billion barrels, enough to last 45 years at current rates of consumption. Known reserves of coal equaled 724 billion tons in 1992, enough to last 200 years. Natural gas reserves totaled 4,378 trillion cubic feet, a 63-year supply at current consumption levels.

At first glance, these estimates might seem to be cause for alarm. The 45-year supply of oil could mean that the difficult transition from oil to other energy sources would take place in our lifetimes. But "proven reserves" are constantly changing, confounding predictions based on them. In 1978, for example, proven oil reserves stood at 648 billion barrels, enough (we were told at the time) to last 29.2 years at then-current rates of consumption. Many environmentalists were sounding the alarm for energy conservation; then-President Jimmy Carter called for passage of a national energy policy to conserve our rapidly depleting oil reserves. During the following 14 years, nearly 84 billion barrels of oil were extracted and burned, yet proven reserves of oil actually *increased* by 351 billion barrels. Today, there is still enough oil in the ground to last

45 years, not the 15 years one might have guessed based on the 1978 information. How is this possible?

The answer to the riddle is that estimates of "proven reserves" of oil, coal, and gas include only those amounts that already have been discovered and are recoverable with present technology at current prices. Vast parts of the world have yet to be explored for fossil fuels, and technological advances are allowing oil to be found and extracted from sites that once were thought to be inaccessible or already pumped dry. Each year, consequently, brings new discoveries that add to the world's known energy reserves.

In 1991, Frances Cairncross, environment editor for *The Economist*, ventured to guess that total fossil fuel *resources* — that is, discovered *and* yet-to-be-discovered reserves — could last *650 years* at current rates of consumption. This is not implausible. Known reserves of oil rose by nearly a factor of 10 during the past forty years, from 103 billion to 991 billion barrels. A similar increase could occur during the next forty years.

If shortages of oil, coal, or natural gas occur in the future, the price of

Growth in Global Oil Reserves

Instead of diminishing over time, as one would expect, known oil reserves are growing. Between 1948 and 1992, proven oil reserves increased by a factor of 14.6. Despite repeated warnings that supplies would run out, reserves in 1990 exceeded one trillion barrels for the first time.

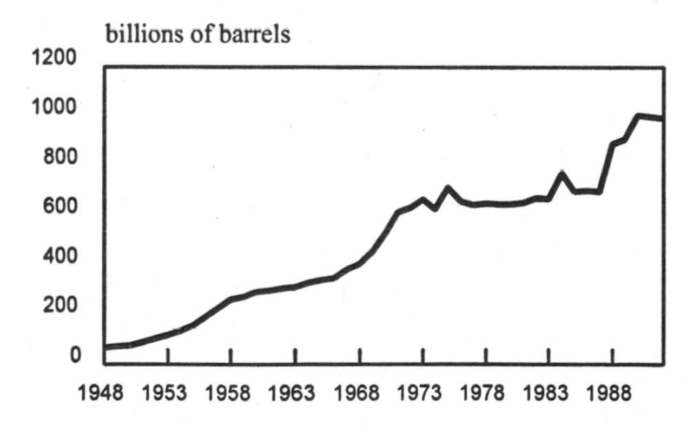

Source: American Petroleum Institute, 1994.

energy will be bid up and more fossil fuels will be found and brought to market. Most people know how this works, even if they can't draw the "supply curves" and "demand curves" used by economists to illustrate the process. At higher prices, producers can hire additional workers and buy more equipment, and therefore create more of the product. Higher prices also send a signal to entrepreneurs, telling them that they can make more profits by producing the higher-priced item, further increasing the product's supply.

Many environmentalists who understand how market processes work in every other part of their lives refuse to believe that they also apply to fossil fuels and other "non-renewable" resources. It is natural to assume that supplies will run out, since they are physically finite, but this point of view is mistaken. The amount of oil and coal in the ground is vast compared to the amounts we use. Even small increases in price can make it profitable to extract deposits once thought too deep or too thin to be worth developing. As paradoxical as it may sound, fossil fuels are unlikely to *ever* be completely exhausted by man, since their rising prices would make alternative energy sources more attractive to consumers long before the last barrel of oil is found or the last ton of coal is mined.

Energy demand considerations

While higher prices stimulate more production of a scarce product, they also encourage consumers to buy less of the product. Consumers have many ways to conserve energy: setting thermostats lower, taking shorter showers, buying more energy-efficient cars, insulating their homes, and so forth. Manufacturers, too, can conserve energy by changing their production methods to capture waste heat and use less energy. Millions of consumers and producers reducing their energy consumption in these ways can have a significant effect on total demand, and consequently on how long fossil fuel reserves can be expected to last.

Many environmentalists assumed that the world demand for energy was driven by population growth and rising standards of living. But during the 1970s, this assumption proved to be wrong. While world population continued to grow and standards of living continued to rise, global demand for energy grew at progressively *lower* rates. World energy consumption rose 64 percent between 1960 and 1970, 33 percent from 1970 to 1980, and only 17 percent between 1980 and 1988. World demand for oil vividly illustrates this pattern. (See the graph on the following page.) After increasing at double-digit rates during much of the 1950s and 1960s, world demand for oil suddenly slowed during the 1970s. During the ten-year period from 1980 to 1989, oil consumption rose just *4 percent.*

Energy conservation and improved energy efficiency made this dramatic change in the rate of global energy consumption possible. These activities are driven by some of the same forces that are leading to cleaner air: improvements in automobile technology that doubled the fuel efficiency of the U.S. fleet between 1973 and 1986, replacement of energy-intensive products with energy-efficient products, and the trend toward overall greater economic efficiency.

Progress in using energy efficiently has been especially dramatic in the U.S. According to Lynn Scarlett, vice president for research at the Reason Foundation, "in the United States, the amount of energy needed to produce a dollar of GNP (in real terms) has been declining steadily at a rate of one percent per year since 1929. By 1989, the amount of energy needed to produce a dollar of GNP was almost half of what it was 60 years earlier. Moreover, since the 1970s there has been a steady decline in the amount of energy used *per person.*"

A complete picture of future energy supplies, in summary, requires that we take into account trends in the global demand for fossil fuels as well as the effect of price increases on energy supplies. The demand situation is dominated by a dramatic reduction in the rate of increase in global energy consumption, and by rising energy efficiency in developed countries. The slower rate of growth in world demand for energy means each gallon of oil and each pound of coal can be "stretched" further and further, pushing forward the hypothetical date at which fossil fuel reserves might finally be exhausted.

Will we run out?

Let's return to our original question: *Is the world in danger of running out of fossil fuels?*

The answer is clearly *no.* World coal and oil resources are huge, enough to last hundreds of years at current levels of consumption. World energy consumption, while still rising, is growing very slowly now and may grow more slowly still in the future due to underlying changes in

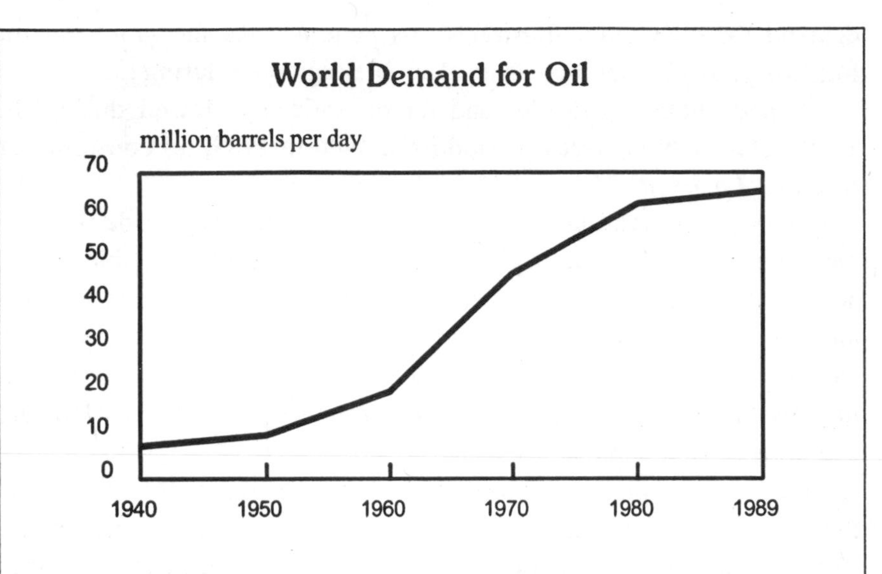

Source: Data prior to 1970 from S. Fred Singer, "World Demand for Oil," in Julian L. Simon and Herman Kahn, *The Resourceful Earth*, 1984, p. 343; post-1970 data from *Statistical Abstract of the U.S.*, 1992, Table 933.

technology and the world economy. If world demand for energy ever threatens to outstrip the supply, higher prices paid by consumers will be swiftly translated into new supplies of conventional fossil fuels and, if necessary, the discovery and use of alternative fuels.

Depletion of fossil fuels will not stop our progress toward making the Earth a cleaner and safer place.

Conclusion

Our world is getting cleaner, not dirtier

Air quality in the U.S. has improved significantly since 1975, and total air pollutant emissions are below the levels that prevailed in 1940. Current levels of air pollution are believed to be too low to have much of an impact on the incidence of human cancer. Other developed nations also have made progress in cleaning their air since 1970.

Water quality in the U.S. has steadily improved since its low point in the 1950s. New technologies and regulations mean factories and municipal sewers no longer foul our rivers and lakes. Fish have returned to many rivers and lakes once thought to be dead.

The tiny traces of additives and pesticides present in our food, once thought by leading environmentalists to pose a major threat to human health, have been found to pose such tiny risks that they are overwhelmed by the hypothetical risks of naturally occurring chemicals in many common foods. Thanks to the expanded use of high-yield seeds, fertilizers, and pesticides, the people of the world have never been better fed. Indeed, an end to the threat of famine around the world is in sight, if only civil wars and corrupt governments did not stand in the way.

Forested areas in America are increasing in size, and logging is now conducted on a sustainable yield basis. The old days of clear cutting and abandonment in forestry are behind us. Gone, too, are the days of open town dumps with their potential for contaminated leachate, vermin, and odors. In their place is recycling, diverting one-fifth of our garbage; the modern landfill with its liner, cap, and other safety features; and clean and safe waste-to-energy incineration.

Our descendants won't blame us for using up all the Earth's energy resources because there is enough oil and coal in the Earth to last hundreds of years at current rates of consumption. The dynamics of supply and demand mean our distant descendants will have plenty of time to find safe alternatives to fossil fuels, should they ever need them.

The Work That Still Needs to Be Done

Environmentalists can celebrate the progress made since the early 1960s, without being blind to the serious environmental problems that remain to be addressed:

- Air pollution remains a problem in some of America's cities. We must find ways to identify and control the remaining sources of air pollution — such as cars that are not properly tuned and other nonpoint sources.

- The battle against water pollution must shift away from point sources, which are now controlled, to nonpoint sources such as farming, construction, and lawn care practices that cause fertilizer and other substances to run off into rivers, lakes, oceans, and groundwater.

- Older landfills should be closed or retrofitted with new and safer technology. Better ways to minimize the effects of landfill operations on local communities still need to be found.

- We must improve our understanding of when recycling makes sense and when it doesn't. Rather than rely on the old rhetoric that "recycling is always good," we need to study and honestly report the trade-offs that sometimes make recycling inappropriate.

- Government policies that subsidize logging in ecologically fragile areas need to be changed, and government management of our forests and public lands could be improved.

This list is only suggestive of the things that need to be done; in Chapter Eight we propose many more specific ways to carry forward the fight to protect the environment. Despite all the work that remains ahead of the environmental movement, our review of available information confirms our initial assertion: Significant progress has been made in protecting the environment. *Our world truly is becoming cleaner over time, not dirtier.*

Americans have less reason today to be afraid of their environment than at any previous moment in human history. Their hard work and major investments of tax dollars have purchased a cleaner environment for them and their children. Elizabeth Whelan, one of the first scientists to speak out against the doomsday rhetoric that fills the popular press these days, said it best ten years ago when she wrote:

> Americans and citizens all over the Western World can be proud of the strides we've taken to improve our environment. The innovative technological breakthroughs of the twentieth century have resulted in the healthiest population ever to live on this planet. While the advances have not come without risks, the ultimate benefits have in fact vastly outweighed the costs, despite what the scaremonger lobby would have us believe.

3. What about cancer?

The cancer scare

ONE OF THE most tragic consequences of the modern environmental movement is that it has made many people *afraid* of the environment. We are afraid to drink water from rivers, to swim in lakes, or to eat fresh fruits and vegetables from our own gardens. Everywhere, the threat of "getting cancer" hangs over us, turning the seeming beauty of nature into a hidden danger.

The cancer scare began in 1962 with Rachel Carson's shocking best-seller, *Silent Spring*. Carson blended fiction with fact to produce a horror story not unlike those produced today by Stephen King or Dean Koontz. Her book is filled with references to "evil spells," "witchcraft," and "devils." In *Silent Spring*, pesticides become "chemical death rain." Hidden forces have caused us all to fall into a zombie-like "mesmerized state," while the scientific community has been inexplicably gripped by a "fanatic zeal" to wipe out entire life forms.

Though the language of *Silent Spring* has more in common with *Night of the Living Dead* and *Frankenstein* than it does with a scientific treatise, the book was presented to the public as objective science. Millions of readers accepted it as such. It didn't take other writers long to note Carson's success and imitate her tactics. Paul Ehrlich, whose record of failed predictions was described in the previous chapter, is one. Others include Ralph Nader, Lester Brown, and Paul Brodeur.

In recent years, the cancer scare message has appeared repeatedly in fundraising letters and newsletters from environmental groups. These *sales pitches* (let's call them what they really are) have raised hundreds of millions of dollars for environmental groups. But they have also spread unnecessary fear to every corner of the country.

It is sad testimony to the power of these scare tactics that the authors of a book on the *environment* should feel compelled to devote an entire chapter to setting straight the record on *cancer*. Yet if we did not, many readers would wonder why, if our world is getting cleaner, they are constantly warned of new and ever-more-deadly sources of cancer in the air, the water, and their food.

What is cancer?

Cancer is the uncontrolled and rapid creation of new cells in the body. Sir Richard Doll and Dr. Richard Peto give the following, more complete, definition:

> The various human cancers are diseases in which one of the many cells of which the human body is composed is altered in such a way that it inappropriately replicates itself again and again, producing millions of similarly affected self-replicating descendant cells, some of which may spread to other parts of the body, and eventually overwhelm it. Some cancers are easily curable, whereas others are almost always completely incurable by the time they are diagnosed.

Cancer is not a single disease, but many diseases known to cause the uncontrolled replication of cells. Different kinds of cancer are triggered by different events, often when anti-risk factors are missing or the body's natural defenses have been compromised. Genetics, viral infections, high-fat diets, tobacco, and occupational exposure to carcinogenic (cancer-causing) substances are now thought to cause cancers. Scientists admit that they are generally unable, at this time, to determine the cause of most specific cancer cases, though our knowledge of how cancers start and how they spread is slowly improving.

Man is not the only creature vulnerable to cancer. Cancer affects all but the lowest forms of animals. Even the bones of dinosaurs over a million years old bear evidence of cancer-like changes. Cancer has existed in humans since the earliest times, long before the Industrial Age. Every known population of man experiences some cases of cancer.

Cancer is especially common among the elderly. There appear to be two reasons why this is so. First, as the body ages it gradually loses its ability to reliably replicate dying cells. As *Van Nostrand's Scientific Encyclopedia* explains, "Over a period of years, the restorative ability of the body generally falls behind as part of the aging process." Second, some cancers are known to have long latency periods, meaning the event that triggered the cancer could have occurred as long as 25 years before the cancer manifested itself. The older a person gets, the more likely it becomes that the eventual cause of his or her death will be diagnosed as cancer.

Is the rate of cancer increasing?

Several authors in the environmental movement have claimed that cancer rates are rising as a result of our exposure to air and water pollution. Evidence to support this claim, however, is seldom presented. The table on the next page shows trends in U.S. cancer mortality rates* over a twenty-year period. Rates are given for women and men and reported by age group. The combined rate for both sexes and all ages has been adjusted to take into account the different number of people in each age group.

---

*The unavailability and unreliability of data on cancer *incidence* leads most experts in this field to rely on cancer mortality rate data, as we do here.

The overall cancer mortality rate reveals a slight increase of 2.4 percent over the past twenty years. Rates for both men and women 54 years and younger fell significantly, while rates for men and women 55 years and older rose. It is also apparent from the table that cancer mortality among the elderly is much higher than among the young. For example, women aged 65 to 74 are *53 times* as likely to die of cancer than are women aged 25 to 34. The figures are not much different for men.

Change in Cancer Mortality Rates 1970 - 1989

(deaths per 100,000 population in specific groups)

Age groups	1970	1980	1989	% Change 1970-1989
Both sexes, all ages, age-adjusted	129.9	132.8	133.0	+ 2.4
Females				
25 to 34 years	16.7	14.0	12.4	- 25.7
35 to 44 years	65.5	53.1	47.7	- 27.2
45 to 54 years	181.5	171.8	151.9	- 16.3
55 to 64 years	343.2	361.7	373.3	+ 8.8
65 to 74 years	557.9	607.1	670.9	+ 20.2
75 to 84 years	891.9	903.1	1010.2	+ 13.2
85 years and over	1,096.7	1,255.7	1,312.9	+ 19.7
Males				
25 to 34 years	16.3	13.4	11.8	- 27.6
35 to 44 years	53.0	44.0	38.4	- 27.5
45 to 54 years	183.5	188.7	162.8	- 11.3
55 to 64 years	511.8	520.8	525.3	+ 2.6
65 to 74 years	1,006.8	1,093.2	1,079.1	+ 7.2
75 to 84 years	1,588.3	1,790.5	1,877.3	+ 18.2
85 years and over	1,720.8	2,369.5	2,563.3	+ 49.0

Source: *Statistical Abstract of the U.S.*, 1992, Tables 117, 121.

Plainly, cancer in the U.S. is primarily a disease of old age.

At first glance, this somewhat mixed record may seem to lend support to those who claim that overall cancer mortality rates are rising (although a 2.4 percent increase over a twenty-year period hardly amounts to an "epidemic"). But this is not how experts interpret these data. They say the rising incidence of cancer among older Americans is *not* the result of a factual increase in their risk of cancer. Rather, it is due to the steep decline in *other* causes of death. For example, the death rate for persons 65 years and older from heart disease, motor vehicle accidents, and all other accidents *each fell by nearly one-third* from 1970 to 1989.

As more and more Americans survive infections, diseases, and accidents, living into their 70s, 80s, and 90s, the percentage of senior citizens dying from cancer necessarily has increased. In other words, more Americans are living long enough to succumb to their body's inability to repair itself. As science writer Michael Fumento comments, "you have to die of *something.*"

Reported cancer mortality rates among the elderly are also known to be extremely unreliable. In the past, doctors and coroners had fewer tools and tests with which to determine the cause of a person's death. Death by cancer, especially among senior citizens with other health problems, was often attributed to other causes. As tests have improved, more and more deaths are correctly attributed to cancer, *and* cancers are being found in elderly patients who die from some other cause. Together, these two trends make it *appear* as though cancer risks are rising, when in reality they have not changed. For this and other reasons, Doll and Peto say:

> It is dangerous to make inferences from trends in overall age-standardized cancer rates if these trends are due chiefly to trends among older people and are not also evident upon examination of the trends in the age-standardized rates among people under age 65. This is not because the deaths of old people are less important, nor because trends among them may be determined by social changes which took place half a century or more ago, but simply because the data on cancer trends among old people are often less reliable.

Overall, the trends in cancer mortality during the past twenty years look very good indeed. Cancer mortality rates for males and females in every age group under 55 have fallen since 1970. The rate of increase in the 55 to 64 year-old groups (8.8 percent for females and just 2.6 percent for males) is sufficiently low to produce a negative rate of change in cancer rates for males and females under 65 years of age. Only rates for males and females 65 and older show significant increases.

The nation's leading experts on cancer and diseases agree with this assessment. Here is a representative sampling of their statements:

- "Overall, cancer mortality among young adults in the United States is decreasing quite rapidly, and much of the decrease cannot plausibly be attributed to improved therapy."
  Sir Richard Doll and Dr. Richard Peto

- "Despite the popular conception that the U.S. is suffering from an 'epidemic' of cancer, the scientific evidence collected to date does not support this view. With the exception of lung cancer, age adjusted cancer death rates for most other forms of cancer have decreased or remained constant for the past fifty years. . . ."
  American Council on Science and Health

- "U.S. cancer death rates, except for lung cancer due to tobacco and melanoma due to ultraviolet light, are not on the whole increasing and have mostly been steady for 50 years."
  Dr. Bruce Ames, University of California - Berkeley

Cancer and pollution

The fact that cancer mortality rates for the nonelderly population in the U.S. are falling casts doubt on the claim that pollution is causing a significant number of cancers. It is also worth noting that Japan, which is as highly industrialized as the U.S. and more densely populated, has cancer mortality rates that are very low by international standards. Still, the relationship between cancer and pollution cannot be so easily dismissed.

Occupational exposure to asbestos during the 1940s and 1950s has been determined to be responsible for higher rates of a particular kind of lung cancer that accounts for about 2 percent of U.S. cancer deaths today. In isolated cases, air pollution, too, has killed people. For example, unusual weather conditions called inversions caused air pollution to rise to toxic levels in Donora, Pennsylvania in 1948, and in London, England in 1952. Twenty people died in Donora and approximately 4,000 in London as a result. Finally, some people with pre-existing health conditions or genetic predispositions are especially sensitive to pollution. While the average person might not be harmed by low levels of exposure to carcinogens, some people appear to be much more vulnerable.

The question, then, becomes a more subtle one. Man-made chemicals and pollution have not increased the overall cancer mortality rate, much less caused a "cancer epidemic." But could they nevertheless be responsible for a smaller but still significant share of cancer deaths? Doll and Peto attempted to answer this question by using epidemiological methods. The results of their study, published by the National Cancer Institute in 1981, is shown in the pie chart on the following page. It shows pollution of all kinds accounted for 2 percent of avoidable cancers, and food additives and exposure to industrial products each were responsible for less than 1 percent.

To interpret Doll and Peto's findings, three things must be noted. First, old age and genetic causes do not appear in the chart because they are not *avoidable* causes of cancer. Doll and Peto estimated that between 20 and 25 percent of all cancers fell into this "unavoidable" category. Recent research attributing some 20 percent of all cancer deaths in the U.S. to a *single gene* (see the box on page 45) suggests that even more cancers than these may be unavoidable.

Second, the data on which the estimates were based reflected the cancer risk 25 years ago, not in 1994. Substantial progress has been made in reducing air and water pollution since that time. It is likely, then, that less than 2 percent of avoidable cancers — and probably less than 1.5 percent of all cancers — are attributable to pollution.

Third, Doll and Peto's "diet" category refers only to naturally occurring substances in food and to over-consumption (obesity), not to food additives or pesticide residues, which are counted separately. It would not be correct, in other words, to assert that some part of the cancer risk associated with "diet" can be attributed to man-made chemicals or pesticides.

Regarding the health effects of pesticides in food, Doll and Peto report that the rate of death from liver cancer, the most likely kind of cancer to be caused by pesticides, has not increased in developed countries since the introduction of long-lasting pesticides, and that clinical

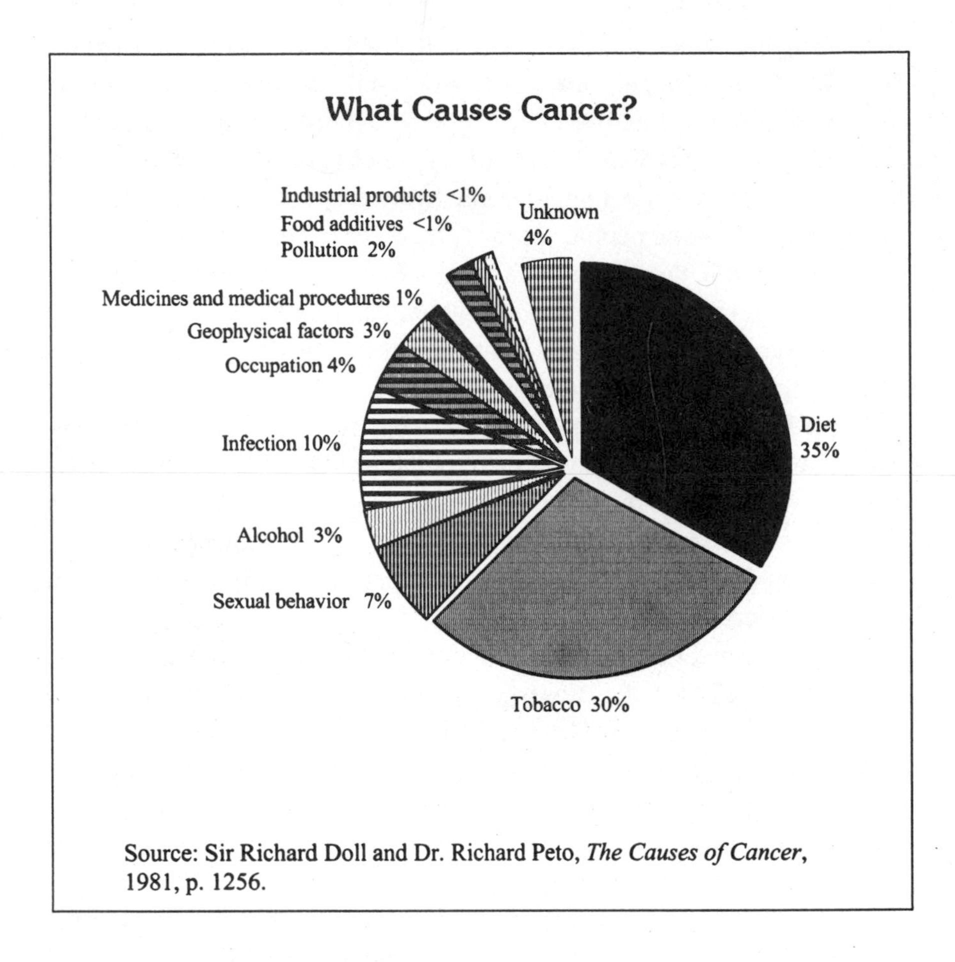

Source: Sir Richard Doll and Dr. Richard Peto, *The Causes of Cancer*, 1981, p. 1256.

and epidemiological evidence linking pesticides to health problems is "limited" and "not compelling." They conclude:

> For our present limited purpose (of estimating the proportion of *current* cancer mortality avoidable in various ways), the occurrence of pesticides as dietary pollutants seems unimportant. However, this does not imply that no modification of current practices is advisable. Obviously, where human exposure can be avoided without undue cost, perhaps by different or more limited pesticide practices or by the use of some alternative methods of control, it would seem prudent to do so.

Doll and Peto's findings are widely supported by toxicologists and epidemiologists and still reflect the position of the National Cancer

Institute. The American Medical Association agrees, reporting: "There is no definite epidemiological evidence that the U.S. has experienced an overall increase in the incidence of cancer related to high levels of pollutants or contaminants in the environment."

Animal testing and false alarms

If man-made chemicals and pollution pose so small a threat to human health, why do we constantly hear of new studies that "prove" that this chemical or that product may cause cancer?

The principal sources of the false alarms are studies involving laboratory animals fed or injected with large amounts (called the "maximum tolerable dose," or MTD) of the substance being tested. If the animals develop more cancerous tumors than animals in a "control" group (which are not fed or injected with the substance), then researchers assume that

Do Our Genes Determine Our Cancer Risk?

In December 1993, two teams of scientists working independently discovered a gene that is believed to be responsible for cancers of the colon, uterus, and ovaries. Such cancers account for some 80,000 deaths in the U.S. every year, or nearly 20 percent of all cancer deaths.

According to Dr. Francis Collins, who heads the federal Human Genome Project, "This is a very huge achievement. There is no doubt this research is going to produce faster, better cancer detection, as well as providing important clues for new ways of treating the cancers."

Growing evidence that vulnerability to cancer is an inheritable trait is forcing a re-evaluation of past research that assumed genetics played little or no role in causing most kinds of cancer. The number of cancer deaths that can be attributed to diet, pollution, or other external causes must now be revised downward to take into account the role played by our genes.

Source: Steven M. Powell et al., "Molecular diagnosis of familial adenomatous polyposis," *The New England Journal of Medicine*, December 30, 1993. See also Michael Waldholz, "Scientists Find Gene That Causes Cancer," *Wall Street Journal*, December 3, 1993.

much smaller doses of the same chemical might be expected to have a similar but smaller effect on humans. The risk to human health is then extrapolated from the laboratory animal data.

Animal testing is a valuable tool for determining the safety of many kinds of chemicals and drugs. All else being equal, conducting tests on mice and rats is better than conducting tests on humans! But animal tests are a poor predictor of whether a substance causes cancer in humans. The following are a few of the reasons why animal tests are unreliable:

- Huge doses of the chemical being tested must be administered to create observable effects in the small and short-lived population of test animals. These high doses often cause trauma, which can give rise to tumors and premature death.

On this point, Bruce Ames says, "Animal cancer tests done at the MTD of a chemical might commonly stimulate all three steps in carcinogenesis and be positive because the chemical caused chronic cell killing and inflammation with some mutagenesis. . . . We postulate that a just sublethal level of a carcinogen causes cell death, which allows neighboring cells to proliferate, and also causes oxygen radical production from phagocytosis and thus chronic inflammation, both important aspects of the carcinogenic process."

- Approximately one-fourth of 427 chemicals tested on both rats and mice caused cancer in mice but not rats, or caused cancer in rats but not mice.

Not only do mice and rats respond differently to the same chemicals and doses, but many chemicals that cause cancer in rats and mice do *not* cause cancer in hamsters. If chemicals have different effects on such closely related animals, how can such tests give us any meaningful information about whether a chemical will be carcinogenic to humans?

- Animal tests often are conducted incompetently.

In her 1984 book, *The Apocalyptics: Cancer and the Big Lie*, Dr. Edith Efron documents case after case of botched experiments that nevertheless formed the basis for important public policy decisions. For example, here is how she describes the science used to justify the banning of Red Dye No. 2:

> Unfortunately, the scientist in charge of the 500 rats left the agency, and the rats were left unsupervised for a long time. When, finally, some scientists picked up the experiment in midstream, their work was slovenly. An unknown number of control rats got mixed up with the test rats, and dead rats, instead of being dissected immediately, were left to rot in their cages.

"But botched or not," says Efron, "the FDA maintained that this study had not proven the safety of the food color, and thus Red Dye No. 2 was banned."

Another botched test was used for some time to argue that DDT, banned in 1972, was a carcinogen. According to Dr. Elizabeth Whelan,

> Later, many flaws were found with this experiment. For example, even though the mice were supposed to be a leukemia-free strain, the disease was found in the control group as well as in the treated group. Tumors were also reported in the breeding stock and the controls. There were other experimental problems. A study undertaken by the World Health Organization suggested that the feed used in the Targan and Kemeny work was contaminated with aflatoxin, one of the most potent natural carcinogens.

Researchers eventually established that DDT is, at worst, a weak human carcinogen posing little threat to human health. (We will return to this point in Chapter Four.) This finding, however, did not receive the same publicity as the flawed Targan and Kemeny test, leaving many people with the false belief that DDT is a potent human carcinogen.

- Few scientists are eager to publish the results of a study that failed to find what they were expecting to find. But if an animal test is repeated often enough, a positive finding will eventually be generated simply by pure chance. Repetition of tests and selective reporting of the results have meant more and more chemicals are falsely labeled carcinogenic.

- One reason for all the false positives is that "laboratory mice have a high spontaneous incidence of tumors — that is, they develop tumors whether or not they are exposed to chemicals," says Efron. It is common practice for experimenters to choose the most sensitive species and sexes for their tests, thereby maximizing the chances of tumor growths.

- Animal testing assumes that a constant linear increase in effects occurs as doses are increased. In fact, it is known that the increase in effects is *not* linear for several suspected human carcinogens (including saccharin and formaldehyde). The absence of a linear relationship can hardly be surprising. Many substances, such as vitamins and certain minerals, are toxic in large doses but beneficial to human health in small doses.

Dr. Jay I. Goodman, chairman of the Board of Scientific Counselors of the National Toxicology Program, a federally funded science program that coordinates toxicologic research and testing activities within the Deparment of Health and Human Services, reported in 1993 the Board's finding that "the implicit assumptions underlying extrapolation from the MTD . . . do not appear to be valid. Therefore, both the criteria for selection of the high dose used and the default criteria that are employed for extrapolation from high-dose to low-dose [i.e., the assumption of linearity] must be reevaluated in a critical manner."

Dr. Ames, in an article published in *Science*, summarized the scientific community's disdain for animal testing:

> Extrapolation from the results of rodent cancer tests done at high doses to effects on humans exposed to low doses is routinely attempted by regulatory agencies when formulating policies attempting to prevent future cancer. There is little sound scientific basis for this type of extrapolation, in part due to our lack of knowledge about mechanisms of cancer induction, and it is viewed with great unease by many epidemiologists and toxicologists.

Keith Schneider, environment writer for *The New York Times*, reported in 1993 that ". . . even scientists who conducted the [animal] studies say that as many as two-thirds of the compounds deemed carcinogenic would present no danger to humans. Yet the standards remain on the books."

Science writer Michael Fumento, who gives lengthy documentation of the shortcomings and abuses of animal testing in his book, *Science Under Siege*, writes:

> The day will come, not too long from now, when dosing animals with massive amounts of chemicals and then declaring that this predicts cancer in humans at low doses will be literally laughed at, in the same way we now laugh at witch doctoring and entrail reading. Our current cancer prevention scheme will be classified alongside leeching with the great medical follies of history. The only question is, how many hundreds of billions of dollars will be spent before then and how many lives will be needlessly cut short by policies focused on the trivial and unlikely, rather than the real dangers and truly preventable risks?

Epidemiology and false alarms

If tests on laboratory animals are unreliable, and tests on humans are unethical, how are we to determine whether or not a chemical is a human carcinogen? An alternative approach is epidemiology, the branch of science that seeks to discover what causes disease. Epidemiologists compare groups of people thought to be the same in every possible way — age, sex, income level, location, etc. — *except* for the one agent under investigation. The population not exposed to the agent in question is called the control group. Playing the role of scientific detectives, epidemiologists helped identify the cause of smallpox, the relationship between rubella in early pregnancy and birth defects, and the association between cigarette smoking and lung cancer. Doll and Peto, whose work we have cited frequently, are among the best-known and most-quoted epidemiologists in the world.

Like animal studies, epidemiologic studies play a vital role in discovering threats to human and animal health. Carefully done studies — involving large populations, authoritative data sources, and cautious statistical interpretation of the results — are extremely valuable and reliable guides for health care and public policy. But also like animal studies, epidemiologic studies have limitations and can be incompetently performed. Unfortunately, this has often been the case with studies purporting to find a link between chemicals, pollution, and cancer.

Inaccuracies are especially common with *case-control studies*, in which information is collected by questionnaires answered by the afflicted persons or, more often, by their relatives or friends. Unfortunately, victims themselves will often provide inaccurate information in order to avoid embarrassment, reinforce a personal conviction, or avoid taking responsibility for past actions. If the victim is deceased and a relative must complete the questionnaire, different but still strong motives exist to conceal or distort information. Who, after all, wants to report accurately the amount of alcohol one's mother drank, or how infrequently one's father exercised? Or a relative may simply lack the knowledge needed to provide detailed information on the victim's eating, drinking, or smoking habits. And each of these problems is made worse when the study involves only a small number of cases: Epidemiologic "studies" with as few as ten cases have been published!

Another limitation on epidemiologic studies is the impossibility of finding genuine control groups. For example, we noted earlier that cancer rates in Japan are very low, despite the country's high degree of industrialization. But this hardly *proves* that industrialization does not cause high cancer rates. Differences in the Japanese diet, genetic background, or personal behavior could offset or counteract the effects of industrial pollution. The two populations — U.S. and Japanese citizens — are too dissimilar for a comparison to have much value. While the differences in this case may be obvious, in many other cases they are very difficult to find and control. As a result, unknown differences between the "case" populations and "control" populations affect the results of every epidemiologic study.

Epidemiologists use statistics to calculate the risk that something is causing a disease. A risk factor of 2 would indicate that people in the exposed population had two times the rate of disease as did people in the control group. Small sample sizes ordinarily produce a wide range of possible risk factors, often ranging from some positive value to zero or even a negative value (which would mean exposure to the agent led to *less* disease). The popular media, having little space or time for long explanations and always searching for a gripping headline, tends to report the biggest positive number in a study's conclusion. By ignoring the equally likely lower risk factors, the media exaggerates the significance of a study's findings, generating dramatic and frightening predictions about rising rates of cancer or other diseases.

Doll and Peto use very large population groups and published health and mortality data to conduct their studies. They consistently conclude that exposure to man-made chemicals and pollution is responsible for only a very small fraction of current cancers. Unfortunately, their findings seldom generate newspaper articles or television specials for much the same reason as airplanes that don't crash don't get covered.

Much of the news coverage concerning chemicals, pollution, and cancer is the result of poorly done epidemiologic studies. Environmentalists, who are right to question the effects of man-made chemicals and pollution on the environment, need to be aware of how such studies are often misrepresented by the popular media.

Conclusion

Man-made chemicals and pollution *could* pose a serious cancer threat to the American people. The question environmentalists must ask, however, is whether a serious cancer threat exists *in fact*. The evidence presented in this chapter shows that the answer is no.

Despite all the hype and propaganda about a "cancer epidemic," the facts show that cancer mortality rates for most age groups are falling. Some cancers are on their way to becoming diseases of only the very old, and at that time they are probably unavoidable. New research shows that our genetic inheritance may account for more of our cancer risk than perhaps anything else in our lives.

So long as the Environmental Protection Agency and other government agencies project human cancer risks on the basis of poorly done animal experiments, public policy will continue to wrongfully condemn many useful products. Huge expenditures will continue to be made to control or ban relatively harmless substances. And so long as the media gives lead-story coverage to poorly done epidemiologic studies, we will continue to be treated to regular reports of the cancer threat posed by this or that substance.

4. The "crisis of the month" club

OUR WORLD IS getting cleaner, yet news about the environment is dominated by terrifying predictions of environmental destruction. When asked about the state of the Earth, more of us think about the threat of global warming than the reality of falling levels of air pollution. The list of supposedly pending disasters is a long one: Besides global warming, there is ozone depletion, acid rain, radiation, pesticides, toxic chemicals, hazardous waste, and many more. These possible hazards attract far more attention than does the *progress* being made in air and water quality. Yet in case after case, as we attempt to show in this chapter, the warnings of impending disaster are exaggerated.

Many environmental "crises" are simply manufactured out of flimsy evidence and marketing puffery. As a result, the three highest priorities of the environmental movement during the 1980s and 1990s — global warming, ozone depletion, and acid rain — each lacked solid scientific evidence of significant harm to either plant or animal life. Federal laws enacted to "solve" these problems are costing consumers and businesses tens of billions of dollars a year, diverting resources from more serious environmental problems, necessary social programs, and job-creating private investments.

Sometimes, a "crisis" identified by the environmental movement is a real problem that merits serious attention. In these cases, the movement should be commended for capturing the nation's attention and mobilizing support for a prompt response. But even here, the movement's tactics often have evoked a false sense of urgency that leads to inappropriate and inefficient public policies. Examples of such cases could include the management of solid waste, toxic chemicals, and pesticides.

Our purpose in this chapter is to provide the balance that is missing from the fundraising letters and popular media coverage of environmental issues. In the process, we rebut some myths and reveal a side of the environmental movement that seldom receives much attention: the more cautious and science-based side. By the end of this long chapter, the reader will have been introduced to a broad sampling of the many respected scientists, well-informed reporters, and dedicated environmentalists who represent this side of the movement.

While we seek to set the record straight on many issues, we hasten to admit that we lack the specialized knowledge to put forward a definitive account of any of the controversies discussed here. We are laymen who have conducted a survey of available research, no more and no less. The value of such a survey is not that it can *end* debate over any particular issue, but instead that it *inspires* a healthy and informed debate. We concur with famed astronomer Carl Sagan, who said in 1993:

> Science is more than a body of knowledge. It's a way of thinking, a way of thinking that looks skeptically. It teaches not blind obedience to those in authority, but vigorous debate.

Judging by the sometimes sharply conflicting views of experts, there is plenty for environmentalists to debate.

We review in this chapter a dozen "crises" — one for each month of the year — and shed some light on the scientific facts that lie beneath the hysteria. Limited space keeps us from giving detailed expositions on each issue, so we focus on the facts that are seldom reported by the popular media. For more detailed treatments of the issues addressed here, please consult the sources identified in the notes to this chapter.

January: Global Warming

Probably the most talked-about environmental "crisis" in America today is global warming, the theory that man-made pollutants are trapping warm air in the Earth's atmosphere and causing a gradual rise in temperatures. In 1989, at the peak of the global warming scare, *Time* magazine departed from its long tradition of naming a "man of the year," and instead declared the "Endangered Earth" its "Planet of the Year." The magazine editorialized that "The possible consequences [of global warming] are so scary that it is only prudent for governments to slow the buildup of carbon dioxide through preventive measures."

The International Panel on Climate Change (IPCC) concluded in 1990 that global temperatures could increase by 0.5 degrees Fahrenheit per decade unless steps were taken to control emissions of greenhouse gases (most importantly carbon dioxide, methane, and chlorofluorocarbons (CFCs)). They postulated that global temperatures could increase 5.4 degrees Fahrenheit by the end of the next century, and that such an increase would have devastating consequences for coastal cities (because melting polar ice caps would increase ocean levels) and negative consequences on agriculture and forests around the world.

How reliable are the forecasts of catastrophic global warming? What steps, if any, should we take to prevent global warming from occurring?

Where scientists stand on global warming

In the course of our survey of the scientific and popular literature, we have discovered considerable dissent from the popular view of global warming, a view based largely on the IPCC report. While some scientists still believe global warming is an urgent threat, many more apparently doubt its existence or believe its consequences will cause more benefit than harm to plant and animal life.

Robert C. Balling, Jr., director of the Office of Climatology at Arizona State University, is among the scientists who believe that the global warming threat has been exaggerated. As early as 1988, he writes,

> [M]any scientists were becoming increasingly skeptical about the apocalyptic view of the greenhouse effect; these "skeptics" were beginning to steal some of the spotlight. . . . [T]here is a large amount of empirical evidence suggesting that the apocalyptic vision is in error and that the highly touted greenhouse disaster is most improbable.

In 1990, three prominent scientists — Dr. Robert Jastrow, founder and director (retired) of Goddard Institute for Space Studies, National Aeronautics and Space Administration (NASA); Dr. William Nierenberg, director emeritus, Scripps Institution of Oceanography; and Dr. Frederick Seitz, president emeritus, Rockefeller University, and past president, National Academy of Sciences — declared that

> [W]ithin the constraints of the limited computing power currently available to climate forecasters, decades of computing will be needed to provide policymakers with the information they require. . . . The forecasts do not appear to be good enough in their present form to provide a sound basis for decisions affecting the economies of the U.S. and other nations.

Marc S. Plantico and three other scientists with the National Climatic Data Center of the National Oceanic and Atmospheric Administration (NOAA) and the Lamont-Doherty Geological Observatory at Columbia University wrote in 1990: "While it is possible that man has already altered the current climate, it is just as likely that the climate changes of the last several decades are dominated by natural long term climate variability."

The following year, Dr. Roger Revelle, one of the first scientists to devote serious attention to the possibility of global warming, said "the scientific basis of greenhouse warming is too uncertain to justify drastic action at this time. There is little risk in delaying policy response."

Dr. S. Fred Singer, a geophysicist, professor of environmental sciences at the University of Virginia, and director of the Science and Environmental Policy Project, is an outspoken opponent of the popular vision of global warming. So is Dr. John Christy, a University of Alabama scientist working with NASA to measure global temperatures. So is Dr. Patrick Michaels, the Virginia State Climatologist and associate professor of environmental sciences at the University of Virginia. And Dr. Richard S. Lindzen, professor of meteorology at the Massachusetts

Institute of Technology, said in 1992 that "as a scientist, I can find no substantive basis for the warming scenarios being popularly described."

These scientists apparently represent mainstream scientific thinking on this topic. A Gallup poll conducted on February 13, 1992 of members of the American Geophysical Union and the American Meteorological Society — the two professional societies whose members are most likely to be involved in climate research — found that 18 percent thought some global warming had occurred, 33 percent said insufficient information existed to tell, and *49 percent believed no warming had taken place.* While this is not the same as stating that global warming *will not* occur in the future, the history of global climate change is an important issue in the global warming debate.

In 1991, S. Fred Singer surveyed two groups of climate experts: the authors and reviewers of the IPCC study, and "The Phoenix Group," a group of 24 scientists convened by Robert Balling for a 1990 conference on global warming. Singer found that 40 percent of the IPCC authors and reviewers believed that their report's "Policymakers' Summary," written by a small steering committee, exaggerated the certainty of upcoming climate change. Nearly all the members of The Phoenix Group agreed with this assessment. Sixty percent of the IPCC group and all of the Phoenix Group members believed that current global circulation models did not accurately portray the atmosphere-ocean system, making it unlikely that they can accurately predict future climate changes.

Confirming the Gallup poll and Singer's findings is a letter dated February 1992 and signed by over fifty scientists, most of whom hold or once held leadership positions in the American Meteorological Society. Part of their letter reads:

> As independent scientists researching atmospheric and climate problems, we are concerned by the United Nations Conference on Environment and Development (to be held on June 1992 in Rio de Janeiro), being developed by environmental activist groups and certain political leaders. . . .
>
> . . . [T]he policy initiatives derive from highly uncertain scientific theories. They are based on the unsupported assumption that catastrophic global warming follows from the burning of fossil fuel and requires immediate action. We do not agree.

Fifty scientists may seem to be a small number, but there are only about sixty climatologists in the U.S. who work with climate histories or global climate models. An even smaller number publish regularly in scientific journals. The surveys and letter described above demonstrate that a large majority of these experts oppose key parts of the popular global warming theory.

If the preceding discussion is accurate, why do most news stories on the subject of global warming imply that the scientific community supports the popular view? We can think of three reasons. First, the aforementioned rule that *bad news sells* means research that seems to document global warming receives much more extensive coverage than research pointing the other way. Second, many intellectuals in fields *other than* climatology are predisposed to believe in global warming, and they are most often quoted and interviewed on this topic. Since these individuals are speaking outside their fields of expertise, their opinions ought to be viewed with caution. And third, leaders of the environmental movement saw in global warming an issue that could serve as a rallying point for the movement. Consequently, the popular view has appeared in countless newsletters, fundraising letters, and position papers, gaining an appearance of validity quite independent of the science that often stands in opposition to it.

While knowing where most scientists stand is an important part of understanding global warming, the reader should also know something of the issues and controversies involved in the debate. Specifically, why have so many scientists concluded that global warming is not as serious a problem as is popularly believed? And what forecasts, if any, are more widely supported by practicing climatologists?

PROBLEMS WITH THE THEORY

We found three principal objections to the popular view of global warming:

- **Records of historical temperatures fail to support the IPCC's predictions of future global warming.**

If a build-up of greenhouse gases leads directly to temperature increases, then temperatures over the past ten years should have increased 0.5 degrees Celsius. In fact, global temperatures rose by only a statistically insignificant 0.07 degrees Celsius. (See graphs below.) During the last century, global temperatures rose just 0.45 degrees Celsius, and 0.34 of that increase occurred before World War II, when man-made

No Global Warming Has Occurred

The graphs below show temperatures predicted by advocates of the global warming theory and actual global temperatures according to highly accurate satellite measurements. The graphs plainly show that actual temperatures are well below those forecast by the global warming theory, and actually have been declining since 1987.

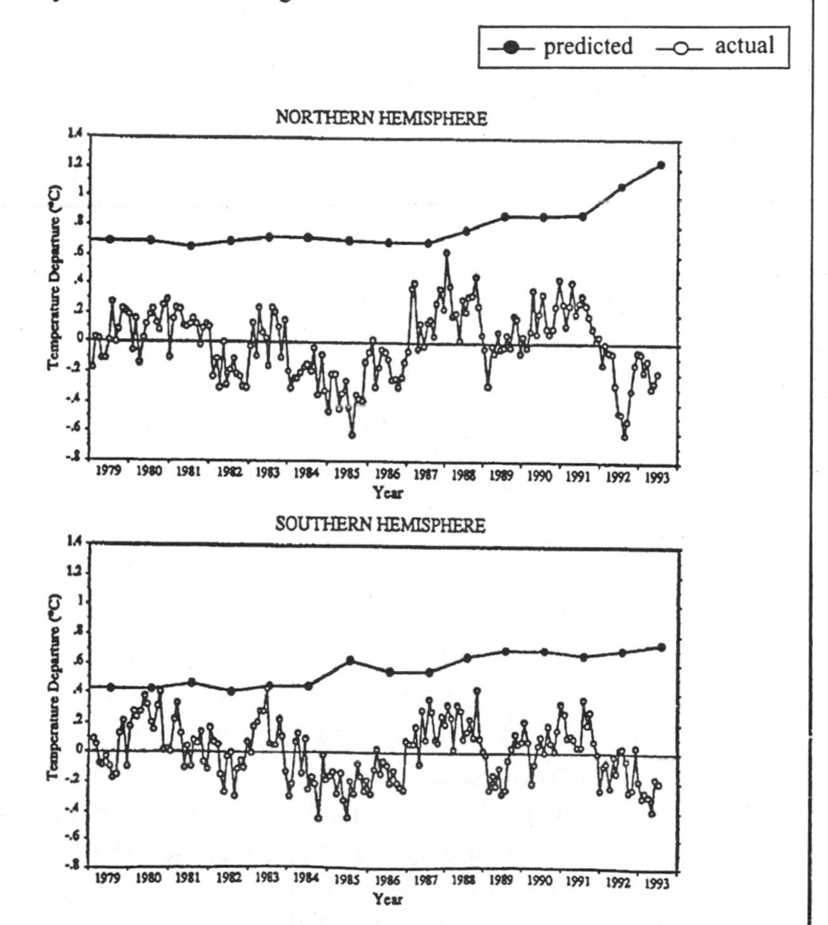

Source: *World Climate Review* 1 (4) (Summer 1993), p. 15. Reprinted with permission.

emissions were lowest. The observed warming in the last 55 years has been so small that temperatures in the Northern Hemisphere — once predicted to see the largest temperature increases — in fact experienced no significant change.

Global temperature changes since 1979 have been recorded by satellites that are accurate to within 0.01 degrees Celsius. These data are acknowledged to be accurate even by advocates of the global warming theory. The discrepancies between the global temperature record and global warming theory raise serious doubts about the reliability of predictions for future climate change.

Critics of the IPCC predictions also note that the amount of carbon dioxide in the atmosphere varied dramatically during the millions of years preceding man's presence on Earth. For example, at the time of the emergence of most land plant species, the amount of carbon dioxide in the atmosphere was ten times greater than it is today. Similarly, studies of greenhouse gases trapped in air bubbles in the Arctic ice pack reveal large and rapidly occurring changes in global climate during this period. Scientists have been unable to explain why these changes in carbon dioxide levels and global climate occurred, or which might have caused the other. Until answers to these questions are found, only limited confidence can be placed in predictions of future climate trends.

■ Computer models used to forecast global warming are very crude and unlikely to produce reliable data.

The computer models used to predict future climate changes have come under heavy fire from the scientific community. Richard Lindzen points out that air currents carry heat upward and toward the poles, having a considerable cooling effect on air at the planet's surface, but climate models "have large errors here — on the order of 50 percent." Jastrow, Nierenberg, and Seitz have demonstrated that small changes in cloud cover caused by increased evaporation could easily cancel out any warming trend predicted by the computer models. Others have documented that temperatures are affected by changes in the level of solar radiation reaching the Earth, sea-air interactions, and stratospheric dust from volcanoes and asteroids. None of these processes is sufficiently well understood to be accurately modeled, weakening the predictive abilities of any computer model.

Critics further explain that the computer models overlook feedback mechanisms that may offset whatever changes in temperature might otherwise be caused by man's activities. In an atmosphere rich in carbon dioxide, for example, plants grow bigger and faster, and as a result absorb larger amounts of carbon dioxide. Some researchers, such as Gordon Bonan of the National Center for Atmospheric Research, believe that the forests of the Northern Hemisphere have already increased their uptake of carbon dioxide each year, helping to explain why there is substantially less carbon dioxide in the atmosphere than would be predicted based on past levels of human emissions.

Dr. Andrew J. Weaver, at the School of Earth and Ocean Sciences at the University of Victoria, summarized in the July 1993 issue of *Nature* the doubt and uncertainty surrounding computer climate models:

> Perhaps the ocean's role in global warming is becoming clearer, but there are still large uncertainties on the atmospheric side. Water vapor and cloud feedbacks are often poorly resolved in course-resolution climate models, and the basic physics is not yet clear. Furthermore, these models do not, as yet, explicitly incorporate oceanic and terrestrial uptake or release of anthropogenic and natural greenhouse gases; and artificial flux corrections must still be used. Even though the most sophisticated models predict global warming in response to increasing greenhouse gases, we are still searching for the signal in our observational network amid a background of natural climatic variability. Climate scientists look likely to have their hands full for the next few years.

The major shortcomings of current climate models are sufficient grounds to hold off any decisions about whether and how to respond to the threat of global warming. At some point in the future, these models may produce information of sufficient quality to be used as the basis for public policy, but clearly this is not the case today.

■ Almost all of the slight warming in this century has occurred at night and during the winter.

Whether global warming would benefit or endanger animal and plant life depends largely on whether the warming takes place during winter or summer months, and during the day or at night. If warming occurs during summer days, it could lead to crop damage, desertification, and possibly other negative effects on plants and animals. But if warming occurs at night and during the winter, plants and animals may *benefit* from the moderating temperatures and longer growing seasons.

The empirical record for the past fifty years is very clear on this point: The small amount of global warming that has taken place has occurred during winter months and at night. According to Patrick Michaels, the historical record shows

> a warming which is confined primarily to nights and winter, therefore lengthening the growing season; and a lack of summer daytime warming, which precludes negative effects on agriculture and melting of large areas of high-latitude land ice. Actual cooling of summer days has been observed across the Northern Hemisphere.

The role that clouds play in global temperatures gives us reason to believe *future* warming, too, will occur at night and during winter months. During the summer, when days are longest, the net effect of clouds is to reduce daytime temperatures by shading the Earth's surface. During winter months, when days are shorter, the net effect of clouds is the opposite, tending to trap and reflect back heat that would otherwise escape during long winter nights. Since most models predicting global warming also predict cloudier conditions, it is likely that whatever warming occurs will be experienced at night and during the winter.

The Emerging Consensus

Robert Balling, writing in 1992, summarized the emerging consensus among experts on historical climates and climate change:

> The empirical evidence suggests that our future will see a rise in temperature of approximately 1.0 degrees Celsius (1.8 degrees Fahrenheit), with most of that warming occurring at night, in higher latitudes, and in the winter season. Extreme high temperatures probably will not increase in the 2XC2 world [that is, a world with two times the current level of carbon dioxide], and the earth will probably be wetter, cloudier, with substantial increases in soil moisture; droughts may diminish in frequency, duration, and intensity.

This summary is consistent with the views expressed by Jastrow, Nierenberg, Seitz, and most of the other experts we have cited here. In many cases, these scientists caution that offsetting natural processes are so poorly understood that future temperatures could actually *decline* as a result of rising levels of greenhouse gases. In other words, our current understanding of global climates is too inadequate to confidently predict that *any* global warming will take place.

In the absence of catastrophic global warming, rising levels of carbon dioxide are beneficial to plant and animal life. As was mentioned earlier, plant growth increases in response to higher levels of carbon dioxide. Sherwood B. Idso, a research physicist with the U.S. Department of Agriculture, has conducted extensive research into the consequences of a high-carbon dioxide world. He finds that today's carbon dioxide levels, while high by human historical records, are in fact very low compared to levels that prevailed when plant life first evolved. Consequently, he believes plants (and animals, too) will thrive in the carbon dioxide-rich future that appears to lie ahead. He writes:

> The increasing carbon dioxide content of Earth's atmosphere is like a breath of fresh air for the planet's close-to-suffocating vegetation. . . . Literally hundreds of laboratory and field experiments have established this fact. In the mean, they suggest that a 330 to 660 ppm [parts per million] doubling of the air's carbon dioxide content will increase plant productivity by about a third, while reducing plant transpiration by approximately the same amount.

Among the many scientists who share Idso's view is James Teeri, director of the University of Michigan's Biological Station. Teeri and five other researchers reported in 1993 that higher levels of carbon dioxide increase the rate of plant photosynthesis and the number and length of roots for a variety of trees. Forest trees growing in poor soil would especially benefit from carbon dioxide-rich air; in experiments they dramatically increased their root, branch, and leaf growth.

With twice the level of carbon dioxide, the world would witness shrinking deserts, fewer droughts, bigger harvests, and expanding wooded areas. Wildlife would thrive as habitats expand in size and richness with every passing year. Fruit, grain, leaf, and bean seed crops, according to one study conducted by the U.S. Department of Agriculture, could increase by approximately 30 percent without any increase in acreage.

Numbers like these suggest that a carbon dioxide-rich world would be a boon for farmers, consumers, and Third World countries.

CONCLUSION

The scientific basis for the theory that man is causing global warming — the "crisis" that dominated the environmental movement in the late 1980s and early 1990s — has unraveled. Its advocates have no answers for difficult questions about their models' inability to account for past temperature changes, cloud formations, or other feedback processes. The emerging consensus within the scientific community supports the position that climate changes will be far smaller and less disruptive than those originally predicted.

By early 1994, even *Time* magazine, which had featured global warming on its cover in 1989, gave up on the theory. In an article titled "The Ice Age Cometh?" the magazine's writers dismissed warnings of global warming as "apocalyptic" and told readers to "start worrying about the next ice age instead."

The rising levels of greenhouse gases in the atmosphere deserve continued study by scientists. But it is too early to know whether man-made emissions were responsible for the very small amount of global warming that occurred in the last century, or whether a continued rise in greenhouse gas levels will affect the climate of the future. Consequently, we should be very skeptical of efforts to adopt policies that could impose substantial costs on consumers and businesses in the name of "ending global warming." At this time, we do not know enough about the problem to prescribe a solution. *We do know, however, that global warming is not an environmental crisis.*

February: Ozone Depletion

Second only to global warming in terms of publicity and calls for a political response is the ominous "hole in the ozone layer." Ruth Caplan, executive director of Environmental Action, a group founded by the organizers of the first Earth Day, describes the threat like this:

> The stratospheric ozone layer is essential to all life — plants, animals,

> humans. Its job in the balance of nature and the environment is to shield our Earth from the destructive ultraviolet rays of the sun. But every day, in fact every minute, we are pumping into the air tons of synthetic chemicals that are efficient and long-lasting destroyers of stratospheric ozone. These are chlorofluorocarbons, the CFCs that we already know contribute to global warming. In the greenhouse equation, CFCs are secondary players. In the depletion of stratospheric ozone, they are the stars of the horror show.

Concern over the effects of CFCs on the ozone layer led to their ban as aerosol propellants in 1978 and removal from the production process of plastic foam products during the early 1990s. (Contrary to popular myth, the use of aerosol sprays and plastic foam products today poses no risk to the ozone layer.) In 1990, 93 countries agreed to a nearly complete phase-out of CFCs by the end of the century. Later, the deadline for the ban was moved up to the end of 1995.

The price of the ban

While replacing CFCs in propellants and plastic foam products was relatively easy, replacing them in cooling systems is proving to be much more difficult and expensive. "The costs to the country for the termination of CFCs are going to be phenomenal," said Melvyn Shapiro, an atmospheric scientist at the National Oceanic and Atmospheric Administration, in 1992. "Globally, it will cost hundreds of billions of dollars. They have alternative substances, but they're flammable. Do I have to worry about the air-conditioning unit in my car turning into a grenade? About my refrigerator blowing up?"

Shapiro exaggerates the danger posed by CFC replacements, although substitutes often are, in fact, both toxic and explosive. However, his forecast of the cost of the ban is in the correct range. In December 1993, owners of the 115 million older cars still on the road in the U.S. were warned that they would each have to pay as much as $1,000 to have their cars refitted with new air conditioning systems. An industry group expects the total cost to car owners will range from $23 billion to $36 billion through the year 2000. According to an analyst with the University of Michigan's Office for the Study of Automotive Transportation, the CFC phase-out "is like taking $1,000 off the sale [price] of a car."

Additional costs will be absorbed by industry, where CFCs are used in manufacturing processes, and also by the service sector. Over 100,000 large office buildings in the U.S. have air conditioning systems that will have to be refitted to use CFC substitutes, requiring an investment likely to exceed that borne by automobile owners. The cost of converting the refrigerated transportation of food is expected to reach more than $150 billion. And some researchers believe Third World countries will suffer greater hunger and poorer nutrition due to the higher cost of refrigeration. While the international CFC phase-out treaty gives China, Brazil, and India an additional ten years to comply with the ban, Africa and other parts of the world will suffer genuine hardship. Substitutes for refrigeration — such as salting and pickling — pose significant health threats.

Were CFCs so dangerous as to justify the hundreds of billions of dollars now being spent to phase them out? Liz Cook, ozone campaign director for Friends of the Earth, didn't seem to mind the expense when she told *The New York Times* in 1993, "There has to be some discomfort. That's the nature of a ban." But was the ban necessary in the first place? And just how much "discomfort" is the environmental movement entitled to impose on everyone else?

The ozone depletion theory

The same characteristics that made CFCs invaluable for refrigeration and other industrial applications make them a persistent presence in the atmosphere after they escape from heating and cooling coils. Because CFCs are transparent, insoluble, and chemically inert, they are not removed from the air by rain or other natural processes. Instead, they are thought to remain in the atmosphere, some for 100 years or longer, gradually working their way upward to the stratosphere where they are broken down by exposure to short-wavelength solar ultraviolet radiation.

Once in the stratosphere, each CFC molecule releases its chlorine atom, which becomes a highly efficient destroyer of ozone molecules. By repeatedly reacting with ozone molecules and free oxygen atoms, a single CFC molecule can destroy thousands of times its weight in ozone molecules. The result is said to be a potentially disastrous thinning of the ozone layer, one of Earth's shields against ultraviolet (UV) radiation.

Public concern over the condition of the ozone layer was dramatically heightened during the 1980s when the media reported a "hole" in the ozone layer above the South Pole. During the 1970s, researchers had discovered (actually, they *rediscovered*, but more about that later) that the amount of ozone above the Antarctic land mass was falling by more than 50 percent each spring and then gradually returning to its previous level by early summer. The amount of the decline and area of the hole was growing, and in 1987 over 90 percent of the ozone over an area equal to 10 percent of the Earth's surface was depleted. Although the hole shrunk the following year, man-made CFCs have been implicated in this annual occurrence and are thought by many to be responsible for the increasing size and "depth" of the hole.

In 1991, the EPA estimated that CFCs would cause ozone depletion of 4 to 5 percent over the next fifty years, significantly less than the 10 percent depletion predicted just a few years earlier. The EPA has claimed that such a depletion of the ozone layer, by allowing more UV radiation to reach the surface, could cause 12 million additional cases of nonmelanoma skin cancers in the U.S. (Nonmelanoma skin cancer is a curable disease that is not generally considered life-threatening. Malignant melanoma, an often-fatal form of skin cancer, does not appear to be caused by exposure to UV radiation.)

Al Gore summarized the popular theory of ozone depletion in 1993 like this: "For every 1 percent decrease in ozone, there is a corresponding 2 percent increase in the amount of ultraviolet radiation bathing our skin and a 4 percent increase in skin cancer."

PROBLEMS WITH THE THEORY

As was true of the global warming theory, serious scientific objections have been raised against the ozone depletion theory. In the discussion that follows, we identify five areas of concern.

■ **Key evidence is missing that CFCs are in fact causing a significant amount of ozone depletion.**

The debate begins over the questions of *how much* ozone depletion is caused by CFCs and whether such depletion is *long-lasting*. The mere fact that CFCs can destroy ozone molecules does not mean they pose a significant threat to the ozone layer.

Satellite records of the amount of global ozone contradict the ozone depletion theory. Between 1962 and the early 1970s, the amount of global ozone *rose* between 4 and 11 percent. Between 1969 and 1986, ozone levels over the Northern Hemisphere decreased between 1.7 percent and 3 percent. Since 1986, global ozone has been on the rebound, increasing steadily at 0.28 percent annually. If the gradual accumulation of CFCs in the atmosphere during these years had a net impact on global ozone levels, it is not apparent from this record.

The reason CFCs can destroy ozone molecules, yet not affect the global supply of ozone, is because the ozone layer is not composed of a static supply of ozone molecules which, once destroyed, are never replaced. On the contrary, billions of tons of ozone are created and destroyed every second all around the world. Huge quantities of ozone are created above the Equator, where bright sunlight stimulates production and warm temperatures slow the process of ozone breakdown. This ozone is then carried by a wave-like action to the middle and higher latitudes and eventually to the poles.

The thickness of the ozone layer varies considerably from place to place and from one season to the next. Concentrations of methane and nitric acid (both naturally occurring and from man-made emissions) seem to slow the process of ozone destruction, while the presence of sulfur dioxide and bromine speed it up. Changes in the amount of solar radiation reaching the outer atmosphere affect the rate at which new ozone molecules are created, and changes in wind patterns affect the distribution of ozone around the globe. Temperature changes, especially at the poles, are known to affect the rate at which ozone is destroyed. According to several scientists, the temporary decline of global ozone levels during the 1980s can be largely explained by natural variation, unusually cold temperatures in the Antarctic, and the ending of an 11-year solar cycle.

The empirical record of changing global ozone levels, plus our knowledge of other factors influencing global ozone, indicate that the impact of CFCs on overall ozone levels has been slight. This effect would not seem to be sufficient grounds for an outright ban on CFCs.

■ The Antarctic ozone hole is a naturally occurring phenomenon that is highly unlikely to occur anywhere else.

Perhaps because the case against CFCs is so weak, advocates of the

Holes in the Ozone Theory
"It's money, purely money"

"A full-blown 'ozone hole' rivaling the one that appears over Antarctica might open up over the U.S., zapping Americans with damaging ultraviolet sunlight during the spring, warned NASA scientists in an ominous early February 1992 press conference. *Time* showcased the story on the front cover of its February 17 issue. . . .

"Although NASA did not acknowledge it, the 'danger' of an ozone hole opening over the Northern Hemisphere had already passed in less than a month after the existence of the putative crisis was announced. By late February, satellite data showed that the levels of ozone-destroying chlorine monoxide had dropped significantly and provided absolutely no evidence of a developing ozone hole over the U.S. NASA waited until April 20, 1992, to announce at a press conference that a 'large arctic ozone depletion' had been 'averted.' In other words, no ozone hole had opened up over the U.S. *Time*, far from featuring the story on its cover, buried NASA's admission . . . in four lines of text in its May 11 issue.

"The NASA revelations were exquisitely timed to bolster the agency's budget requests for its global climate change program, whose funding is slated to double by fiscal 1993. One NASA atmospheric scientist even wondered if it was only a coincidence that Senator Gore's new book of apocalyptic environmentalism, *Earth in the Balance*, was published just days before NASA held its ozone press conference. After all, Gore chaired the subcommittee on Science, Space and Technology, which oversees NASA's budget.

"'What you have to understand is that this is about money,' Melvyn Shapiro, the chief of meteorological research at a NOAA laboratory in Boulder, Colorado, told *Insight* magazine. 'It's money, purely money.'"

Source: Ronald Bailey, *Eco-Scam: The False Prophets of Ecological Apocalypse*, 1993, pp. 119-120.

ozone depletion theory have focused on the Antarctic ozone hole (AOH). NASA in 1992 warned that a similar hole might develop over the Northern Hemisphere, though one never did. (See the sidebar above.) The nature of the AOH, however, reveals that it existed long before man-made CFCs could have played a major role; it cannot grow much beyond its current size; and similar holes in other parts of the world are extremely unlikely to occur.

During the cold and dark Antarctic winter, swirling winds called the Antarctic vortex cause temperatures to drop to minus 112 degrees Fahrenheit. Clouds, which in more ordinary conditions cannot form due to the low levels of water vapor present in cold air, appear in the eye of the vortex. The resulting ice crystals act as surfaces on which complicated chemical interactions take place. When sunlight appears in spring, more chemical reactions occur, creating a veritable killing field for ozone and producing the annual hole. By early summer, the Antarctic vortex breaks up, temperatures rise, and ozone created in warmer regions fills the hole.

The popular view of ozone depletion imagines that CFCs are solely responsible for the AOH, yet the hole was first observed in 1956 by G.M.B. Dobson, inventor of the machine now used to measure ozone. Dobson wrote about his discovery in a book, titled *Ozone in the Atmosphere*, published in 1968. The AOH was found again in 1957 and 1958, long before man-made CFCs could have played a major role in destroying ozone.

The popular view also imagines that the AOH will expand beyond Antarctica and perhaps be replicated in other areas of the world. The unique combination of wind patterns, temperatures, and chemistry at the South Pole, however, make this scenario highly implausible. The hole cannot expand beyond the Antarctic vortex, and wind and temperature conditions similar to those at the South Pole simply do not occur anywhere else on the globe. Dr. Hough W. Ellsaesser, a distinguished meteorologist and participating guest scientist at the Lawrence Livermore National Laboratory, summarizes the science this way:

> The ozone hole, if due to man, reflects a process which can occur only in those portions of the atmosphere which are maintained at temperatures below about minus 80 degrees Celsius (-112 degrees Fahrenheit) for two to three months, during at least the latter half of which they must also be exposed to sunlight. Such temperatures occur only in restricted vertical layers, roughly 12 to 20 km, within the polar vortices which develop due to radiative cooling when sunlight is absent over the pole in winter, and at the tropical tropopause. . . . The phenomenon does not occur to any appreciable extent over the North Pole because the north polar vortex breaks up and rewarms about the same time as the sun comes up there. Also, ozone loss is unlikely to ever be detected at the tropical tropopause both because there is little

> ozone there to be destroyed and because the air there is being constantly flushed out by a slow updraft. . . .

Ellsaesser concludes, "Thus, unless there are changes other than the simple addition of more chlorine to the stratosphere, the ozone hole does not appear likely to become any more important than it was in 1987."

- **The amount of ultraviolet radiation reaching the Earth's surface is not increasing.**

The theory that ozone depletion will cause an increase in human cancer rates is based on the assumption that ground-level UV radiation will rise twice as fast as atmospheric ozone levels fall. In fact, the amount of ultraviolet radiation reaching the Earth's surface has not increased as predicted, and in recent years has fallen.

Dr. Joseph Scotto and others write in the February 1988 issue of *Science*:

> Recent reports of stratospheric ozone depletion have prompted concerns about the levels of solar ultraviolet radiation that reach the earth's surface. Since 1974 a network of ground-level monitoring stations in the United States has tracked measurements of biologically effective ultraviolet radiation (UVB, 290 to 330 nanometers). The fact that no increases of UVB have been detected at ground levels from 1974 to 1985 suggests that meteorological, climatic, and environmental factors in the troposphere may play a greater role in attenuating UVB radiation than was previously suspected.

Scotto found that UVB radiation at the Earth's surface *fell by an average of 0.7 percent per year* since 1974. Even measurements taken from Mauna Loa, Hawaii, far away from urban sources of air pollution, showed no increase in the amount of UVB. The accuracy of these measurements has been affirmed by researchers for the NOAA and the National Cancer Institute.

If the ozone depletion theory were correct, then the decline in ozone levels between 1969 and 1986, estimated at between 1.7 percent and 3.0 percent in the middle latitudes, should have translated into increases in ground-level UV in the range of 3.4 and 6.0 percent. Instead, UV levels consistently *fell* during this period. Once again, the ozone depletion theory fails to conform to known facts.

■ Small increases in UV levels are harmless to plant and animal life.

It now appears that CFCs may be causing increased UV levels in only one area of the world: Antarctica. It is not clear whether, even here, the effects are harmful. Ellsaesser notes that "the ozone hole merely causes ultraviolet fluxes at the surface over Antarctica in spring, comparable to what is experienced there every summer." Other scientists agree. Dr. John Frederick, an atmospheric scientist at the University of Chicago, says "All the ozone hole does is bring summer-like ultraviolet radiation levels a couple of months early." An editorial in *Science News* in 1991 notes that even with reduced springtime ozone levels, Antarctica experiences UV levels typical of cities like Chicago. Obviously, this is a far cry from popular images of UV "poisoning" caused by the AOH.

One researcher has estimated that higher UV levels at Antarctica may reduce phytoplankton growth rates each spring by as much as 6 to 12 percent, though other researchers have been able to confirm growth reductions of 5 percent or less. Even the higher estimate would translate into an annual reduction in growth of approximately 2 to 4 percent in the course of a year. This is well within natural variations, and in fact may itself *be* one of those natural variations: As a naturally occurring event, the AOH is part of the Antarctic ecosystem.

The claim that the AOH may cause more extensive injury to animal and plant life was given a boost by reports of rabbits and sheep in Chile being blinded by high UV levels. Researchers at the University of California, however, conducted analyses of the eyes of blinded sheep and found the affliction to be the result of a common eye infection completely unrelated to ultraviolet light. "The sun angle is so low at the tip of South America, and the atmosphere is so cloudy and cold, that sunbathers freeze before they tan," writes Dr. Patrick J. Michaels. "Even the peak amount of daily radiation ever measured down there . . . was equivalent to the amount usually observed in Buenos Aires, a city of approximately 10 million sighted individuals."

If little or no damage to plant and animal life is occurring in Antarctica, where depletion of 50 percent of ozone each spring is routine and depletions of over 90 percent have been known to occur in the past, what basis is there for supposing that injury will result from the much lower levels of ozone depletion predicted for the middle latitudes? Very little indeed.

According to Dr. S. Fred Singer, the 5 percent decrease in ozone projected by the EPA to occur during the next fifty years "would increase UV exposure to the same extent as moving about sixty miles south, the distance from Palm Beach to Miami, or from Seattle to Tacoma. An increase in altitude of one thousand feet would produce the same result."

Ellsaesser expresses the same facts this way:

> The National Academy of Sciences (NAS) found that over the U.S. the doubling distance for skin cancer incidence is 8 to 11 degrees latitude, or roughly 600 miles. This means that skin cancer incidence increases roughly 1 percent for each 6 miles of displacement towards the equator. The NAS also concluded that a 1 percent decrease in the ozone layer was equivalent to a 2 percent increase in skin cancer incidence; that is, to a displacement of 12 miles toward the equator.

Few of us would worry about moving sixty miles south, yet the increase in UV exposure caused by such a move equals the total increase in UV exposure projected to result from CFC-caused ozone depletion during the next fifty years. This remarkably small "danger" propelled the U.S. to support an international ban on the production of CFCs.

■ CFCs are no longer a global threat.

There is one final issue concerning the ozone depletion theory that merits mention. In August 1993, NOAA researchers found that the initial phase of replacing CFCs had already resulted in a virtual halt in the growth of CFC-11 and CFC-12 concentrations in the atmosphere, as shown by the graphs on the following page. This accomplishment occurred much sooner than was expected by proponents of the CFC ban or by scientists working for industry. What happened?

Part of the answer appears to be that a natural mechanism for removing CFCs from the atmosphere exists after all. It is well known that CFCs are several times heavier than air, and that when spilled or leaked they tend to flow along the ground. Two scientists studying termite colonies reported in 1989 that soil microbes are capable of speedily

Growth Rate of CFC Concentrations in the Air

Researchers for the National Oceanic and Atmospheric Administration (NOAA) reported in August 1993 that the growth of CFC concentrations in the Earth's atmosphere has dramatically slowed. The slow-down is attributable in part to the early stages of the CFC phase-out. Natural processes, too, are likely to play a role in removing CFC concentrations from the atmosphere.

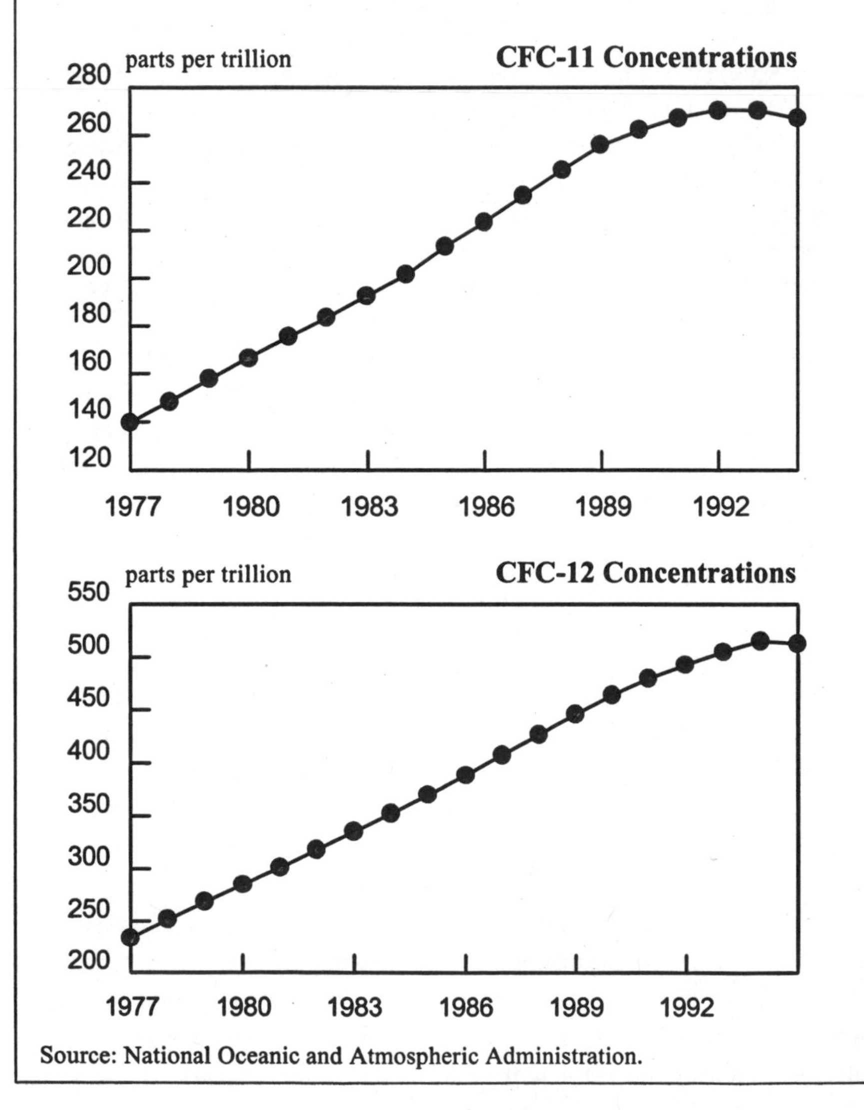

Source: National Oceanic and Atmospheric Administration.

destroying several kinds of CFCs, including that notorious ozone killer, CFC-12. Their work, reported in the *Journal of Geophysical Research* and other authoritative journals, suggests that the lifespan of CFCs in the atmosphere may be much less than the 100 years or more originally estimated. The existence of this natural "sink" would help explain the sudden stop in CFC accumulation in the atmosphere.

If, as seems unlikely, CFCs were ever a threat to the ozone layer or to plant and animal health, then the progress *already made* in halting their accumulation in the atmosphere makes the international ban on CFCs doubly unnecessary. It is not too late to avoid wasting hundreds of billions of dollars replacing CFCs in existing appliances and automobiles.

Conclusion

If ever the environmental movement abandoned common sense, it did so in its campaign against CFCs. If the Antarctic ozone hole was opening and closing each year *before* man-made CFCs were invented, then CFCs cannot be responsible for creating it. If the total amount of ozone in the upper atmosphere is not declining, and if UV levels at the Earth's surface are not rising, then something must be wrong with the ozone depletion theory.

Even if we grant the theory and evidence showing that CFCs cause ozone destruction, we still find that their contribution pales into insignificance when compared to natural variations caused by winds, temperatures, and solar radiation. And even if we grant one of the key predictions of the ozone depletion theory — that ground-level UV levels will rise by 10 percent during the next fifty years — we find the likely impact on plant and animal health to be negligible.

In short, ozone depletion is not an environmental crisis. The threat exists in the minds of many people only as a myth associated with aerosol cans, plastic containers, and the decidedly unscientific image of poisonous radiation raining down on the plants and animals of Antarctica. To the extent the environmental movement exploits these myths, it is engaging in tactics that may fairly be called unethical.

In addressing the possible threat of CFCs, the environmental movement ignored good science, relied on media hype and exaggeration, and made no effort to minimize the costs its actions would impose on others.

Far from representing a victory for the environmental movement, the ban on CFCs may represent the movement's most embarrassing moment.

March: Acid Rain

WHAT IS ACID RAIN?

Rain, snow, and fog that are relatively acidic are called acid precipitation, or more commonly, acid rain. Rain can be made acidic by lightning and other natural causes, and scientists have determined that rain that fell thousands of years ago was, at times, more acidic than rain today. But the contemporary debate concentrates on the degree to which man-made pollution causes rain to be more acidic than it otherwise would be. It is well established that mankind causes *some* acid rain: Emissions of sulfur dioxide and nitrogen oxides can be converted by exposure to bright sunshine into molecules of sulfates and nitrates, and these particles then interact with water vapor to form sulfuric or nitric acids, which return to Earth in rain, snow, or fog.

The original fear was that wind was carrying sulfates and nitrates many miles from their sources, and that their return to Earth in acid rain was killing wildlife and forests, endangering human health, and injuring crops. To some people, acid rain was a symbol of pollution and greed in the 1980s. Typical of such views was that of pop philosopher Fritjof Capra, expressed in his 1983 book, *The Turning Point*:

> [Coal-fired plants] . . . generate one of the most insidious and completely invisible forms of air pollution, acid rain. . . . Eastern New England, eastern Canada, and southern Scandinavia are heavily affected by this type of pollution. When acid rain falls on lakes it kills fish, insects, plants, and other forms of life; eventually the lakes die completely from acidity they can no longer neutralize. Thousands of lakes in Canada and Scandinavia are dead or dying already; entire fabrics of life that took thousands of years to evolve are rapidly disappearing. At the heart of the problem, as usual, lies ecological shortsightedness and corporate greed.

This image of environmental destruction remains deeply embedded in the minds of many Americans, even though extensive scientific research has failed to document even one of the assertions in this supposedly factual statement. Fear of acid rain helped to shape the enormously expensive Clean Air Act Amendments of 1990, legislation that economists predict will cost consumers an extra $29 billion to $39 billion a year in return for environmental benefits worth less than half as much.

Harm caused by acid rain

To find the truth about the many conflicting claims about damage caused by acid rain, Congress in 1980 authorized a ten-year, $500 million study of acid rain. The research effort, called the National Acid Precipitation Assessment Program (NAPAP), involved hundreds of scientists conducting extensive laboratory and field investigations around the country. In 1987, NAPAP issued an Interim Assessment, but release of the final report was delayed until after passage of the Clean Air Act Amendments of 1990.

The NAPAP final report, titled *Acidic Deposition: State of Science and Technology*, was finally published in four immense volumes in July 1990. An extraordinary research effort, the report examines every side and aspect of the acid rain problem. Specifically, the researchers found:

- **Acid rain has not injured forests in either the U.S. or Canada.**

"The popular notion that forests throughout the U.S. and Canada are in a state of decline due to 'acid rain' is contradicted by available scientific information," says the NAPAP report. It continues,

> The literature reviewed in this report indicates that most forests in the U.S. and Canada are apparently healthy and growing without obvious symptoms of unusual or pollutant-related stress. . . . Acidic deposition has not been shown to be a significant factor contributing to current forest health problems in North America, with the possible exception of spruce die-back and mortality at high elevations in the northern Appalachians.

In the case of red spruce, the researchers noted that "red spruce is a species which is known to be particularly prone to winter injury," and that foresters attributed much of the die-back to severe droughts and extensive winter damage in Vermont and New York during the 1960s. Significantly, NAPAP was unable to find any correlation between estimated levels of exposure to air pollution and any changes in the health or productivity of eastern forests.

■ **Acid rain has had no observable effect on human health.**

NAPAP searched both for direct and indirect effects of acid rain on human health. To evaluate the direct effects, it examined laboratory and epidemiologic studies of exposure to sulfur dioxide, nitrogen dioxide, and acidic aerosols. None of the three was found to pose a significant threat to human health at current levels of exposure.

Regarding sulfur dioxide, the NAPAP report concludes: "Current U.S. 24-hour and annual average air quality presents a small risk of adverse health effects from sulfur dioxide in all but a few limited areas," and "Given that the annual standard [i.e., the National Ambient Air Quality Standard (NAAQS)] is attained virtually everywhere in the U.S., the magnitude of the health risk from long-term sulfur dioxide exposures is relatively small in the U.S. today."

Regarding nitrogen dioxide, the NAPAP report reviews evidence showing that exposure of children to relatively high *indoor* levels of the gas (produced by gas stoves and heating units) has been associated with higher rates of infection, but no evidence exists of human injury at typical levels of *outdoor* exposure. "Because gas use or other indoor sources are a major determinant of peak nitrogen dioxide exposures," the report concludes, "reducing outdoor nitrogen dioxide levels is unlikely to significantly affect peak exposures for residents exposed to these indoor sources."

The NAPAP report expresses concern that evidence linking acidic aerosols to lung disease among children may be emerging, but

> given the inherent uncertainties in the studies and lack of acidic aerosol exposure information, the reported associations are quite uncertain. . . . In any case, any effects of sulfates or acidic aerosols are not readily separated from other pollutants at this time, such as ozone or general particulate matter, or from other nonpollutant factors that may influence the results.

NAPAP then asked whether acid rain might threaten human health indirectly by corroding exterior surfaces, in the process releasing into the air small amounts of copper, lead, asbestos, and other possibly hazardous materials. After an exhaustive survey of the literature, NAPAP concludes that "Incremental exposures to metals due to acid precipitation alone are not likely to be associated with any notable increased risk of human health effects, expect possibly for lead and mercury." They continue,

> Even assuming the most extreme plausible combinations of multiple exposure scenarios for any given individual (e.g., those persons with shallow wells and consuming large quantities of wild game or fish), the expected incremental levels of exposure estimated for metals other than lead and methylmercury would still be relatively negligible and not generally likely to cause exposures to reach or exceed concentrations associated with lowest observed adverse effects.

Lead and mercury are noted as exceptions because background levels for some groups are known to already be near or at levels where adverse effects occur. For such persons, even extremely small increases in exposure that would not generally be thought to endanger human health could produce an observable negative effect. Lead and mercury are known, too, as highly active chemicals that can cause sickness at very low levels. The possible hazard that acid rain poses to such vulnerable people is described in the NAPAP report as a hypothetical possibility requiring additional research.

■ Acid rain has not injured crops, and may even have a positive effect on some crops.

"Acute injury to vegetation as a result of exposure to present day levels of acidic deposition in North America are [sic] virtually unknown," write the authors of the NAPAP report. In fact, "acidic deposition appears to be beneficial to soil fertility, acting as a supplement to fertilizer by providing sulfur and nitrogen. Even when the cost of neutralizing by liming the acidity added by wet deposition is considered, it is likely that such deposition has a net benefit to the soil."

The NAPAP surveyed hundreds of studies of the effects of acid rain on common field crops, finding "no convincing evidence that there are effects of ambient levels of rain acidity on the yield of soybean or any other crop species that has been studied." At one point, the NAPAP authors approvingly quote a 1983 study that found "the effects of acid deposition on crops are minimal and . . . when a response occurs, it may be positive or negative."

- **Acid rain has acidified only a very small number of lakes, and these can be restored to health by liming.**

To study the effect of acid rain on lakes, NAPAP used data from the National Surface Water Survey (NSWS), a randomized systematic sample representing a population of 28,300 lakes in acid-sensitive regions in the U.S. The first task was to determine how many lakes were actually acidic, defined as having a pH level of 5.5 or less. (Acid lakes are frequently incapable of supporting fish populations, although their clarity and lack of leeches and algae make them popular swimming sites.) The results of the survey are shown in the table below.

The survey found many fewer acid lakes than expected in the Northeast, where acid rain was thought to be a serious problem, but many more

Acid Lakes in Acid-Sensitive Regions
(percent of lake surface area rated acidic)

Region	**pH <5.5**
Northeast	4%
Interior Southeast	0
Florida	24
Upper Midwest	<1
West	0
All National Surface Water Survey lakes	3%

Source: NAPAP, *Acidic Deposition: State of Science and Technology*, July 1990, Volume II, p. 9-340.

in Florida, where rainfall is much less acidic. In fact, half of the surface area of acid lakes in the U.S. was found to be in Florida. Regarding other parts of the country, NAPAP reported that "No acidic lakes were sampled in the Interior Southeast or Minnesota, and only one, a geothermal spring, was sampled in the West. Based on NSWS results and other studies, it appears that there are virtually no acidic lakes in these areas." Overall, only 3 percent of the total surface area of lakes in the U.S. was found to be relatively acidic.

NAPAP next attempted to determine whether the acidic lakes received their acidity from natural causes or from acid rain. Here, NAPAP reported great uncertainty regarding the role of acid rain. Many natural sources of acidification were reported, including: the natural acidity of forest soils; the absence in lake and river bottoms or in watersheds of minerals that would naturally buffer water; the complicated and highly variable role that forests and vegetation play in absorbing and releasing nitrogen, sulfur, and other chemicals; and the presence of chlorine ions from sea salts in areas near oceans. Various combinations of these natural sources of acidity explain why many lakes and rivers in the U.S. and around the world have been naturally acidic for hundreds of years, long before man-made emissions could have had any effect on them.

In addition to natural sources of acidity, NAPAP identified several ways human activity contributes to acidification of lakes *other than* by contributing to acid rain. Such activities include: draining peatlands, which causes rapid acidification by releasing the stored sulfur deposited on the soil over the course of many years; removing forests or in some cases replanting forests; and diverting water flows from streams or wetlands into downslope drainage ditches that prevent water from making close and repeated contact with soil, a process that would otherwise buffer the water.

The high number of acid lakes in Florida, where acid rain deposition is relatively low, testifies to the role of natural and human causes unrelated to acid rain. NAPAP estimated that 38 percent of Florida's acid lakes draw their acidity primarily from peaty soil and an absence of erodible minerals in river and lake beds to serve as natural buffering agents. Additional acidity is produced by sea salt spray, which is carried by winds to all parts of the Florida peninsula. It further seems likely that the extensive and rapid development occurring in Florida has caused some peat bogs to release their sulfur loads, and has changed the flow of water in ways that reduce the amount of natural buffering that otherwise would take place.

While Florida's acid lakes can be explained without evoking man-made acid rain, the causes of acidity in Northeast lakes is less clear. Dr. Edward Krug, a soil scientist with the Illinois State Water Survey at the time of the NAPAP study, has been a prominent advocate of the view that natural causes of acidity in lakes overwhelm human causes even in the Northeast, but his views are controversial. NAPAP confirms the science and reasoning behind the research of Krug and others who share his views, but cautions that "it is difficult to determine how many systems those studies represent."

Krug has studied lakes in the Adirondack region of the Northeast, where NAPAP found some 10 percent of all lakes to be highly acidic. The sediments of many such lakes, Krug says, "reveal that high-altitude Adirondack lakes, including Lake Colden and Woods Lake, have been fishless for most of their history. They also reveal that these lakes temporarily lost some of their *natural* acidity during the mid-to-late 19th and early 20th centuries — and during this period were filled with fish." The causes of the natural acidity were pine needles and peat moss on the lakes' banks and nearby watersheds, and the relative scarcity of lime-like substances in the lake bottoms. The lakes lost their natural acidity for short periods of time because ashes produced by slash-and-burn logging in the area reduced the acidity of run-off water entering the lake.

"These findings are consistent with what we know from history," continues Krug. "The Indians never lived in the Adirondacks. The Iroquois word 'Adirondack' means 'bark eater,' telling us that the food supply, including fish, was never plentiful."

The natural acidity of many of the lakes in the Adirondacks poses a dilemma for environmentalists. Adding lime to these lakes could lower their acid levels to where they could sustain populations of fish. This would *not*, however, return these lakes to their natural state, since for hundreds of years these lakes have been highly acidic and without fish due entirely to natural causes. Our intervention would not reverse the effects of human pollution, but reverse instead a *natural* process that has failed to produce a result — sustainable fish populations — that some environmentalists mistakenly identify with unspoiled nature.

For under $500,000 a year, the acidity of every acid lake in the Northeast could be reduced to levels that would support fish populations, simply by adding lime to lakes and rivers in the area. NAPAP included in its report a half-dozen case studies of where lime was added to lakes from airplanes or by dumping slurry solutions from shore, with apparently beneficial effects on fish and plant life. If our goal is to make these lakes suitable for fishing, then liming the lakes is a much more cost-effective approach than spending billions of dollars reducing sulfur and nitrogen dioxide emissions.

Conclusion

In the scientific community, the NAPAP findings are accepted as authoritative. But the environmental movement, having sold acid rain as an *urgent* problem requiring your *immediate* financial contribution, chooses simply to ignore the study. The acid rain provisions of the Clean Air Act Amendments will add billions of dollars a year to the utility bills of homeowners and businesses, yet the benefits in terms of environmental protection and human health will be negligible.

The story of acid rain demonstrates a painful truth about the modern environmental movement: Too often, *good science simply doesn't matter*. According to one insider interviewed on *60 Minutes* in 1990, "The environmental community has spent almost no effort attempting to even monitor the progress [of NAPAP]. . . . We have been working on trying to get legislation in Washington." Politicians, under heavy pressure from media and the environmental lobby, also chose to ignore the NAPAP report. The U.S. Senate spent just *one hour* discussing the report for which it spent $500 million in taxpayers' money. Incredibly, the report was never even presented to the House of Representatives.

Senator John Glenn (D-Ohio) scolded his colleagues with words that could have been directed to the environmental movement as well:

> We spend over $500 million on the most definitive study of acid precipitation that has ever been done in the history of the world and then we do not want to listen to what [the experts] say.

The NAPAP study, to summarize, found that claims of the destructive effects of acid rain are much exaggerated. *Acid rain poses little or no threat to forests, crops, human health, or lakes.* Once again, billions of dollars are wasted battling a problem that doesn't exist.

April: Deforestation

In Chapter Two we reported that net tree growth in the U.S. is consistently outpacing tree harvests, resulting in a steady increase in both the number of wooded acres in the U.S. and annual tree growth. We explained that forestry in the U.S. and other developed countries is now conducted on a *sustainable yield basis*, with a growing share of lumber and wood pulp coming from commercial forests planted and maintained expressly for these purposes.

In parts of Africa, Asia, and South America, however, forestry is not yet conducted on a sustainable yield basis. On these continents, trees are being cleared for cattle ranches and crops or harvested for lumber and firewood at rates that are not sustainable. Ecologically sensitive areas, particularly *rainforests* on all three continents, have been damaged, often permanently, by these practices. Because rainforests absorb carbon dioxide (and release it when they are burned) and are home to uncounted but enormous numbers of bird, insect, and wildlife species, rapid deforestation would pose a global ecological threat.

Forestry in temperate regions

During the past fifty years there has been very little net change in the total wooded area of the world's temperate regions — Europe, North America, and parts of Asia — which together account for approximately half the wooded area of the world. This is true despite a dramatic growth in the amount of wood taken from temperate forests, testimony to the success of plantation forests and sustainable yield forestry techniques.

Sustainable yield forestry requires planning, proper harvesting techniques, and reforestation follow-up. Canadian Pulp and Paper Industry and the American Forest and Paper Association, the two leading trade associations for the forest products industry in North America, have established Principles for Forest Management that attempt to codify these policies and achieve voluntary compliance by members.

Claims have been made that deforestation is taking place in the temperate forests of Canada, but this appears to be a problem only of the past. Tough policies are now in place to prevent deforestation. "Over 50 percent, or about 225,000,000 hectares of Canada's land area are still covered with the original forest. This is an area five times the entire country of Sweden," says Dr. Patrick Moore, a founder and director of Greenpeace. "In British Columbia, the Forest Alliance has developed 21 Principles of Sustainable Forestry and these have been adopted by all the major forestry companies."

British Columbia Forests Minister Dan Miller said in 1993, "We have a law requiring that every area harvested is replanted, and it's followed to the letter." Extensive research by the British Columbia Ministry of Forests shows that Canada's second-growth forests support tree species diversity as high or higher than existed in the old growth forests they replace. Continuous improvement in forestry methods ensures that Canadian forests will be protected in the future.

Deforestation in tropical regions — how much?

So how much deforestation is taking place? Roger A. Sedjo and Marion Clawson of Resources for the Future, writing in 1984, estimated that the rate of tropical deforestation during the second half of the 1970s was 11.3 million hectares per year* — just 0.58 percent of the area of tropical forests worldwide. In 1992, the United Nations' Food and Agriculture Organization estimated that the annual rate of tropical deforestation was approximately 17 million hectares — still less than 1 percent of the area of tropical forests worldwide.

Importantly, even these small numbers overstate the deforestation problem. As Sedjo and Clawson reported, "undisturbed or 'virgin' broadleaved closed forests have a lower rate of deforestation than the total, being only 0.27 percent annually as compared with 2.06 percent annually for logged-over secondary forests." They concluded:

> This figure indicates that deforestation pressure on the more pristine and generally more genetically diverse tropical forests is quite low. These findings are in sharp contrast to the conventional view that the tropical forests "are disappearing at alarming rates," and suggest that concerns over the imminent loss of some of the most important residences of the world's diverse genetic base, based on rates of tropical deforestation, are probably grossly exaggerated.

---

*A hectare is the metric equivalent of 2.471 acres.

An example of "grossly exaggerating" the deforestation problem is found in *The Rainforest Book*, published by the Natural Resources Defense Council (NRDC) in 1990. At one point, the book's author tells us:

> Already, half the Earth's tropical forests have been burned, bulldozed, and obliterated. The rest are being wiped out at a shocking rate of 35.2 million acres a year. That's 67 acres a minute — a football field a second. If this pace continues, most of the rainforests will be gone before the end of the century.
>
> As the forests are destroyed, so are the myriad species that depend on them for survival. Recent studies estimate that tropical deforestation wipes out 17,000 species of plants and animals per year — species that exist nowhere else. That's about 48 species made extinct every day, or 2 an hour.

The "shocking rate" of 35.2 million acres a year equals about 14 million hectares a year — about three-quarters of 1 percent of the area of tropical forests. Moreover, the author says, but then appears to forget, that this estimate was the suspected rate of deforestation for *all* tropical forests, not just the more ecologically sensitive rainforests. Finally, the author makes no attempt to distinguish between deforestation of *virgin* forests versus second-growth forests. In other words, there is no way that the author's reported rate of deforestation could have led to the destruction of "most of the rainforests" by the end of the century, or even the end of the next century.

Today, we know that even the 1984 Sedjo/Clawson deforestation estimate, 11.3 million hectares per year, was too high. David Skole, an ecologist at the University of New Hampshire, and Compton Tucker of NASA examined in 1993 satellite photos of the Amazon rainforest to determine how much deforestation occurred between 1978 and 1988. After painstakingly examining 210 such photos, they concluded that the average rate of rainforest loss was 3.7 millon acres (just 1.5 million hectares) per year. If deforestation in Brazil accounted for half of all rainforest deforestation in the world, as is generally assumed, then the new estimate means the *global rate of rainforest deforestation was just 3 million hectares per year* during much of the 1980s. As a percentage of existing rainforests, the annual loss was less than a tenth of 1 percent.

How could so great an error in measurement have occurred? Original estimates of deforestation rates, such as Norman Myers' 1980 estimate of 20 to 24 million hectares, were little more than guesses based on a small number of case studies. Later estimates relied on the work of a researcher who used satellite data to count the number of fires burning in the Amazon at one time in 1988, at the very height of government-subsidized deforestation in that country (more about this later). The researcher guessed at the number of acres being cleared by each fire, then assumed that 40 percent would never return to their forested condition, and finally doubled this number to arrive at an estimate of global deforestation. Incredibly, this was the "science" behind a widely publicized 1990 report by the World Resources Institute; this "science" also led Vice President Al Gore to declare U.S. support for a Biodiversity Treaty being considered at the 1992 Earth Summit.

Tropical deforestation and species extinction

Deforestation in tropical regions, while not taking place at "shocking rates," nevertheless poses problems that merit environmentalists' concern. First, tropical forests that have been cleared do not recover as easily as do forests in temperate regions. In the tropics, high levels of heat and humidity cause rapid plant growth, and organic material quickly biodegrades. As a consequence, most available nutrients are in use at any given time, contained in growing plants rather than stored in the soil. Nutrients return to the soil when a plant sheds leaves or dies, but they are quickly taken up again by another living plant. When the protective canopy of a tropical forest is removed by clearing or burning, the nutrients, too, are removed. The soil is almost immediately exhausted of the few nutrients it has stored, and then it is baked by intense sunshine and eroded by heavy tropical rainfall. As a result, natural recovery after clear-cutting or "slash-and-burn" agriculture in the tropics occurs very slowly or not at all.

Secondly, if tropical deforestation were occurring on a large scale, it could have devastating effects on thousands and possibly millions of species of insects, plants, and animals. The delicate ecology of the rainforest, in particular, is easily disrupted by slash-and-burn clearing. As many as 50 percent of all the species on Earth are thought to reside in moist tropical forests (although this is only a guess). Some evidence suggests that many species have extremely limited ranges, perhaps measured in acres; thus the destruction of even a small plot of rainforest might result in the extinction of several animal and plant species.

There is enough truth in this popular view of tropical deforestation to alarm us greatly when it occurs. In a moment we will discuss why deforestation takes place and what can be done to prevent it. But first, we need to confront once again the exaggeration and false fears cultivated by some environmentalists, this time regarding the degree to which species are being made extinct by the deforestation taking place today.

The best estimate we have of rainforest deforestation — the Skole and Tucker work reported above — suggests that deforestation is destroying less than one-tenth of 1 percent of global rainforests each year. It is difficult to imagine how this rate of deforestation could "wipe out 17,000 species of plants and animals per year," as the NRDC claimed. And indeed, Julian Simon and Aaron Wildavsky, among others, have commented on how such estimates are derived from little more than guesswork and pure speculation.

Estimates that thousands of species are being driven to extinction each year can usually be traced to one of two sources: Dr. Norman Myers, a British ecologist who in 1978 predicted the loss of one million species by the year 2000; and Dr. Edward O. Wilson, a Harvard biologist who variously claims that 4,000, 30,000, or 50,000 species are lost each year.

The Myers claim was pure speculation, put forth without documentation or even some explanation of the theory he might have used to arrive at the number. Simon and Wildavsky attempted to follow his reasoning:

> Observe that an upper limit for the present [rate of species extinction] that is pure guesswork, and that is 100 times the observed rate in the recent past, has become the basis for a forecast for the future, which is 40,000 times greater than at present, and which has been published in newspapers to be read by tens or hundreds of millions of people and understood as a scientific statement.

Wilson bases his claim on a supposed relationship between the area of tropical forests and the number of species they can support. The asserted relationship is much disputed among ecologists and wildlife experts, however, and has been found to have little or no predictive value. For example, Brazilian zoologists have been unable to identify a single species that was made extinct by the massive deforestation of Brazil's coastal forest. "Despite extensive inquiries," says Dr. Vernon Haywood, former chief scientist of the World Conservation Union, "We have been unable to obtain conclusive evidence to support the suggestion that massive extinctions have taken place in recent times."

The potential for tropical species extinction is troubling, even if it may not occur on as large a scale as predicted by Myers or Wilson. Rather than further dispute the extent of the problem, we would prefer to focus on finding a solution to deforestation.

Why deforestation occurs in tropical areas

Approximately 80 percent of the deforestation taking place in tropical areas is the result of clearing land for agricultural use. The wood that results from such activity is generally burned during the clearing process, or used for cooking or construction of local housing. Wood for the production of paper is no longer taken from natural rainforests. Instead, it is taken from eucalyptus plantations planted and harvested especially for paper production. (See the sidebar on the following page.) Hardwood logs are still harvested from the rainforest, however, and to a small but important extent this contributes to deforestation.

In the past, considerable deforestation of tropical regions occurred because little value was placed on conservation, property rights were ill-defined, and replanting and sustainable yield forestry were unaffordable. The day-to-day struggle for survival was the most real and pressing concern for generations of lumberjacks, sailors, and dockhands. For over a century, the tropical forests were thought to be a limitless supply of forest products from which hard-working men and women could derive a living. The idea that this supply of trees might one day run out, or that paychecks should be reduced to set aside funds to plant more trees or protect endangered wildlife, would have been considered ludicrous — like worrying about the supply of sand on beaches.

Thanks in part to rising levels of prosperity, and thanks once again to the environmental movement, attitudes toward the rainforests changed dramatically during the 1960s and 1970s. Today, the greatest barrier to the adoption of sustainable yield forestry in tropical regions is not the "greed" of Western corporations but a dramatic social and economic upheaval taking place in many of the world's developing countries. West Africa, in particular, is besieged by war, massive migration to cities, tribalism, drugs, AIDS, and government corruption. The result is acute

Bringing Sustainable Yield Forestry to the Tropics

Increasingly, lumber and pulp are taken from plantation forests, where trees are planted specifically to be harvested at a later date. Plantations can yield up to thirty times more usable wood per acre than natural forests, enabling the world's wood fiber needs to be met without logging ecologically sensitive areas. Some experts predict that by the year 2000, more than half of all industrial wood production in Latin America will come from plantation forests. Already, such forests account for 20 percent of the world's industrial wood.

Plantation forests using fast-growing eucalyptus trees have recovered hundreds of thousands of acres of land in the tropics that once were severely degraded. Such forests demonstrate that sustainable yield forestry techniques can work even under the difficult conditions present in tropical regions.

Aracruz Celulose, a wood pulp producer operating in southeastern Brazil, has planted eucalyptus trees on 326,000 acres of formerly devastated land along the coast of the Brazilian state of Espirito Santo. The company plants an average of *100,000 trees per day*, using its own "bank" of 100 different eucalyptus clones.

Besides planting eucalyptus trees on its own plantation, Aracruz reports that it has planted *1.5 million native trees* and distributes a remarkable *9 million* free eucalyptus seedlings to local farmers every year. For every 2.4 acres of eucalyptus plantation it plants, the company preserves one acre of natural forest. The preserved areas are strategically positioned within the plantation to create migration trails for animals and birds, thereby minimizing the impact of the plantation on wildlife.

Thanks in part to companies like Aracruz Celulose, virtually all wood pulp (used for making paper) produced in Brazil now comes from plantation forests, not from natural rainforests. Eucalyptus plantations are, admittedly, imperfect substitutes for the rich diversity of the rainforests, but the fact of the matter is that they are not *replacing* rainforests, but instead are being used to *reclaim* land that is often severely eroded and abandoned. Eucalyptus plantations prevent soil erosion and provide suitable habitat for many forms of rainforest wildlife.

Sources: Roger Sedjo and Marion Clawson, in Julian L. Simon and Herman Kahn, *The Resourceful Earth*; Christina Lamb, "Chopping Down Rainforest Myths," *Financial Times*, January 8, 1992; and information provided by Aracruz Celulose.

poverty and an increasingly desperate search for food, firewood, and shelter. Hundreds of millions of people rely on a form of "cut and run" forestry: A section of rainforest is cleared, the thin soil is used for a few years to grow crops or run cattle, and then, when the soil is exhausted, the cycle begins again with the clearing of a new section of rainforest.

Because property rights cannot be enforced in the present state of lawlessness that pervades Western Africa, no one has the motive or the ability to protect wooded areas for later harvest or other less-immediate uses. The current incentive structure encourages just the opposite sort of behavior: Exploit every natural resource as rapidly as possible, with little or no regard for the effects on others or on future generations. In the absence of secure property rights, one person's delay is another person's opportunity to exploit the resource first. Payment for the right to use a resource is a wasted and costly gesture, since no one has legal recourse against anyone else even if property rights are flagrantly violated.

While social and economic chaos explains much of the deforestation of African nations, slash-and-burn forestry has taken place in South America — especially Brazil — for a different reason: Government policies once rewarded, and even *required*, the practice. Before 1989, tax credits, subsidies, and inexpensive loans were given to people who carved farms out of the Amazon rainforest. Laws required owners to clear their properties in order to receive title to the land, encouraging property owners to clear much greater areas than they expected to farm. Moreover, raging inflation in Brazil made land a good investment; as a result, millions of acres were purchased and cleared even though the inability of the land's soil to sustain agriculture for more than a few seasons was well known.

Many of these policies have been repealed or reformed since 1989, and inflation has slowed. The rate of deforestation in Brazil thus has fallen dramatically. Overall, the damage to the mighty Amazon rainforest was not great: Even the usually panic-stricken Worldwatch Institute reported in 1992 that "with nearly 90 percent of its groves still standing, by national or international standards the Brazilian Amazon is relatively untouched."

In summary, the causes of deforestation today are much different than a century ago, or even twenty years ago. The transformation to sustainable yield forestry is underway, featuring eucalyptus plantations and better management of remaining natural forests. The greatest barriers to this successful transformation, more significant even than the climate and poor soil, are the cultural and economic dislocations occurring in the developing countries that host the planet's rainforests. In the grip of wars and economic collapse, even the most conscientious consumer or businessperson may be forced to use natural resources unwisely, or to exploit a precious community asset before someone else does. The only way we in the West can protect the rainforests, then, is by helping to end the social and economic conflicts that plague these nations, and by trying as best we can to hold ourselves and the businesses that hail from our countries to high environmental standards.

Conclusion

Let us state plainly that deforestation *is* taking place in some parts of the world, and it *is* resulting in the extinction of some plant and animal species. Some of the deforestation is unquestionably thoughtless and unnecessary . . . but stopping it may not be within our power. We can, however, take comfort in the knowledge that deforestation is less serious a problem than was once thought: Current rates of deforestation are not likely to destroy more than a barely perceptible fraction of the Earth's remaining rainforests.

We concur with Roger Sedjo and Marion Clawson, who concluded their analysis of global forests in 1984 with these words:

> . . . [W]hile the local effects of the rapid deforestation may be severe, the evidence does not support the view that either the world or the tropics are experiencing rapid aggregate deforestation. Furthermore, the evidence shows that current rates of deforestation are quite modest in much of the world's virgin tropical forests, for example, those of the Amazon (Brazil); and therefore they are probably in little danger of wholesale destruction in the foreseeable future.

May: Pesticides

Rachel Carson called them "chemical death rain." Lewis Regenstein called them "the most potent cancer-causing chemicals known to man." As recently as 1992, Worldwatch Institute president Lester Brown was still predicting they would cause a world-wide cancer epidemic.

When use of synthetic pesticides expanded rapidly during the 1940s, 1950s, and 1960s, there was good reason to be concerned about their potential effects on human health and the environment. Many of these new chemicals had not been thoroughly tested for their long-term effects on humans. To have remained silent about them would have been like burying our heads in the sand and ignoring a potentially major new risk. Rachel Carson, Barry Commoner, and others rightly called for a thorough evaluation of the effects of pesticides.

Today, an objective assessment produces a mixed picture. On the one hand, environmentalists were proven right about the effects of some pesticides on eagles, hawks, and other birds of prey. The dramatic fall in raptor populations during the 1960s and 1970s is now generally believed to have been caused, at least in part, by several specific pesticides. The continued presence of DDT and other persistent pesticides in lakes, rivers, and coastal waters has negative effects on some fish and raptor populations even today, many years after the use of such substances was banned in the U.S.

On the other hand, claims that *all* pesticides are persistent or highly toxic have been found to be wrong, as have claims that pesticides pose a serious threat to human health. Indeed, the use of pesticides in some countries has dramatically *improved* human health, and has also indirectly benefited many forms of wildlife by reducing the acreage that would otherwise have been cleared for farming.

Pesticides and wildlife

There is now little doubt that some pesticides — including DDT, dieldrin, chlordane, and toxaphene — have hurt wildlife. Although these substances are now banned in the U.S., they continue to be detected in small amounts in coastal waters, lakes, and rivers. These pesticides share several traits that make them especially threatening to wildlife. They are *persistent*, meaning they resist biodegradation and can remain in water or lake sediment for many years after their initial use. They are also *toxic* to many kinds of wildlife at relatively low doses. Finally, these pesticides tend to be stored in animal fat, meaning predators high on the food chain (such as eagles) get heavier doses than do animals (such as fish) that are lower on the food chain. This process is called *bioaccumulation*.

While it is now common to blame pesticides alone for the loss of some bird and fish populations between 1940 and 1970, in fact pesticides were only one of several factors at work, and they may not have been the most important. The populations of many raptors, including eagles and peregrine falcons, were falling steadily during the decades *before* synthetic pesticides were widely used. Causes included bounties on eagles, paid by state governments such as Alaska and not repealed until 1952; rapid loss of habitat in the Northeast; mercury, PCB, and lead poisoning; and aggressive hunting and egg collecting. Generally forgotten now is the fact that many conservationists killed raptors and destroyed their nests because they preyed on the more popular song birds. (See sidebar on this page.)

The Story of Hawk Mountain

During the 1920s and 1930s, killing hawks, falcons, and eagles was considered good sport even by conservationists, who believed doing so helped protect song birds. The government of Pennsylvania paid a bounty for dead hawks because hawks killed farmers' chickens.

Hawk Mountain, located in the Appalachian Mountains in eastern Pennsylvania, was an especially popular place among hunters. Huge flocks of hawks and eagles passed over the mountain each Autumn during their migration south; at times, hundreds and even thousands of birds were shot down in *a single day*. Each year, that is, until 1934, when Rosalie Edge purchased Hawk Mountain for $3,500 and strictly prohibited hunting. Government officials and even the conservationists of the time thought she was crazy to stand up for the raptors, but there was little they could do to stop her.

Over the years, the Hawk Mountain Sanctuary has probably saved more hawks, falcons, and eagles than any piece of legislation. It is not unlikely that several avian species would have disappeared from North America if not for the protection of this crucial point in their migration path. Today, the Hawk Mountain Sanctuary Association stands as a remarkable testimony to the role of private action in protecting rare and endangered species.

Source: Robert J. Smith, "Private Solutions to Conservation Problems," in Tyler Cowen, *The Theory of Market Failure: A Critical Examination*, pp. 358-359.

Pesticides, too, played a role in the decline of raptor populations. Dieldrin is now known to have killed adult birds, including peregrine falcons, eagles, and owls, during the years from 1946 to 1964. DDT and its derivative, DDE, are believed to have slowed reproduction rates for many of the same species during the 1960s and 1970s by causing the thinning of egg shells. The two pesticides combined to keep raptor populations from recovering, even after hunting and other threats diminished. The decision to ban general use in the U.S. of DDT, along with other pesticides that also were persistent and toxic to wildlife, appears to have been merited on environmental grounds.

Thanks to the bans and to conservation efforts, some raptor populations are recovering. Bald eagle populations have increased from 417 nesting pairs in 1963 to 3,000 in 1992, leading the U.S. Fish and Wildlife Service to propose changing their protected status from "endangered" to "threatened." Peregrine falcon populations have grown rapidly, making their recovery in eastern North America, in the words of wildlife experts, "one of the most striking of the recent success stories in conservation." This accomplishment, they add, "would have failed had environmental levels of DDE been too high to permit successful breeding in the wild. Such is still the case in Central California, where DDE levels are high and shell thinning exceeds critical levels."

Evidence that persistent, toxic, and bioaccumulative pesticides are gradually being removed from the environment is found in the Great Lakes region, which was especially hard-hit by pesticides during the 1960s and 1970s. Levels of DDE and dieldrin in starlings, coho salmon, and freshwater fish all show dramatic rates of decline since the mid-1970s or, in the case of coho salmon, since records began to be kept in 1980. The chart on the following page depicts the striking fall in DDE levels in herring gull eggs since 1974.

Unfortunately, the persistent nature of these pesticides means small amounts of contamination will continue to exist, probably for decades to come. For example, ocean sediments off the coast of Los Angeles contain on the order of 200 tons of DDT. The pesticide will continue to make its way into the region's food chain, harming a variety of marine fish, birds, and mammals.

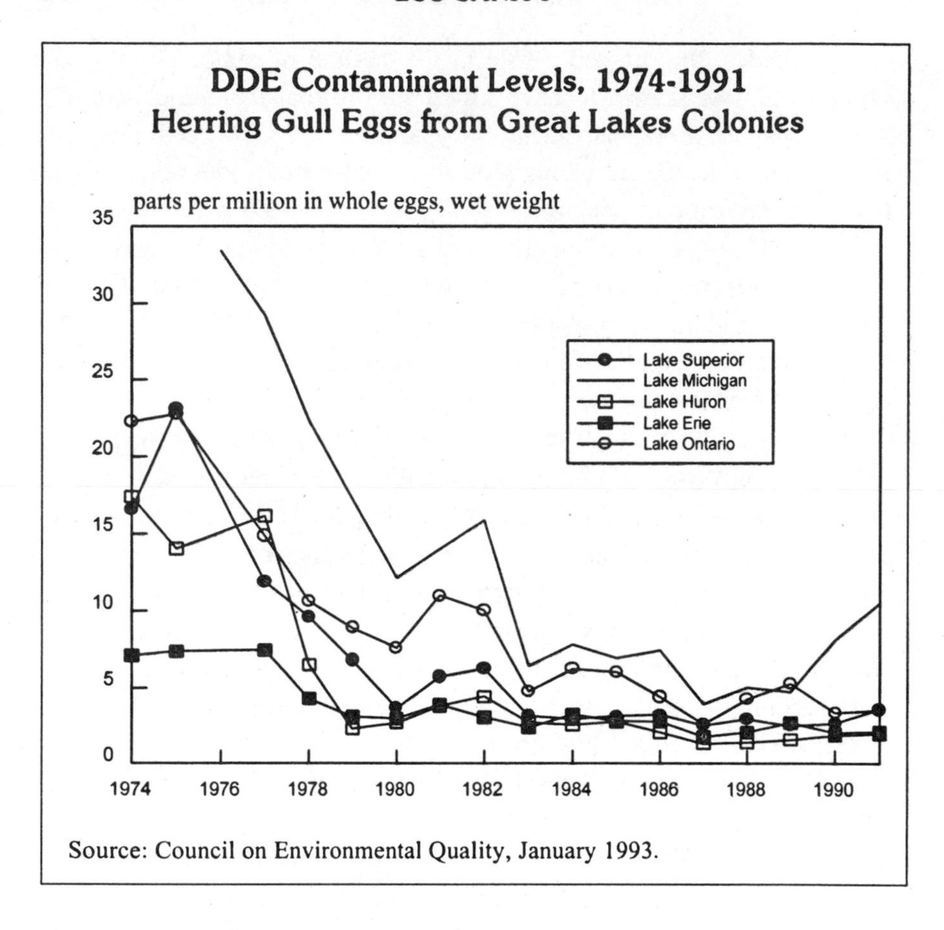

Source: Council on Environmental Quality, January 1993.

Risk of future injury to wildlife

The negative effects of pesticides on wildlife were the result of a small number of now-banned pesticides that were persistent and highly toxic, and tended to bioaccumulate. These pesticides, in particular DDT, were often applied to fields and lawns in excessive amounts and without regard for the effect of run-off into neighboring streams or lakes. Simple ignorance of the injury being caused to wildlife, and the very low cost of the pesticides involved (DDT cost just 15 cents a pound in 1969), explain this neglect.

After the ban of DDT in 1972, significant changes took place both in the chemistry of pesticides and in their use. Highly persistent and toxic pesticides have been replaced with compounds that have shorter lifespans and more limited biological effects. According to Dr. George Werezak, director of environment, health, and safety for Dow Chemical Canada and a member of the Virtual Elimination Task Force of the International Joint Commission, none of the pesticides in current use is thought to have adverse effects on wildlife at current levels of use. In a 1993 report to the Commission, Werezak wrote:

> Studies on chlorinated compounds presently in use indicate that at concentrations detected in the environment, wildlife and human exposures are far below those exposures noted in animal studies to produce toxic effects. . . . Any adverse effects noted in wildlife in the Great Lakes region have been associated with a limited subset of chlorinated compounds, such as PCBs, DDT and several other cancelled pesticides. The distribution of these chemicals in the environment was due to their historical use or unintended generation. No such adverse effects have been reported for the chlorinated alkanes, alkenes, or lower chlorinated monoaromatics, nor would any be expected based on their inherent toxicity, fate and partitioning in the environment. The toxicological effects observed in some wildlife relate to past exposures to select chlorinated compounds. This pattern is not reflective of use patterns or environmental loading rates of chlorinated compounds in use in the Great Lakes region today.

Patterns of pesticide use also have changed since the 1960s. Overall use of pesticides in the U.S. is falling and is, by international standards, now quite low. The U.S. uses just one-third as much pesticide per acre of farmland as does the European Community, for example. Japan uses up to 24 times as much pesticide per acre as does the U.S. Farmers are now alert to the dangers of run-off, and they use planting and tilling patterns that help prevent pesticides from reaching waterways. Farmers also typically use integrated pest control techniques, including crop rotation, naturally resistent crop strains, and natural pest predators such as "ladybugs" and praying mantises. Finally, a wider variety of short-lived pesticides is now available; many are designed to attack only a particular pest and minimize collateral injury to other creatures.

While it will take decades for the last traces of DDT and other long-lived pesticides to be removed from the environment, it appears that important lessons have been learned and past mistakes are not being repeated. What injury to wildlife may have been caused by pesticides in the past was the result of a small number of especially toxic and persistent chemicals that are no longer used in the U.S. The responsible use of newer, less toxic, and less persistent pesticides does not pose a significant threat to wildlife.

Pesticides and cancer

Since pesticides are poisonous to insects and have been known to kill fish and birds, we are right to worry about their effects on our own health. Originally, attention was focused on the possibility that pesticide residues were causing an increase in cancer rates. For a number of reasons, we now know that this risk is very small.

- The Food and Drug Administration (FDA), which tests foods to ensure that pesticide residues do not exceed federal standards, uses a World Health Organization measurement of Acceptable Daily Intake (ADI) that assumes humans are 10 times more sensitive than the most sensitive animal tested, and that some humans are 10 times more sensitive than the average human population. In other words, the FDA standard is set 100 times lower than the lowest amount known to cause tumors in laboratory mice.

- Dr. Sandra Archibald of the Stanford University Food Research Institute, and Dr. Carl Winter of the University of California - Riverside, have compared FDA measurements of likely levels of consumption of specific pesticide residues with ADI levels for each substance. They found that actual consumption only rarely rises above 1 percent of ADI and is often less than a hundredth of 1 percent.

- The EPA estimates that the risk of cancer from ingesting pesticide residues is about three in one million. A risk this low is indistinguishable from no risk at all.

- To arrive at its risk assessment, the EPA assumes that every food item being tested is consumed daily for 70 years, and that every food item has the maximum allowed amount of residues — although less than 1 percent of foods actually have this much. Dr. Richard Hill, who in 1989 was science advisor to the EPA's assistant administrator for pesticides and toxic substances, said at the time that this policy overstated pesticide risks by a factor of between 10,000 and 100,000.

- If the EPA risk assessment — about three in one million — is adjusted downward by a factor of just 2,000, as is recommended by Archibald and Winter (and is significantly less than the overstatement of risk according to Richard Hill), a more accurate risk estimate is produced of 0.0015 in one million, or 1.5 in one *billion.*

Dr. James Wells, of the California Department of Food and Agriculture, said in 1989: "Pesticide residues present negligible risks to the consumer because the dose isn't there. This is a principle of toxicology: The dose makes the poison. If you're not exposed to something, it can't cause you any harm."

Epidemiologists Sir Richard Doll and Dr. Richard Peto, whose work is reported in Chapters 2 and 3, found that pesticides contribute so little to our cancer risk that they do not merit even a token risk factor. Also in those chapters, we described how Dr. Bruce Ames, a biochemist, found that naturally occurring pesticides (found even in organically grown food) are present in the human diet in concentrations *10,000 times greater* than man-made pesticides.

Most cancer rates in the U.S. have *not* increased since the widespread use of pesticides began, directly contradicting many predictions made by pesticides' critics. In fact, cancer rates for the under-65 population have actually fallen. To this mountain of evidence, and at the risk of appearing to be "piling on," we add three more expert opinions:

- "Consumer advocates, however well intentioned, continue to tell us that dangerous, cancer-causing pesticides are present in our food and that we and our children are at extreme risk. *This is simply not true.* There is no food safety crisis. While some pesticides are known to have caused tumors in laboratory animals when exposure occurs in concentrated doses, the residues which may be present on some foods occur at such minute levels that they present no risk of harm to human health. . . . Indeed, U.S. food supplies contain less than one quarter of one percent of the allowable intake of pesticides."

  Dr. C. Everett Koop
  former Surgeon General of the United States

- "The risk of pesticide residues to consumers is effectively zero. This is what some fourteen scientific societies representing over 100,000 microbiologists, toxicologists and food scientists said at the time of the ridiculous Alar scare. But we were ignored."

Dr. Sanford Miller
Dean of the Graduate School of Biomedical Sciences
University of Texas at San Antonio

- "I don't know of any evidence that one person in the United States has ever been injured by consuming food treated with pesticide residues. Not a single person."

Dr. Robert Hollingsworth, Director
Michigan State University Pesticide Research Center

The conclusion is difficult to miss: Pesticides don't cause cancer. On this score, the predictions of many leading environmentalists of the 1960s and 1970s were wrong.

Pesticides and other illnesses

Denied their cancer scare by scientific research, some critics of pesticides have attempted to show other possible health effects. Particular attention has focused on possible effects on the human immune and endocrine (hormone) systems and possible *in utero* injury to the unborn. These hazards are hypothesized because of observed reactions of laboratory animals, aquatic animals, and wildlife to mixtures of toxic substances, including (but not limited to) pesticides.

As we are writing this book, convincing evidence that such harms are occurring is missing. An often-mentioned study of the offspring of women who regularly ate fish from the Great Lakes has been heavily criticized by scholars for its small sample size, questionable data-gathering techniques, and failure to adequately control for confounding factors. Since the fish that were eaten presumably contained traces of mercury, PCBs, lead, and other contaminants, this study sheds very little light on the health effects of *pesticides* even if its findings are supported by future researchers. Finally, such a study might at best illustrate the health effects of remaining traces of banned pesticides. Such information reveals little about newer, shorter-lived, and less-toxic pesticides.

Whether pesticides might have subtle effects on human health is only an hypothesis. At the end of this chapter we will revisit the broader questions of whether toxic chemicals and hazardous wastes are having such effects, and what would constitute sufficient proof of these effects.

How necessary are pesticides?

By making it possible to produce more food per acre of land under cultivation, pesticides have saved millions of acres of wilderness in the U.S. and around the world. "Had our country tried to achieve the 1980 [food] production employing the yield and technology of 1940, it would have required the cultivation of an additional 437 million acres of land," says Dr. Norman E. Borlaug. This is an enormous area, larger than the entire land area of the U.S. east of the Mississippi River. Borlaug further estimates that such an expansion of cultivated lands would have required that over 60 percent of all the forests and woodlands in the U.S. be converted to cropland.

Borlaug's estimates take into account *all* the changes in "yield and technology" between 1940 and 1980, not only those involving pesticides. Cross-breeding (and more recently, genetic engineering) and improvements in fertilizers and cultivation techniques contributed significantly to increasing yields during those years. But few experts doubt that pesticides played a major role in this process. Some crops, such as cotton, are virtually impossible to grow commercially without the use of pesticides.

Dr. Alvin Young, director of the U.S. Department of Agriculture's Office of Biotechnology, predicts that "if we wipe out pesticide use, we will slash U.S. food output by at least 40 percent." The National Academy of Sciences estimates that crop harvests would fall by 30 percent, farm prices would rise by 70 percent, and U.S. agricultural exports would fall to zero.

Once a crop is brought in from the field, pesticides are used to protect it from insects and fungus during storage and shipping. An estimated 32 percent of fruit, 21 percent of vegetable products, and 6 percent of food grains would never make it to grocery store shelves without synthetic fungicides, according to a 1991 report by GRC Economics, a Washington-based consulting firm. Beyond the economic value of these food products, there is a human health benefit: One common mold contaminant in grain, aflatoxin, is a dangerous human carcinogen. Thanks to pesticides, it is held in check.

But probably the most remarkable demonstration of the health-preserving powers of pesticides was the use of DDT to kill malaria-carrying mosquitos. Thanks to DDT, countries such as Zanzibar (an island off the east coast of Africa) reduced the percentage of their populations infected with malaria from 70 percent in 1958 to under 5 percent in 1964. Then, the DDT spraying program was suspended, and by 1984 the malaria rate was back up to 50 to 60 percent. Robert L. Turner, chief malariologist for the U.S. Agency for International Development (AID) at the time, observed:

> If Zanzibar's [DDT spraying] program hadn't been suspended in the 1960s, malaria would now be 98 percent eradicated. DDT is a dirty word in the States. There were many abuses when it was considered an end-all insecticide. *But we don't put it into the environment, we spray it on walls.* It doesn't cause health problems for humans.

An estimated three million Africans, a third of them children, died of malaria in 1984 alone. It is probably fair to say that Zanzibar and other African countries would not have suspended DDT spraying if environmentalists had not claimed, without evidence, that DDT posed a significant risk to human health. DDT is still used to combat malaria in some parts of the world, and the decision to suspend spraying in Zanzibar and other areas reflected the judgments of health officials and political leaders as well as environmentalists. Still, the environmental movement must take partial responsibility for halting the use of what many health experts considered to be the greatest life-saving chemical ever discovered — so great that its inventor, Dr. Paul Muller, was awarded the Nobel Prize in medicine in 1948.

Robert D. Kaplan reports in the February 1994 issue of *The Atlantic Monthly* that the death toll from malaria continues unabated. "Virtually everyone in the West African interior has some form of malaria," he writes. He goes on to deliver this grim description of conditions there:

> It is malaria that is most responsible for the disease wall that threatens to separate Africa and other parts of the Third World from more-developed regions of the planet in the 21st century. Carried by mosquitoes, malaria, unlike AIDS, is easy to catch. Most people in the

> sub-Saharan Africa have recurring bouts of the disease throughout their entire lives, and it is mutating into increasingly deadly forms. "The great gift of Malaria is utter apathy," wrote Sir Richard Burton, accurately portraying the situation in much of the Third World today.

DDT's essential role in protecting human health in Third World countries does not mean its agricultural use in the U.S. should have continued unabated. But the suffering in Africa is a vivid reminder of the trade-offs that must be made when the environmental movement enters the public arena and demands action. Sometimes, our victories can impose tremendous losses on those around us.

CONCLUSION

Some pesticides, used carelessly and in excessive amounts in the past, caused significant harm to wildlife. The residue of that use continues to haunt our environment, depressing the reproduction rates of birds and fish in coastal waters and lakes around the country. Banning the most persistent and toxic pesticides made good sense.

Industry has responded by creating a new generation of pesticides that biodegrade more quickly, harm fewer kinds of wildlife, and do not bioaccumulate. Farmers have responded by using fewer pesticides and avoiding the practices that led to run-off into nearby lakes and streams. For these reasons, the danger to wildlife posed by pesticides today is much less than it was twenty and thirty years ago.

Synthetic pesticides do not pose a serious health threat to people in the U.S., and probably never did. The possibility that pesticides contribute to cancer rates is very unlikely: We are exposed to extremely low levels of pesticide residues, and there is no evidence that this level of exposure is sufficient to cause cancer. New fears that pesticides, along with other man-made chemicals, might be causing more subtle kinds of illnesses should be carefully investigated, but there is no convincing evidence at this time that they do.

Doing without pesticides would require an enormous expansion of cropland, requiring millions of acres of wilderness to be cleared and cultivated. The price of food would go up and supplies would fall. The amount of food lost to insects and fungus would increase enormously, meaning many of the acres of wilderness cleared to make way for crops would have been lost for no reason. Finally, the story of DDT and malaria in Africa illustrates how pesticides also play a vital role in protecting public health in the Third World. The campaign against DDT by environmental groups led to the suspension of DDT spraying in many African countries, leading in turn to the deaths of millions of people every year. The environmental movement needs to acknowledge its role in this tragedy and learn from it.

Unaware of the facts, many environmentalists support proposals by more radical elements of the movement to ban or severely restrict all pesticides. We believe a complete understanding of the pesticides controversy shows such proposals to be unnecessary, dangerous to human health, and in some ways destructive of the environment.

June: Nuclear Power

Nuclear power is frightening. It is the direct descendant of the nuclear bomb, the ultimate weapon of mass destruction, the sword held over our heads and the heads of our children. For many in the environmental movement, nuclear power is an icon representing out-of-control technology and the power and arrogance of an industrial-military complex. The issue seems to be beyond debate, above even facts. It involves war and peace, and even man's inner nature.

The early books setting forth the environmental movement's principles — books like Fairfield Osborn's *Our Plundered Planet* (1948), Barry Commoner's *Science and Survival* (1963), and Paul Ehrlich's *The Population Bomb* (1968) — all discuss the implications of nuclear weapons and their potentially lethal impact on the Earth. The Bomb was the preeminent environmental threat. It pushed bird-counting and tree-planting into the background, making them things to do because they were enjoyable and made some small difference. The real battle to *save the planet* had shifted to politics and the halls of the nation's capitol.

Due to the major role that opposition to nuclear war played in the early days of the environmental movement, speaking in favor of nuclear power may be the fastest way for an environmentalist to tarnish his or her reputation. Even to ask for a fair hearing of nuclear power's potential as a safe and clean fuel is to risk ridicule and condemnation. *Have you forgotten Hiroshima and Nagasaki?* we are asked.

We haven't forgotten, nor do we have an inflated trust in man's ability to resist temptation or always do the right thing. We are compelled by the facts to believe that: (1) nuclear power has served enough time in the whipping house for the sins of its father; (2) we owe it to ourselves and future generations to evaluate this energy source on its own merits; and (3) one can honestly denounce war, and especially nuclear war, while also defending the peaceful uses of atomic energy.

Natural vs. man-made radiation

In Chapter Two we described Dr. Bruce Ames' research showing that *natural* pesticides in plants are thousands of times more numerous and potent than the traces of man-made pesticides in our food. Ames made a very telling point: "Natural" and "man-made" pesticides are chemically very similar and have similar effects. If people are commonly exposed to high concentrations of naturally occurring chemicals without apparent harm, why should very small amounts of similar chemicals, different only in that they are man-made, have harmful effects?

The same question arises in the case of nuclear power. Every person on Earth is exposed to *natural* radiation coming from the ground, from space, and even from the food we eat. Trace elements that naturally exist inside our own bodies produce small amounts of radiation. Compared to all this background radiation, exposure to man-made radiation is very slight.

"This radiation we are exposed to from natural sources," writes Dr. Bernard L. Cohen, professor of physics and radiation health at the University of Pittsburgh, "is hundreds of times larger than the well-publicized radiation we may someday receive from the nuclear power industry." Elizabeth Whelan provides the following breakout of the various sources of radiation:

> The principal single contribution to our radiation exposure is natural background radiation, which accounts for over half of the total. The next largest source of radiation is *medical procedures*, which contribute 42 percent. The manufacture and testing of nuclear weapons accounts for 3.5 percent; mining and burning coal, 3 percent; and the entire nuclear power process, including mining, fuel preparation, and waste disposal, contributes less than 1 percent of the total radiation present in our current environment.

What about living *right next door* to a nuclear reactor? Federal law requires that radiation from nuclear power plants not exceed five millirems *per year*; most nuclear facilities do better than the law requires, emitting less than one millirem per year. (A millirem is a unit of measurement representing the effect of radiation on the human body.) The legal limit amounts to just 1.4 percent of the 350 millirems of natural background radiation to which the average American is exposed each year. Moreover, background radiation levels are known to reach twice the average level depending, for example, on local geography, elevation, and whether a person lives and works in brick rather than wood buildings. Finally, a single coast-to-coast airplane flight subjects its passengers to five millirems of radiation in a single day, an amount equal to a full year's exposure caused by living next door to a nuclear reactor.

The evidence that background levels of radiation overwhelm the emissions of nuclear power plants is compelling. Natural variations in background radiation are many times as large as the contribution made by nuclear power.

Radiation and cancer

In the discussion of pesticides that preceded this section, Dr. James Wells observed that "the dose makes the poison. If you're not exposed to something, it can't cause you any harm." The same reasoning must apply to radiation: Exposure levels are so small that we should not expect to find any adverse effects on human health. In fact, this is exactly what scientific research has found.

If you turn back to page 42, you will see that Sir Richard Doll and Dr. Richard Peto estimated that 3 percent of all avoidable cancer deaths can be attributed to "geophysical factors," by which they meant primarily radiation from all sources. If nuclear power accounts for 1 percent of radiation from all sources, then nuclear power may be responsible for approximately .03 percent of avoidable cancer deaths each year, and even a smaller fraction of *all* cancer deaths.

The National Cancer Institute (NCI), the federal agency charged with conducting research on cancer risks for the EPA and other government enforcement agencies, reported in 1993 that "NCI epidemiologists looked at cancer deaths in populations living around nuclear facilities and found no increased risk due to living near such facilities." Bernard Cohen says "the average exposure from a nuclear power plant to those who live closest to it is about 1 percent of their exposure to natural radiation; hence, if they live there for a lifetime, there is one chance in 100,000 that they will die of cancer as a result of exposure to radiation from the nuclear plant."

Evidence that low levels of radiation are of little consequence comes from clinical studies as well as epidemiologic studies comparing cancer rates among populations living in areas with high levels of natural background radiation and populations living in areas with low levels of radiation. The clinical research is extensive: One recent survey of over 1,000 separate studies of plants, animals, bacteria, and cell cultures found strong and repeated support for the proposition that radiation below a certain threshold (approximately 100,000 millirems) is either harmless or actually beneficial.

Epidemiologic studies of persons living in Colorado, Wyoming, and New Mexico, where background radiation levels are as much as twice the national average, have found that cancer rates there are significantly *lower* than the national average. Similarly, a study published in 1980 in *Science* examined 140,000 Chinese, about half living in areas with very high natural background radiation levels, the other half in areas with relatively low levels of radiation, and failed to find any significant difference in cancer rates. Dr. Ben Bolch and Dr. Harold Lyons conclude:

> The China radiation study illustrates . . . [that] the effect of radiation exposure is probably nonlinear. In other words, an incremental halving of exposure, say, does not necessarily lead to an incremental halving of the number of occurrences of diseases such as lung cancer. . . . In fact, some recent animal investigations also tend to show that the health effects of low levels of exposure are much less than would be predicted linearly from higher levels of exposure.

In short, there is no evidence to support the position that radiation from nuclear power generation is causing cancer in the U.S. Even variations in background radiation, which are many times larger than the contribution from nuclear facilities, have not been shown to cause any increase in cancer rates. A possible explanation for the absence of association is the presence of a threshold below which increases in radiation have either no effect or beneficial effects. This threshold appears to be far above current average levels of exposure to radiation.

How safe are nuclear reactors?

Saying nuclear power causes few, if any, cancer deaths in the U.S. each year doesn't completely answer the critics. What is the risk of explosion? Or of meltdowns or major leaks of radiation? And what about the disaster at Chernobyl, in the former Soviet Union, or the near-disaster at Three Mile Island?

Obviously, human errors can always occur. No matter how many safety measures and systems exist, it is always *possible* that an accident could occur and result in the release of significant quantities of radiation. Unfortunately, many environmentalists end their investigations at this point and declare themselves opposed to nuclear power. Instead, we should ask *how possible* are such accidents, and how likely is it that they will harm human health and the environment.

First, nuclear power plants *cannot* explode like nuclear bombs. As Bolch and Lyons explain, "A nuclear bomb requires a very high percentage of uranium 235, far higher than the maximum of 3 percent found in a nuclear power plant. In addition, a bomb must be triggered by a special explosive device not found in a nuclear power plant." What *can* occur is a failure of the systems that moderate the reaction process and cool the core. When water is used both to moderate and cool, the failure of one or both systems has the effect of slowing the rate of nuclear reactions taking place in the pile. This is what took place on March 28, 1979, at the Three Mile Island nuclear power plant near Harrisburg, Pennsylvania.

The thick concrete and steel containment domes that cover nuclear reactors in the U.S. prevent the release of radiation even if a cooling system fails. This, too, was demonstrated during the accident at Three Mile Island. The maximum level of human exposure to radiation resulting from the accident at Three Mile Island was approximately 70 millirems, and the average exposure was just 1.2 millirems. Not surprisingly, researchers have been unable to find any increase in cancer rates among persons living within a twenty-mile radius of the plant in the 15 years since the accident occurred.

While the accident at Three Mile Island demonstrated the safety of American nuclear power plants, an accident seven years later in the former Soviet Union demonstrated what can happen when certain safety features are missing. Nuclear power plants in the Soviet Union typically do not have containment shells, and nuclear reactions are moderated with graphite rods instead of water. On May 26, 1986, at a nuclear power plant near Chernobyl, an experiment intended to test the facility's back-up systems instead led to the disabling of the reactor's cooling systems. The graphite rods melted and steam produced by the core's rising temperature blew apart the reactor pile and the surrounding building.

The accident at Chernobyl resulted in 31 immediate fatalities and later deaths numbering in the hundreds from fire and radiation exposure. Over 100,000 people were evacuated from the area, and many thousands more were exposed to high levels of radiation or unknowingly consumed food contaminated with radioactive fallout. (The Soviet government failed to warn its citizens of the consequences of the accident until after many of them were injured or exposed to risk.)

The Chernobyl accident demonstrated how human and environmental harms can arise from the mismanagement of nuclear power. But fundamental differences between the U.S. and the former Soviet Union, both in technology and government policy, cannot be assumed away. The chain of events leading to the Chernobyl disaster simply cannot be repeated in the U.S. Different technologies make it highly unlikely that an uncontrolled rise in core temperatures could take place, or that significant amounts of radiation could be released despite the presence of the containment shell. The accident at Three Mile Island, while unfortunate in many ways, nevertheless demonstrated the inherent safety of nuclear power plants in the U.S. The lesson for environmentalists from these two accidents is that the safety precautions taken in the U.S. should be put to use in other countries, *not* that nuclear power is unsafe here at home.

The safety of nuclear power plants in the U.S. has been closely studied by independent scientists and, in 1979, by a respected commission appointed by the Nuclear Regulatory Commission (NRC). These studies repeatedly confirm the finding that the risks to life and the environment posed by nuclear power, while not zero, are considerably less than what is posed by burning coal, oil, and other fuels. The report commissioned by the NRC, for example, found a serious radioactive leak from a single nuclear reactor could be expected to occur only once in 10,000 years.

Reaction to the accident at Three Mile Island, in retrospect, can only be called *hysterical*. The plant's cooling towers were featured on the evening news around the country night after night as the nation was told how the accident *might* cause widespread injury and death, *might* have been much bigger, and *might* "prove" that nuclear power is inherently unsafe. Headlines in newspapers put the entire nuclear industry on trial. Residents of Harrisburg at the time of the accident experienced fear far beyond what most of us will ever have to face.

Once again, the fear was needless. The accident at Three Mile Island hurt no one (except through hysteria and stress) and, if it "proved" anything, it proved that even major malfunctions and human errors are unlikely to lead to the release of radiation or cause other risks of injury to the neighbors of nuclear power plants in the U.S. Already-strict regulations concerning nuclear power safety were stiffened further in 1979, making the likelihood of serious accidents smaller still.

Disposing of nuclear waste

The final hazard posed by nuclear power plants arises from the radioactive waste they generate. Spent fuel rods from nuclear reactors are currently being stored in shallow ponds on the property surrounding the plants. Because most of the elements in the rods have short lives, their radioactivity diminishes quickly, leaving those elements with longer lives (primarily uranium and plutonium) to be reclaimed by reprocessing. The remaining waste can be converted into a solid substance and bonded with glass, and then encased in stainless steel canisters and embedded in stable rock formations or stored above-ground for later recovery and recycling. Reprocessing is used in France (which generates 65 percent of its electricity from nuclear power), Britain, and other countries that use nuclear power. The feasibility of glass bonding has been demonstrated by several scientific commissions assigned to study the problem of nuclear waste disposal.

Probably the most important aspect of the nuclear waste problem that is often overlooked by members of the environmental movement is the very small amount of it that is produced. A large nuclear power generator will produce just six cubic yards of waste per year, about one dump truck's load. With reprocessing, even this amount could be reduced: All nonmilitary reactors now operating in the U.S. would produce a cube of high-level wastes with sides measuring just 35 feet.

The extremely long life of radioactive waste rightly makes it of special concern to environmentalists. But this concern should not lead to unthinking opposition to safe disposal plans. Many common kinds of waste persist in the environment for decades and even centuries without injuring either human life or the environment. The way to *ensure* that harms don't arise is to segregate the waste from contact with plant and animal life. The process of fusing nuclear waste with glass and encasing it in stainless steel achieves this segregation completely, resisting any known natural process of corrosion or dissipation.

A related concern that is sometimes expressed is that our distant descendants might unknowingly disturb a nuclear waste storage site, in the process releasing still-dangerous substances into the environment. Avoidance of this scenario is part of all nuclear waste disposal plans, and it is not so difficult as opponents of nuclear power believe. Storage above ground makes visual inspection of the canisters easier and also makes them available for recycling when new technologies emerge to make this feasible. Alternatively, burial deep in bedrock makes the odds of accidental discovery and violation by man extremely remote. If, at some distant time in the future, our descendants forget all that preceded them but nevertheless retain the technologies required to dig or drill to these great depths, then it is also likely that they will possess the kinds of technology already available today that allow long-range detection of nuclear wastes.

The radioactive waste disposal problem is much less one of missing technology than of the persistent and ill-informed opposition to implementation of *any* solution by anti-nuclear activists. Seeking to prevent the expansion of nuclear power, they have expertly manipulated public opposition to waste disposal of any kind — the often-mentioned NIMBY (Not In My Backyard) syndrome. Unfortunately, environmentalists have been taken along for the ride, adding their numbers to a campaign that no longer has much to do with protecting the environment.

Conclusion

The environmental movement's disaffection with nuclear power is based on the past, not the present or future. It has more to do with ideology and fear than with facts and science. As was true of pesticides, breaking away from current dogma will be difficult for many environmentalists who grew up fearing and opposing these modern inventions. But such a break with the past will be good for the environment and good for the movement.

The peaceful use of nuclear power to generate electricity has been placed under intense scrutiny since it first arrived on the scene. The effects of radiation on humans, for example, have been studied more closely than any other substance, either natural or man-made. Accidents occurring at nuclear power plants, whether major ones like the accidents at Three Mile Island and Chernobyl or minor ones bound to occur in big factories employing hundreds of workers, are given widespread coverage in newspapers and on television. The result is a degree of fear and concern that greatly outweighs the real risks involved.

An honest evaluation of nuclear power shows it to be a safe and clean source of energy. Instead of opposing it, environmentalists should consider encouraging its expanded use in order to avoid the air and water pollution and solid waste generation that accompanies the use of other kinds of fuel.

July: Automobiles

How serious a threat to the environment do automobiles pose? According to Al Gore:

> We now know that their cumulative impact on the global environment is posing a mortal threat to the security of every nation that is more deadly than that of any military enemy we are ever again likely to confront.

Whew! Cars are a highly visible source of pollution and conspicuous consumers of a nonrenewable energy resource, petroleum. And their concentration in urban areas, where they contribute to the formation of ground-level ozone and smog, makes them a favorite target of environmentalists. But they are also an essential source of mobility for millions of Americans, making possible hundreds of millions of trips to jobs, relatives, and parks and national forests each year. Are they really a "mortal threat" to our nation's security?

Cars and air pollution

Automobiles and other forms of transportation are responsible for approximately one-third of man-made nitrogen oxide and volatile organic compound emissions, one-fifth of particulate emissions, two-thirds of carbon monoxide emissions, and less than 5 percent of sulfur dioxide emissions. These numbers are large enough to warrant serious attention by environmentalists, and no one disagrees that cleaning up auto emissions would help improve urban air quality. Less widely acknowledged, however, is the considerable progress that already has been made in reducing the rate at which individual cars produce pollution. Indeed, this record is one of the most dramatic and unsung environmental *success stories* of the 1980s and 1990s. Consider the following accomplishments:

- Today's new cars emit 97 percent less hydrocarbons, 96 percent less carbon monoxide, and 90 percent less nitrogen oxide than those built twenty years ago.

- Cars purchased in the 1990s will emit about 80 percent less hydrocarbons and 60 percent less nitrogen oxide during their lifetimes, even though they will be owned longer and driven farther.

- Between 1970 and 1991, total highway vehicle emissions of hydrocarbons dropped 66 percent, carbon monoxide emissions by 59 percent, and nitrogen oxide emissions by 21 percent — despite the doubling of vehicle miles traveled.

- Emission standards for the U.S. auto fleet are more strict than those of other countries. For example, for the model years 1981-1988, the *average* emissions for cars sold by General Motors in the U.S. equaled emissions of the *lowest-emitting* Japanese cars sold in the U.S.

- In the European Community, catalytic converters were required in most new cars beginning in 1993; *the U.S. has required them in new cars since 1975.*

- Use of unleaded gas in the European Community ranged from 0.5 percent to 44.5 percent of all gas sold in 1988, compared to 82 percent in the U.S. (See table on next page.) Today, leaded gasoline has been completely phased out of the U.S. market.

Current trends in technology and public policy ensure that air pollution from cars will continue to decline through the 1990s and beyond:

- Since it takes about 15 years for a passenger car fleet to turn over, fewer than one-third of all the motor vehicles on the road today were built to meet stricter air-pollution standards.

- Between 1987 and 2000, the natural rate of turnover in the domestic auto and truck fleet will produce further reductions of 50 percent in hydrocarbon emissions, 52 percent in carbon monoxide emissions, and 34 percent in nitrogen oxide emissions, *without* any changes in current emission standards for cars and trucks.

- Beginning in 1995, in accordance with the 1990 Clean Air Act

Market Penetration of Unleaded Gas, 1988

Country	Unleaded gas as percent of total gas market
United States	82.0
Belgium	0.5
Denmark	33.0
West Germany	44.5
Greece	0.0
Spain	0.1
France	0.2
Ireland	0.0
Italy	0.7
Luxembourg	10.2
Netherlands	26.0
Portugal	0.0
United Kingdom	1.1

Source: EPA, *State of the Environment in the European Community*, Vol. III, p. 73, reprinted in Global Climate Coalition, *The U.S. versus European Community: Environmental Performance*, August 1993, p. 8.

Amendments, oil companies will begin selling reformulated gasoline in the nine cities with the worst ozone problems. The new gasoline will cut vehicle emissions of hydrocarbons and air toxins by at least 15 percent, and all lead and other heavy metals will be removed.

How clean is clean enough? The goal of zero emissions may be attractive, but attaining it could be extremely expensive (more on this in a moment). More importantly, why should we even reach for this goal? Other products have less social and economic value than do cars, and yet they are allowed to produce some pollution.

Automobiles, after all, play a critical role in American society and in the economy. They give parents a broader choice of neighborhoods and schools, workers more choice among jobs, and consumers a greater choice of stores. Automobiles enable us to experience nature by driving to the country, to go off to college and still make it home for special occasions, and even to keep alive the family ties that would probably disappear if frequent travel to the homes of relatives weren't possible. Since automobiles produce all these benefits, is it fair to expect them to be absolutely pollution-free? After all, we don't ask the same of newspaper publishers, toy manufacturers, or basketball teams.

Often forgotten in the debate over automobiles and the environment is the pollution created by the modes of transportation that cars replaced. Prior to motorized travel, Americans didn't ride bicycles: They rode (or sat in carriages pulled by) horses. Fred L. Smith, a former senior policy analyst for the EPA and now president of the Competitive Enterprise Institute, gives this vivid and unpleasant description of the impact horses had on American cities less than one hundred years ago:

> Cars create pollution. But it's also true that cars may well have dramatically decreased overall pollution. . . . A horse produces approximately 45 pounds of manure each day. In high-density urban environments, massive tonnages accumulated, requiring constant collection and disposal. Flies, dried dung dust, and the smell of urine filled the air, spreading disease and irritating the lungs. On rainy days, one walked through puddles of liquid wastes. Occupational diseases in horse-related industries were common.

Smith goes on to report that New York City in the 1890s had to dispose of *15,000 dead horses every year*, a huge public health and environmental problem. Often, these rotting corpses were hauled in open-air wagons to the edge of town, where they were dumped into huge kettles and heated over coal fires (without emission controls) until they were "reduced" into grease, later to be sold to the manufacturers of candles and lubricants. The remains of the dead animals that couldn't be sold were dumped, untreated, into the nearest river or lake. Today's automobile looks pretty good by comparison.

Still, all is not fresh air and roses with regard to autos, either. In some areas of the country, such as southern California, unique geography and weather have combined with heavy automobile traffic to make air pollution a persistent problem. The biggest barrier to reducing auto emissions even further is that removing the final few grams of exhaust emissions from new cars is much more expensive than were the initial reductions. Here, as in many other areas of environmental protection, the *law of diminishing returns* applies. (See sidebar on the following page.) This rule of common sense says that the closer we come to the goal of zero emissions, the more costly it becomes to eliminate each unit of pollution.

With between 90 and 97 percent of emissions already removed from car exhausts since 1970, and with fleet turnover bringing the level of reductions to 99 percent or higher by the year 2000, it may be time to declare victory and move on. Ford estimates the tighter emission standards already contained in the 1990 Clean Air Act Amendments will increase the cost of each of its cars by $1,125, yet this investment will buy a reduction in exhaust emissions so tiny it will have no measurable effect on urban air quality. The "clean fuels" provisions of the Clean Air Act will require the U.S. refining industry to spend $37 billion more (in 1990 dollars) during the next ten years meeting regulatory requirements and retooling. Consumers will be spending $18 billion a year more by the year 2000 buying the new "clean fuels" mandated by the law.

These are huge sums of money to buy so little improvement in air quality. It is a safe bet that applying this money to other, more serious, environmental problems would produce "more bang for the buck." *Should we give up on reducing auto emissions even further?* No, but further progress requires that we adopt new tactics.

How well a car's engine is tuned determines how much pollution it generates. Nine out of ten cars on the road, regardless of their age, barely pollute at all, while the remaining one car is responsible for half or more of all auto emissions. The smart way to reduce air pollution from automobiles is to identify the one car in ten that is actually polluting and to compel its owner to have the vehicle tuned or its pollution control equipment fixed.

A promising way to target polluting automobiles has been proposed by Dr. Donald Stedman, a chemistry professor at the University of Denver. Stedman has designed a portable device that can test the exhausts of *moving vehicles* and instantly identify the heaviest polluters. Equipped with a camera, the device can photograph a car's license plate, making it possible to issue by mail a warning or a fine to the owner. One device can test up to 1,500 cars per day at a cost of just pennies per car. A team of researchers led by Stedman has tested the device by reading the emissions of more than 250,000 cars in motion. The device is now being

The Law of Diminishing Returns

The closer we get to the goal of zero emissions of a pollutant, the more costly it becomes to eliminate each unit. The reason is that the first control methods used will usually be the most cost-effective and easiest to implement, and will produce the largest benefits. Continued progress, however, requires using methods that are more and more expensive, and remove smaller and smaller amounts of pollutants. At some point, the costs outweigh the benefits.

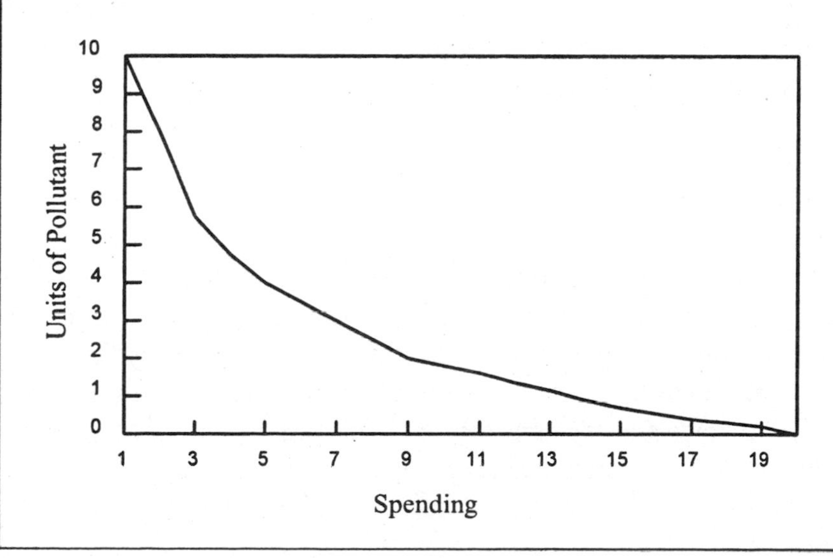

tested by the EPA in several states.

Another promising idea is to charge "congestion fees" to discourage heavy use of roads during rush hours. A significant part of the urban air pollution problem is caused by automobiles caught in heavy traffic. If drivers were charged a premium for using busy highways during rush hours, a financial incentive would exist to take alternate routes, drive during non-peak periods, or carpool. Any of these actions would reduce congestion and therefore the amount of air pollution. Some collection of fees could be done using conventional toll booths, but more efficient systems now exist that do not require drivers to stop to pay tolls. One system, which uses electronic sensors built into roads or overpasses to read the "electronic license plates" of passing vehicles, calculates the charges owed by each vehicle and automatically sends each car and truck owner an itemized monthly bill.

To reduce auto emissions in the future, we must admit that not all cars, at all times, are polluters. Since just *one car out of ten* is a gross polluter, we should target its owner rather than the nine other owners who are innocent of this particular environmental crime. Stedman's portable emissions testing device gives us a way to identify offending vehicles and to compel their owners to get them fixed. Similarly, since a moving car pollutes less than a car trapped in traffic, we should penalize drivers who contribute to traffic jams, not those who take alternate routes or limit their driving to weekends. Congestion fees that make traffic move faster can significantly reduce total auto emissions. By enacting policies such as these, the "mortal threat" posed by automobiles can be addressed simply and inexpensively.

Cars and energy consumption

In Chapter Two we explained that the world's petroleum resources may last for hundreds of years. This fact alone should put to rest concerns that automobiles might cause us to "run out" of oil. In addition, the automobile industry once again has a very impressive record in this regard: Average fuel economy for cars in the U.S. rose from 14 miles per gallon in 1973 to nearly 30 miles per gallon in 1992.

During the 1970s, improvements in fuel economy were driven by consumer demand. High gasoline prices led consumers to prefer cars with better gas mileage, and foreign car manufacturers expanded their market share during these years partly by filling this need. During the 1980s, however, declining gasoline prices and the overall improvement in fuel economy left little market demand for further progress. From this time forward, improvements in fuel economy have been driven by government regulations requiring that car and truck manufacturers achieve fuel economy levels called CAFE standards (Corporate Average Fuel Economy).

To meet CAFE standards, car manufacturers have made most of the major technological changes likely to significantly improve fuel economy, including downsizing, lightweighting, reducing engine size, adding fuel injection, and converting to front-wheel drive. As was the case with auto emissions, further improvements in fuel economy will come at a steep price. Reducing the weight of cars still further may make some cars too unsafe to drive. Research by Robert Crandall at the Brookings Institution and John Graham at Harvard University estimates that 2,200 to 3,900 lives are lost and 20,000 serious injuries occur each year in traffic accidents due to the downsizing and lightweighting of cars.

If government CAFE standards are raised still higher, manufacturers may attempt to comply with the law by producing more small cars and light trucks and fewer big cars and heavy trucks. But here is what is most likely to happen:

- Many people will choose not to buy the smaller cars. Already, CAFE standards on passenger vehicles have increased the sales of small trucks and minivans, which usually get lower gas mileage. Truck sales now account for approximately 40 percent of the U.S. vehicle market.

- Or, people will hold onto their big cars longer, slowing down turnover in the car fleet and once again defeating the purpose of CAFE.

- Even *if* people buy smaller cars, higher fuel economy lowers the cost of each mile traveled, meaning many people will choose to drive more often and for longer distances, resulting in little if any actual reduction in the amount of gasoline consumed.

All of these shifts and changes in consumer behavior work to cancel whatever energy savings might otherwise be achieved by raising CAFE standards. Meanwhile, complying with higher standards would impose major costs, inconveniences, and risks on consumers and business. Ironically, these expenses would be incurred because of an unsuccessful attempt to conserve a resource that is in little danger of being exhausted for many decades! Michael Sykuta and Kenneth Chilton, of the Center for the Study of American Business, recently summarized the case against higher CAFE standards like this:

> Increasing CAFE standards by 40 percent would decrease gasoline demand by less than one-fourth of 1 percent — less than one day's consumption of gasoline per year. And what would be the cost of this tiny reduction in gasoline use? A 1990 study by Andrew Kleit of the Federal Trade Commission found that the cost of raising CAFE standards by about 1 mile per gallon in one year could cost as much as $11 for every gallon of gasoline saved.

Plainly, we have reached a point of diminishing returns: The end of our ability to mandate higher fuel economy through CAFE standards. Consumers are right to resist a government program that penalizes car and truck manufacturers for building products that reflect consumer demands. The goal of energy conservation may have seemed desirable during the 1970s, but during the past twenty years we have learned that energy supplies are much larger and more reliable than once thought. The campaign for higher CAFE standards is unnecessary, increasingly expensive, and bound to be unsuccessful.

Other environmental impacts of cars

If nine out of ten cars pollute hardly at all, and if cars today are about as fuel efficient as consumers want them to be, what is left for environmentalists to object to? Well, what about:

- **Disposal of used oil?** Large quantities of used oil once were routinely dumped in city sewers, leading to contamination of waterways. (This is an example of the *nonpoint* water pollution we discussed earlier.) But the oil industry has responded to the problem by creating a national oil recycling program. Collection sites number over 7,100 and operate in 47 states and the District of Columbia. During the second quarter of 1993, nearly two million gallons of used oil were collected.

- **Toxic byproducts from manufacturing?** The auto manufacturing industry has participated in the economy-wide trend toward less waste and more efficient manufacturing processes. The amount of lead in a typical Delco battery, for example, fell from nearly 30 pounds in 1974 to 20 pounds in 1990. A reformulation of alloy materials from antimony arsenic to calcium tin eliminated more than one million pounds of antimony and arsenic from Delco Remy's 1990 production. GM claims it reduced the amount of electrical energy required for each vehicle produced in the U.S. by 44 percent between the years 1972 and 1990.

- **Depletion of natural resources?** Building a car requires considerable amounts of steel, glass, and plastic, so environmentalists who want to conserve natural resources may still wish to avoid buying or operating cars. But the good news on this front is that cars are *recycled* at about the same rate as they are produced domestically and imported each year. (See the box on the next page.) Much of the metal, plastic, and glass in the car you now own will eventually be recycled into future cars and other consumer products.

A typical car contains about 60 pounds of recycled paper in its doors, seats, and floor. In addition, individual automobile companies and their subsidiaries report that considerable amounts of recycling are taking place at their facilities. For example, in 1990 alone the five Delco Remy facilities involved in battery production recycled more than 4.2 million pounds of lead, 730,000 gallons of sulfuric acid, and 250,000 pounds of polypropylene. The U.S. Council for Automotive Research (USCAR), founded in 1992 by Chrysler, Ford, and General Motors, has a project called the Vehicle Recycling Partnership committed to finding ways to recycle and re-use cars and their components. The partnership also promotes the increased use of recyclable and recycled materials in motor vehicles.

Conclusion

Several lessons can be learned from the automobile's declining impact on the environment during the past twenty years. One is that the environmental problems of the 1960s and 1970s are not the same as the problems of the 1990s. *This is good news,* because it generally means we are making progress. Environmentalists can congratulate themselves on the role they played to help clean up the American automobile. Without their pressure it is unlikely that such stringent emission and CAFE standards would have been imposed.

Another lesson to be learned is that the techniques used to reduce pollution in the past aren't the most effective methods to use today or in the future. Continued tightening of emission and CAFE standards, for example, would waste billions of dollars to achieve very little real environmental protection. Mobile automobile exhaust testing and congestion fees, on the other hand, promise real improvements in air quality at an affordable price.

Some environmentalists seem to imagine that the Earth will be placed in grave danger unless most Americans begin using bicycles rather than cars to commute to their jobs and visit family members. Such flights of fancy are unnecessary. The automobile is not incompatible with

Your Car Will Be Recycled!

"In 1990, members of the Institute of Scrap Recycling Industries (ISRI) recycled some nine million automobiles — only slightly fewer than the number of new cars registered in the U.S. that year. Collectively, the members of ISRI process and sell some sixty million tons of nonferrous metals, and thirty million tons of waste paper, glass, and plastic — almost 100 million tons of material in all. The size of their operation in the aggregate dwarfs that of all recycling programs run by governments at the city, county, and state level taken together."

Source: William Rathje and Cullen Murphy, *Rubbish! The Archaeology of Garbage*, 1992, p. 202.

a clean and safe environment. As the progress already made continues into the next decade, it is clear that we can have both clean air *and* the essential mobility that automobiles give us.

August: Resource Depletion

Some of the leading thinkers in the environmental movement warn that mankind is in danger of using up, or *depleting*, the Earth's natural resources. Kirkpatrick Sale, for example, wrote in 1980:

> In the last decade we have come to realize not only that these resources are finite and irreplaceable but that our rapacious use of them . . . has serious economic and social effects. Petroleum is a familiar example — it used to be you could stick a pipe into any part of Texas to get oil, but now we have to spend $10 billion to get it from the Alaskan North Slope — and though there is a lot of blather about just how much of the stuff we really have, the authoritative *Science* magazine has asserted, "There is no longer much argument with the conclusion that U.S. resources of conventional oil will be seriously depleted by the year 2000." Iron ore, too, has been rapidly exhausted in this country. . . . Water is even more serious. . . . Forests have been consistently depleted, especially in the West. . . .

Fritjof Capra issued a similar warning in 1983:

> We may find alternatives to energy production from fossil fuels, but this will not stop the depletion of our other resources. If we continue the current patterns of undifferentiated growth, we will soon exhaust the reserves of metals, food, oxygen, and ozone that are crucial to our survival. To slow down the rapid depletion of our natural resources we need not only to abandon the idea of continuing economic growth, but to control the worldwide increase in population.

One basis for these and many other warnings of impending resource depletion was *The Limits to Growth*, published in 1972 by The Club of Rome. According to this report, the world would run out of gold by 1981, mercury by 1985, tin by 1987, zinc by 1990, petroleum by 1992, and copper, lead, and natural gas by 1993. Quite obviously, none of these predictions came true.

Not only can these minerals still be bought, but in many cases their real prices are *below* what they were in 1972. Known reserves, in most cases, are higher than they were in 1972, despite two decades of rising global consumption. Why were these predictions so far off the mark? Why do some prominent thinkers still predict that exhaustion of the world's natural resources lurks "just around the corner"?

PRICES AND RAW MATERIALS

In Chapter Two we concluded that there is enough coal, oil, and natural gas in the ground to last hundreds of years. We described how tight supplies lead to higher prices, which prompt higher levels of production by suppliers and lower levels of consumption by consumers. Let's revisit this idea and see how it applies to other raw materials.

When a shortage of a product emerges, consumers bid against one another for the limited supply, thus bidding up its price. This bidding activity sends a signal to current producers of the product and to entrepreneurs who might get into the business. They produce more of the product, and a new balance of supply and demand is created at a higher price. Consumers eventually respond to the higher price by consuming less of the product. They may reduce unnecessary use or waste, or substitute lower-priced products. This process is continuous: It fuels the discovery of new raw material reserves, invention of new technologies, and substitution of new products for existing products in short supply.

Through this market process, *prices* give us valuable information about whether or not a product is becoming scarce or is relatively abundant. High and rising prices are signs of shortage; lower and falling prices are signs of ample supply.

Prices are more accurate indicators of the supply and demand situation than projections based on past trends or estimates of how much of a mineral lies buried in the ground, because only prices reflect the collected knowledge and plans of countless buyers and sellers. Those who believe a commodity may be in short supply sometime in the future are likely to bid more for it today, in order to beat future price increases and perhaps to set aside some amount for future consumption. Those who believe future supplies will be plentiful will exert a downward influence on prices by refusing to pay higher prices. "Futures markets," which allow buyers and sellers to agree now to do business at a certain price sometime

How Much Do Raw Materials Cost? Not Much.

Even if raw materials suddenly became scarce, the resulting price increases would hardly be noticed by most consumers. The reason is that each of us pays very little each year for the minerals we consume, paying instead for the labor used in shipping, handling, and selling products derived from raw materials. The figures below are for 1980.

Use of Raw Materials
Per-capita use (pounds) and cost (dollars) in U.S.

Material	Amount (pounds)	Average cost per person per year
Fuels	16,000	$950.00
Food	2,000	500.00
Metals	1,000	60.00
Wood	2,000	40.00
Miscell. minerals	2,000	40.00
Stone and gravel	20,000	30.00
Total	45,000	$1,620.00

Source: Max Singer, *Passage to a Human World*, table on p. 83 and notes on pp. 368-369.

in the future, give us even better information about the future supply and demand for many commodities.

The record of raw material prices has been one of almost continuous decline since the turn of the century, suggesting that such commodities are becoming plentiful, not scarce. According to Dr. Max Singer of The Hudson Institute, "from 1919 to 1957 the relative price of extractive products fell by 13 percent compared to other products. The relative prices of minerals declined by 10 percent in the generation before 1919 and then fell by half from 1919 to 1957. These data have been extended to take into account prices up to 1973. They continue to give little support to the . . . hypothesis of scarcity."

According to the World Resources Institute, the real price of all metals and minerals fell by more than 40 percent between 1970 and 1988. And according to economist Stephen Moore, between 1980 and 1990 real prices for agricultural products fell by 38 percent; for minerals and metals, by 31 percent; for energy, by 25 percent; and for forest products, by 15 percent. "Natural resources have been growing more plentiful over the course of the past two hundred years, as measured by their price," wrote Moore in a 1992 report for the Institute for Policy Innovation. He continues:

> The decade of the 1980s, contrary to popular belief, was no exception to this long term trend. Indeed, thanks to steep across the board declines in natural resource prices in the 1980s, today many natural resources are at their lowest price ever. Even as a growing population and a more economically developed society use more resources than ever before, the introduction of new technologies and innovations, which make us more efficient in consuming and producing natural resources, have meant that the earth's resources have continually become less of a limit to growth over time, rather than more so.

In 1980, Dr. Julian Simon challenged Dr. Paul Ehrlich, perhaps the most notorious of environmentalists predicting future resource depletion, to put some of his own money behind his predictions. Simon challenged Ehrlich to *place a bet* on whether or not the price of natural resources would rise or fall in the future. Ehrlich accepted the challenge.

Ehrlich himself chose quantities of five metals — chrome, copper, nickel, tin, and tungsten — with a total price of $1,000, and chose a ten-year period. If the price of the metals was higher than $1,000 in 1990, after adjusting for inflation, Simon agreed to pay Ehrlich the difference; if the price fell, Ehrlich would have to pay Simon. *Ten years later, in 1990, Ehrlich sent Simon a check for $576.07.* The real prices of the metals *had fallen* by this amount since the bet was made. In fact, prices had fallen so steeply that Simon would have won the bet even if prices were not adjusted for inflation.

This record of declining prices is so compelling that the Worldwatch Institute, long a source of doomsday forecasts, concluded in 1992 that "scarcity of mineral deposits does not appear likely to constrain the production of most important minerals in the foreseeable future."

Population growth

Driving many of the 1970s' doomsday predictions was the rapid rate of global population growth. World population was growing at the rate of about 2 percent a year during the 1960s, the fastest in recorded history. Simple arithmetic (performed, in this case, by Paul Ehrlich in 1968) showed that if this rate continued for nine hundred years, there would be *sixty million billion people* on the Earth, or one hundred persons for each square yard of the Earth's surface, both land and sea. Obviously, something would have to "give" between now and the year 2868.

And something did give, much sooner than experts predicted. The world's population growth rate slowed to 1.75 percent per year during the

World Population is Stabilizing

During the 1960s and 1970s, it was common to assume that world population would keep growing until the world's natural resources were exhausted. Today, population growth is expected to stabilize sometime in the next century. The graph below shows this pattern of rapid growth followed by stability.

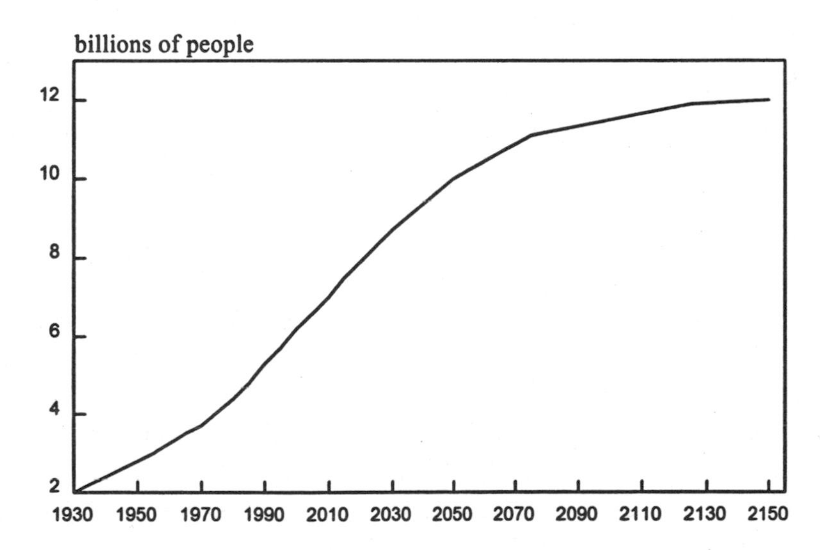

Source: World Bank, *World Population Projections 1992-93 Edition* (Baltimore, MD: The Johns Hopkins University Press, 1992).

1980s, and is now expected to drop to 1.0 percent by the year 2025. Even a 1 percent annual growth rate means the world's population would double every seventy years, but the news gets even better. The United Nations, the World Bank, the U.S. Bureau of the Census, and the Population Reference Bureau all now predict that world population *will stop growing altogether* in approximately one hundred years. World population could peak at between ten and twelve billion around the year 2100. (World population now stands at about 5.7 billion.)

Why is the world's population growing more slowly? How do we know if the new predictions are reliable?

The generally accepted theory, supported by twenty years of declining population growth rates, goes like this. In poverty-stricken societies, many children die before reaching adulthood. Parents therefore value big families in order to ensure that enough sons and daughters live to support them in their old age. Retirement programs, either private or public, usually don't exist in very poor countries, making children an essential part of retirement plans. The low status of women and their general lack of education in poor countries mean they are usually excluded from the cash economy, which reduces the value of their time; time spent on childbearing and childrearing activities consequently does not represent lost earnings. Women thus are encouraged to bear children, who can help in the fields, perform menial tasks, and provide assistance and security in their parents' old age.

As a country grows wealthier, all these reasons to have many children become less important. Infant mortality rates fall, so the need to have many children in order to ensure that a few survive declines. Greater wealth means a comfortable retirement can be purchased from savings rather than relying on children for financial support. As women's productivity in the workplace rises, lost income due to time spent raising children rises as well, making childrearing in effect more expensive. Mechanization gradually replaces the kind of labor children are able to provide, making children a less likely source of family income. Environmental awareness, too, seems to rise with income as attention need not be riveted to the requirements of day-to-day survival.

Much to the distress of would-be grandparents, many couples in wealthy nations such as the U.S. now postpone having children or forego having children altogether. As a result, some developed countries have reached such low rates of population growth that they either are not growing in population size (excluding immigration) or have *negative* population growth rates. If Third World countries gradually join the ranks of the wealthy nations, as was the pattern during the 1970s and 1980s, then their population growth rates, too, will fall.

This explanation of declining population growth rates is *robust* (that is, *strong* because it is supported by many different underlying trends) and therefore reliable. It means environmentalists can approach the question, *will we run out of natural resources?* in a more realistic way than they could during the 1960s and 1970s.

Running out of room?

Before discussing the implications of rising population, it may be valuable to pause in order to give our minds a chance to grasp the difference between 5 billion people and 10 billion people. These are huge numbers. What do they really mean?

In terms of the physical space people occupy, it may be useful to picture this: If all the people in the entire world today came to the U.S., they could all stand inside the city limits of Jacksonville, Florida — an area less than 0.03 percent the size of the U.S. If every man, woman, and child in the world was given a *house* the size of the average U.S. house, they could *all* live in the State of Texas.

These images sound gimmicky, and maybe they are. But they should help dispel from our minds the notion that population growth is leading to *crowding*. Crowding is a different problem having to do with wealth, culture, urban planning, and where people prefer to live, and it can be largely unrelated to population growth. Proof of this is the fact that, by many measures, the U.S. is *less crowded* today than it was when its population was much smaller. For example, our houses keep getting bigger over time; there are fewer people per room in the average home and more square feet of space per worker in office buildings. There is more land designated as parks, and each year Americans report more trips to parks than in previous years. Do these trends suggest that the U.S. is becoming more or *less* crowded over time?

Returning to world population facts, human settlements (cities, towns, and villages) occupy less than 1 percent of the land area of the world, according to Max Singer. If the world's population doubles before finally stabilizing at 10 or 12 billion, human settlements will still cover less than

2 percent of the Earth's land area (assuming no major changes in technology or preferences that might affect population densities).

What about roads? They are not counted as "human settlements," but they do occupy space. The continental U.S. is much more heavily paved than the rest of the world; it has about 3 million miles of paved roads. The area of the U.S. (not counting Alaska) is about 3 million square miles. Since a mile is 5,280 feet, and a typical road (including shoulders) is less than 50 feet wide, the width of an average road is less than 1 percent of a mile. (Interstate highways are wider, but they account for less than one-half of one percent of the total mileage of roads in the U.S.) So for every square mile of the U.S., paved roads cover less than 1 percent of the land area. Globally, then, roads must cover an even smaller percentage of land areas, probably on the order of 0.1 or 0.01 percent.

The relatively tiny size of our cities, towns, villages, and roads suggests that there is little danger we will "run out of room" any time soon. And the steadily declining rate of growth in global population means human settlements and roads will probably never occupy more than 2 or 3 percent of the Earth's land area.

POPULATION AND FOOD

Running out of room is hardly the most serious concern generated by rising population levels. What about room to grow food for 12 billion people? What effects would doubling the world's demand for food have on the environment?

Two teams of researchers have examined these questions. The first was the U.S. President's Science Advisory Committee; the second, a group of Dutch scientists, led by Dr. P. Buringh at the Agricultural University of Wageningen. The two studies came very close to the same overall results, though they used very different methods.

The Buringh work, the more rigorous of the two, involved direct study of ten thousand soil samples from around the world and careful analysis of climate, availability of water, grade, and land uses. The Buringh researchers set aside at least 30 percent and usually over 50 percent of each region they studied for nonagricultural use, regardless of the land's suitability for farming. They found 8,500 million acres of potential farmland in the world, of which 3,500 million (about 40 percent) is currently being used for farming. (Farmland now occupies less than 10 percent of the Earth's land area.) This means food production could be more than doubled, with no changes in current agricultural practices, by doubling the number of acres being farmed.

If the yield of each acre of land now being farmed were increased, sufficient food could be produced to feed the growing population with a much smaller increase in acres farmed, or possibly even fewer acres than are now farmed. One way to increase yields is *sequential cropping* in warmer climates, whereby two, three, or even four crops are harvested from the same field each year. The Buringh study figured sequential cropping could add the equivalent of *5,000 million acres* of farmland to the world's food supply each year. Applying existing technologies (fertilizer, pesticides, high-yield plant varieties, and irrigation) to land already under cultivation in developing countries could *double again* current yields without any expansion of acreage. Even small advances in agricultural technology — such as the ability to produce feed for livestock from paper pulp or other non-crop sources — would boost these numbers even higher.

All told, says Max Singer, "with conventional agriculture we can at least triple the number of acres harvested for food, and we can at least triple the effective yield of the average acre. New science may add to our ability to grow food — as well as providing protection against unforeseen problems — and our ability to manufacture new kinds of nutrients for animals provides further insurance."

Tripling the number of acres harvested and tripling the effective yield per acre means food production could be multiplied by a factor of nine without any breakthrough discoveries. This level of food production far exceeds any realistic forecast of human needs in the future.

Population growth, society, and environmental quality

Aside from the possibilities of crowding and hunger, population growth poses a third threat: social and economic displacements that can result in environmental destruction. This problem cannot be denied. In much of Africa and parts of South America and Asia — where 90 percent of population growth during the next forty years is expected to occur — population growth and acute poverty are combining to produce high levels of water and air pollution, locally severe deforestation, and sometimes severe loss of topsoil to erosion. A 1993 report on conditions in

Pakistan illustrates the problem:

> In Pakistan, the environmental problems faced are enormous. Pakistan is not a resource-rich country, although once it may have been so. Whatever little resources we had, have been squandered partly through misuse, partly through overpopulation. As a result, we have started to run out of cultivable land, forests, irrigation water, and clean urban air. . . . The waste and contamination of the ground water by agricultural runoffs, industry effluent, human excrement and hospital waste is increasing daily. The air in the urban areas is being polluted at a rapid pace by vehicular and industrial emissions.

Robert Kaplan, whose description of malaria cited earlier gave us a glimpse of conditions in western Africa, paints an equally dismal picture of conditions in India. "Given that in 2025 India's population could be close to 1.5 billion, that much of its economy rests on a shrinking natural-resource base, including dramatically declining water levels, and that communal violence and urbanization are spiraling upward, it is difficult to imagine that the Indian state will survive the next century."

What is taking place in these countries, and in many African countries as well, is the absence or collapse of institutions that might otherwise accommodate the pressures of population growth and provide protection of the environment. Massive migration to cities has destroyed family institutions that were better suited to the pastoral life of the countryside; gangs, unemployment, and drug abuse have been the result. Property rights, which must be defined and enforced if users of natural resources are to be held accountable for their actions, have been virtually abandoned in parts of Pakistan, India, Sierra Leone, the Ivory Coast, and a long list of other Third World countries. The process of economic growth, which will be discussed in further detail in the next chapter, has stopped in these countries, leaving in its place desperate poverty and complete disregard either for the rights of others or for the surrounding environment.

An example of the complexity of the social and cultural processes at work is the role played by education in reducing the rate of population growth. In many developing countries, girls are usually kept out of school to assist their mothers in the fields. As adults, women are encouraged to bear many children to assist them in the fields. This pattern can be seen plainly in the African country of Chad, where adult women have an average of less than one month of education, but bear an average of six children.

Giving Third World women access to education increases their value in the workplace and starts the process of voluntary population control. One estimate suggests that $6.5 billion a year would be enough to raise the education of Third World women to a level equal to that of men. This is a big expense, yet it pales in comparison to the hundreds of billions of dollars spent here in the U.S. battling acid rain, CFCs, and other exaggerated or unproven environmental problems.

The United Nations has called the status of women the "root cause" of population growth, poverty, and environmental degradation in Third World countries. But merely improving the status of women will not lead to economic growth or end environmental degradation. Other institutions must be changed or built to stop the violence and lawlessness that is destroying human life and damaging the environment.

Population growth and resource depletion are genuine environmental problems in Third World countries, even if they do not appear to be major threats for developed countries or on a global level. Serious thought must be given to ways of addressing the underlying causes of these problems.

Conclusion

Those who repeatedly warn of resource depletion have been wrong too often to be trusted any longer. Known reserves of most minerals are rising, not falling, and declining real prices are proof that these resources are becoming increasingly abundant rather than depleted. Global population growth, the main force behind the resource depletion predictions, is gradually slowing and is expected to stop entirely in approximately one hundred years.

It now appears that the Earth will have little difficulty supporting a population of 10 or 12 billion people, about twice the current world population. There is ample room for human settlements, and food supplies could be expanded sufficiently using existing technologies. The *real* problems concerning resource depletion in the world today occur in Third World countries where civil war, lawlessness, and a culture that deprives women of status and education are perpetuating problems that developed countries solved long ago. Unless social order and civil and economic rights are restored, these countries will continue to experience rapid population growth, severe poverty, and mismanagement of their natural resources.

September: Plastic

Plastic is often labeled a villain by environmental activists. Because it is used in packaging and single-use products (such as disposable diapers and cups), plastic seems to symbolize our "throw-away" culture. Say Will Steger and Jon Bowermaster,

> Our garbage problem worsens because most consumer goods are designed, in the words of the Worldwatch Institute's Cynthia Pollock, "for a one-night stand." They are bought, used, and tossed with little regard for their lasting potential. America's biggest misconception was that the limits on dumping were endless — a näiveté that encouraged history's biggest throw-away society.

Disposable plastic products may be difficult to love, but the evidence suggests they do not deserve to be singled out for harsh criticism by environmentalists. While more needs to be done to encourage plastic recycling, plastic is only a small fraction of the nation's solid waste stream, and its unique qualities make substantial contributions to health and the environment. In the end, plastic packaging and disposable items may be no better but also no worse than most of the other products that become part of our country's solid waste stream.

Plastic and the Garbage Problem

In Chapter Two we rebutted the notion that the U.S. has a "solid waste crisis." There is no danger of running out of room for landfills. And thanks to major advances in landfill and incineration technologies, the disposal of solid waste has never been safer or better managed. With these facts in mind, we question whether it is worth the time and energy of environmentalists to campaign against a particular class of products that contribute to the nation's solid waste stream. Surely there are more important issues to address than whether polystyrene cups are better or worse than paper cups?

According to a report for the EPA prepared by Franklin Associates, Ltd., a respected consulting firm, plastic accounts for 9.8 percent by weight and 21.1 percent by volume of municipal solid waste sent to landfills. These estimates are probably too high, however, because they exclude construction and demolition debris and are based on controversial input/output models that over-estimate the amount of plastic that actually finds its way into a landfill.

Dr. William Rathje, professor of archeology at the University of Arizona and America's preeminent "garbologist," appears to have a more reliable estimate of plastic in solid waste. Dr. Rathje and his students have conducted archeology-style "digs" in landfills around the country to determine what they *really* contain. He has found that plastic of all kinds constitutes about 7 percent by weight and 16 percent by volume of a typical landfill, less than the Franklin Associates estimates but still a large enough fraction to merit attention.

Rathje further estimates that polystyrene plastic — the stuff used to make disposable cups, plates, and hamburger "clamshells" — accounts for no more than 1 percent of landfill volume. Fast-food packaging, according to Rathje, amounts to no more than one-third of 1 percent of a typical landfill's volume. Other studies and surveys support Rathje's findings. The Oregon Department of Environmental Quality, for example, found in 1993 that plastic of all kinds accounted for 7.75 percent (by weight) of Oregon's total municipal solid waste stream. Plastic packaging in Oregon accounted for slightly more than half of this total (4.35 percent); rigid plastic containers just one-sixth (1.37 percent); and polystyrene plastic, a mere 0.26 percent of Oregon's total solid waste stream.

The plastic cups and plates that environmentalists love to hate account for about 0.2 percent of the nation's solid waste; discarded telephone books alone account for more than this. Similarly, discarded towels, sheets, and pillowcases account for three times as large a share as plastic plates and cups (0.6 percent), and discarded clothing and shoes represent eleven times as much (2.2 percent). (See table on the following page.) Why do environmental groups not protest the disposal of towels, sheets, or old shoes?

Franklin Associates found that plastic soft drink bottles account for 0.2 percent of total national solid waste discards; milk jugs, 0.2 percent; and other plastic containers, 1.1 percent. Plastic packaging accounted for

Nondurable Goods in the Municipal Waste Stream, 1990

(Percent of total discards)

Type of product	Percent of total discards
Newspapers	4.6
Office papers	2.9
Junk mail	2.2
Clothing and footwear	2.2
Disposable diapers	1.6
Magazines	1.5
Towels, sheets, and pillowcases	0.6
Books	0.5
Trash bags	0.5
Paper plates and cups	0.4
Telephone books	0.3
Plastic plates and cups	**0.2**

Source: Franklin Associates, Ltd., *Characterization of Municipal Solid Waste in the United States 1992 Update*, July 1992, Table 17, p. 2-31.

4.1 percent of all discards, compared to 4.6 percent for wood packaging, 5.7 percent for glass, and 12.7 percent for paper and paperboard. (See table on page 137.) Once again, it is puzzling that environmentalists should make plastic containers and plastic packaging the focus of their attack on solid waste.

Grade school students are frequently asked to write letters to lawmakers and corporate CEOs protesting the use of plastic cups and plates by fast-food restaurants. How many of these students know that disposable plastic food and drink containers make up just 0.26 to 0.33 percent of all municipal solid waste? How many know that plastic packaging of all kinds accounts for a smaller fraction of the solid waste stream than wood, glass, or paper and paperboard packaging? More disturbingly, why haven't they been told?

Containers and Packages in the Municipal Waste Stream, 1990
(Percent of total discards)

Type of packaging	**Percent of total discards**
Paper and Paperboard	12.7
Glass	5.7
Wood	4.6
Plastic	**4.1**
Steel	1.4
Aluminum	0.5
Other	0.1
Total containers and packaging	29.2

Source: Franklin Associates, Ltd., *Characterization of Municipal Solid Waste in the United States 1992 Update*, July 1992, Table 23, p. 2-40.

Plastic and recycling

Prior to 1985, the amount of plastic recycling that took place was negligible, giving environmentalists a reason to single it out for criticism. Since then, however, that situation has changed.

The recycling rate for polyethylene terephthalate (PET) soft drink bottles rose from zero in 1980 to 40.6 percent in 1992. These bottles are now recycled at a higher rate than either glass or steel beer and soft drink containers, though at a lower rate than aluminum cans. Overall recovery of plastic bottles and containers in 1992 was 15 percent, compared with 22 percent for steel, 22 percent for glass, and 53 percent for aluminum packaging materials.

A breakthrough in recycling polystyrene cups and clamshells was about to be announced shortly before McDonald's, under pressure from environmental organizations, announced it would replace polystyrene products with paper products. Dow Chemical and seven other plastic manufacturers had formed the National Polystyrene Recycling Company to recycle polystyrene from 450 McDonald's restaurants. The "successful" campaign against McDonald's was a serious blow to this effort, and thus to the plastic recycling movement. While environmentalists around the country declared victory against the evil plastic clamshell, it is difficult to share their enthusiasm when the facts are known.

Three problems have confronted efforts to expand plastic recycling:

- Different kinds of plastic that might appear to consumers to be the same cannot be mixed to produce new plastic products with the same strength or clarity as the original containers. Including even one container made out of the "wrong" kind of plastic can ruin an entire batch of recycled plastic. This makes sorting a very expensive and tedious task. Mixed plastic *can* be used to make park benches, trash bins, and other products, but this market is relatively small.

- Whereas foreign objects (such as gum wrappers or cigarette butts) sometimes left in glass or metal containers collected for recycling are incinerated at the high temperatures used to melt these containers, plastic recycling uses a lower temperature that can leave traces of these contaminants behind. The result, once again, is a lower quality recycled plastic product. The need for visual inspection and hand cleaning of plastic containers to avoid this problem can make recycling uneconomical.

- Finally, the characteristics of plastic that make it attractive as a packaging material — its light weight and rigidity — also make empty containers extremely voluminous and therefore relatively expensive to transport.

To overcome these problems, the plastic industry is experimenting with a process called "thermal decomposition," whereby used plastic is placed in an oxygen-free chamber and heated to about 1,000 degrees, roughly the same temperature required to melt aluminum. The absence of oxygen prevents the plastic from burning, and instead it breaks down into the liquid petroleum products from which plastic is made. These liquid products are then refined and transformed into new plastic, synthetic fibers, lubricants, and gasoline.

Thermal decomposition could be an important breakthrough for plastic recycling because it does not require the labor-intensive sorting, cleaning, and grinding techniques now used to recycle plastic. Environmentalists ought to be the first in line to welcome the commercialization of this technology.

Plastic and biodegradability

Although some plastics are now being developed that use corn rather than petroleum as a basic feedstock, it is true that virtually all plastics in use at this time do not biodegrade. But in this regard plastic is not alone: Paper, wood, and even discarded food do not biodegrade in the dry and dark interiors of landfills. Rathje's landfill excavations routinely discover newspapers published forty years ago that are so well preserved they still can be read with ease. Alongside such papers are frequently found the remains of the dinner that may have been eaten the same day, also remarkably well preserved.

The absence of biodegradation inside landfills may be unfortunate, on the one hand, since natural processes cannot be relied on to gradually reduce the volume of our garbage. But there is much less need to reduce the volume of our garbage — given how very little room it takes compared to available space, and given our ability to build golf courses, factories, and other developments on top of old landfills — than there is a need to *protect ourselves and the environment* from the results of biodegradation of large amounts of waste.

The byproducts of degradation can have serious environmental consequences, including toxic leachate reaching rivers and groundwater, and methane gas emissions. Because plastic doesn't degrade into potentially toxic substances, it may be superior to other substances put into landfills. On balance, plastic and modern landfills work well together to protect the environment *and* human health.

Energy, petrochemicals, and plastic

One of the criticisms of plastic is that it is made from petroleum, a nonrenewable natural resource. The charge is true, but unimportant. Less than 2 percent of the world's petroleum is used to produce petrochemicals of all kinds, including plastic. Reducing our use of plastic would require substituting other packaging materials, such as paper, metal, and glass, which generally require more energy to create. As a result, reducing the use of plastic would increase, not reduce, the consumption of petroleum.

A comparison of polystyrene and paper cups addresses the energy consumption issue as well as other issues of environmental safety. Dr. Martin B. Hocking, in a 1991 article in *Science* magazine, reported:

> Because 6 times as much wood pulp as polystyrene is required to produce a cup, the paper cup consumes about 12 times as much steam, 36 times as much electricity, and twice as much cooling water as a polystyrene foam cup. About 580 times the volume of waste paper is produced for the pulp required for the paper cup as compared to the polystyrene requirement for the polystyrene cup. The contaminants present in the wastewater from pulping and bleaching operations are removed to a varying degree depending on site-specific details, but the residuals present in all categories except metal salts still amount to 10 to 100 times those present in the wastewater streams from polystyrene processing.

Hocking also found air emissions from the production of polystyrene cups to be about 60 percent less than those created during the production of a paper cup. Dr. Hocking's article generated a lively exchange of letters to the editor of *Science*, and some of Hocking's original statements have been amended with more current information. But his original thesis has been upheld: Paper cups are not clearly superior to plastic cups when energy use and other manufacturing side effects are taken into consideration. Research on plastic versus paper grocery bags has produced similar results. A German study of a proposal to ban all plastic containers and packaging in that country estimated that such a ban would increase the volume of waste containers by 256 percent and almost exactly double the amount of energy consumed for the manufacture of packaging materials.

None of these studies necessarily tells us whether paper, plastic, or some other material is best for a particular use. The fact that many different materials continue to be used for different purposes is the best evidence that no one material is best for every use. We should recognize this reality, and recognize too that the simplistic reasoning that says "plastic is always bad" does consumers *and the environment* a disservice.

Disposable diapers

Only 8 or 9 percent of a disposable diaper is plastic, but such diapers have joined polystyrene cups, clamshells, and plastic grocery bags as symbols of our "throw-away society." Jeanne Wirka, in an article graphically titled "Choking on Disposables," recently wrote, "The 18 billion disposable diapers Americans throw away each year — enough to fill an Islip-style garbage barge every six hours — are choking up the nation's rapidly filling landfills and increasing the need for other disposal options like incinerators."

Francesca Lyman, writing in *Garbage* magazine, recently summed up the case against disposable diapers like this: "Many agree that encouraging the use of cloth diapers over disposables makes sense socially — it saves landfill space, cuts down on litter, keeps human waste out of the garbage, and saves trees and petrochemical-based plastic."

The campaign by some environmental groups against disposable diapers, once again, leaves much unsaid. Here is what is *really* known about disposable diapers:

- A 1990 study by the consulting firm of Arthur D. Little found "neither disposable nor reusable diapers are clearly superior in the various resources and environmental impact categories considered in this analysis." They *did* find that disposable diapers provide "better protection against diaper dermatitis," better known as diaper rash.

- Franklin Associates Ltd. studied the issue in 1990 and again in 1992 and found that cloth diapers use more water, cause more overall water pollution, consume more energy, and cause more air pollution, but generate less total solid waste by volume than do disposables.

- William Rathje's excavations of recent strata in nine landfills found the volume taken up by disposable diapers varied from 0.53 percent to 1.82 percent. "Disposable diapers may be a big ticket item in landfills compared with toothpicks and check stubs," writes Rathje and coauthor Cullen Murphy, "but they are simply not in the same league with paper of various kinds (newspapers especially) or items such as food waste, yard waste, and construction and demolition debris, all of which fill up landfills at a rate many times greater than that of diapers. . . . It is certainly an illusion to believe that eliminating disposable diapers would have anything but an imperceptible effect on the larger garbage picture."

While disposable diapers don't show up as an environmental threat, they do play a big role in protecting health. Disposable diapers are such a boost to the sanitation of day-care centers that both the American Academy of Pediatrics and the American Public Health Association endorse their use and discourage the use of cloth diapers by day-care centers.

Patricia Poore, publisher and editor of *Garbage* magazine, recently expressed her frustration with fellow environmentalists who continue to campaign against disposable diapers despite being aware of these facts:

> I feel angry and betrayed by tactics, used by those supposedly preaching nurture, which take unfair advantage of a mother's concern. . . . Because it touched me personally, the bogus diaper debate has focused my attention on *vigilante environmentalism*: "Ignore the facts! We've got a good Cause here, and if you don't get in step, we'll make you pay."

Conclusion

Plastic may symbolize a part of our culture that is not very attractive. So inexpensive that it can be used once and thrown away, plastic packaging makes highly visible litter. Plastic products often reflect the latest fads and fashions, making them a constant reminder that things today are fast-moving and ever-changing. As a result, we tend to react against plastic more for what it *represents* than for what it actually is. We label it a *villain* and campaign against it without checking all the facts and thinking through all the implications.

The facts are that containers and packaging make up only a few percent of the content of a typical landfill. Because of its chemical stability, plastic doesn't contaminate the environment. Progress is being made to increase the amount of plastic that is recycled. Arguments about saving energy or scarce resources seem to tilt decidedly *toward* plastic rather than toward its more politically correct alternatives.

Plastic has received a bum rap from the environmental community. The time is right for a re-assessment, and perhaps a change in tune.

October: Electromagnetic Fields

Can overhead power lines and common household appliances cause cancer? Many people, and more than a few environmentalists, live in fear of this possibility. The story of electromagnetic fields tells us a lot about how the popular media covers environmental issues, what constitutes good science, and how we should view risk.

THE CASE AGAINST ELECTROMAGNETIC FIELDS (EMFS)

Electric and magnetic fields (usually lumped together and called electromagnetic fields (EMFs) or extremely low frequency fields (ELFs)) are similar to background radiation: They are invisible, cannot be felt, and exist in abundance in the natural world. The Earth is enveloped by a gigantic natural magnetic field which makes needles on compasses point north. Additional temporary fields are created by solar flares and lightning. Inside our bodies, little EMFs are generated by our muscles and nerves.

Man creates artificial EMFs by using electricity. Every appliance, tool, or other device that uses electricity generates a low-level EMF. Our use of electrical devices is so extensive that we are virtually always in the presence of multiple man-made EMFs. These fields exist at very low levels, measured in units called milligauss (mG). The intensity of the fields diminishes rapidly with distance from the source, so moving just a few feet away from an appliance can often remove you from the range of its EMF. However, your home's electrical wiring (if grounded to the plumbing) forms EMFs that are likely to be stronger than what is produced by any one of your appliances.

During the 1970s, various researchers began to study the effects of man-made EMFs on plant and animal life. Laboratory tests were conducted and eventually showed that EMFs can produce measurable responses from animal cells, though it is not known whether these responses are harmful. The first epidemiologic study claiming to find a relationship between man-made EMFs and human health was published in 1979 by Dr. Wendy Wertheimer (a psychologist) and Dr. Ed Leeper (a physicist). Wertheimer and Leeper compared the incidence of childhood cancer with the location of power lines in residential neighborhoods of Denver. They found a statistically significant relationship. In 1986, the two authors published a second study claiming to find an association between fetal development and electric blankets.

Paul Brodeur, a writer for *The New Yorker*, publicized the EMF threat in his 1989 book, *Currents of Death*; in a series of articles in *The New Yorker*; and later in such popular women's magazines as *Woman's Day* and *Family Circle*. As the title of his book suggests, Brodeur is convinced that EMFs pose a serious threat to human health. He calls EMFs "the most pervasive — and covered up — public health hazard Americans face." He further claims there are "32 published studies demonstrating ELF effects" on animal tissue, and he contends that as many as 15 percent of childhood cancers are caused by exposure to overhead power lines.

What scientific research has found

Science writer Michael Fumento examined Brodeur's claim that 32 studies support his position on EMFs. Fumento found that "these 32 studies are in contrast to hundreds of animal and cellular studies showing no effects. More important, the strong implication is that these are harmful effects. But that assumption is simply false."

As we noted in Chapter Three, studies that *fail* to find a positive relationship between a substance and cancer are seldom published or reported, whereas a *single* study finding even a weak positive relationship often attracts widespread attention. Even this imbalance in the reporting of scientific studies, however, has not been enough to sustain the case for linking EMFs to cancer or other illnesses. Here are highlights of recent scientific research:

- The 1979 Wertheimer and Leeper study was heavily criticized as being an amateur investigation. Rather than take actual measurements of EMFs inside homes, the researchers relied on their own visual determination of whether power lines near the homes were high-current. Later researchers would find that these estimates were not supported by on-site measurement. Also, Wertheimer and Leeper did not control for exposure to potential confounders such as cigarette smoke and fumes from traffic. Finally, the researchers knew beforehand which homes had children with leukemia, providing an obvious source of bias.

- The 1979 Wertheimer and Leeper study was repeated in Rhode Island a short time later, but no relationship between EMFs and childhood cancer was found. Dr. David Savitz, at the time with the University of Colorado at Boulder, repeated the Wertheimer and Leeper study in Denver in 1987. After controlling for many of the factors that invalidated the Wertheimer and Leeper study, he found no statistically significant correlation between power levels and childhood cancer.

- The federal government's Office of Technology Assessment in May 1989 issued a report saying there was "not enough evidence to judge the possibility of an association" between residential exposure to electric and magnetic fields and adult cancers, and "collectively, the studies do not provide good evidence that ELF exposure increases the risk of leukemia."

- Dr. Eleanor R. Adair, a fellow at the John B. Pierce Laboratory in New Haven, Connecticut, and a senior research associate and lecturer at Yale University, says "no study, whether laboratory research or epidemiological survey, has demonstrated a causal link between low-level ELF fields and human cancer."

- Dr. Edwin L. Carstensen, a physics professor in the Department of Electrical Engineering at the University of Rochester and author of the book, *Biological Effects of Transmission Line Fields*, says "If you look at the scientific basis for the whole thing, there's nothing there. A few studies seem to give a borderline indication of an effect, someone else tries it, and it disappears."

- The Connecticut Academy of Science and Engineering, responding to public fears raised by Brodeur that an electrical power line substation was responsible for a cluster of child cancer cases in the town of Guilford, issued a report in June 1992 saying "There is no evidence that there are any health effects" from the Guilford power station.

Physicists, medical doctors, and epidemiologists agree that there is no reliable evidence that EMFs are dangerous. This does not mean that research ought not to continue, and indeed it is: In 1992, Congress authorized a public/private five-year research effort funded to the tune of $65 million to study the effects of EMFs. As of today, however, evidence is still lacking of an association between EMFs and cancers of any kind.

Problems with the Theory

Logically, there are two big problems with the EMF scare.

- First, if EMFs cause cancer, then cancer rates (especially childhood cancer rates) should have soared during the past thirty years as electric power line construction surged and use of electrical appliances grew. In fact, as we have noted elsewhere, no such increase was experienced.

The rates of childhood leukemias, according to Dr. John Boice, Jr., chief of the National Cancer Institute's Radiation Epidemiology Branch, "have been relatively stable, not what one would expect to see if increasing EMF exposure were having a major effect." The evidence presented in Chapter 3 reinforces this view: There has been no cancer epidemic.

But what about all the cases of illness and even death that Brodeur documents? Half-a-million people die of cancer each year in America, and millions of homes are located near electric power lines and substations that emit EMFs. If there were no association at all between EMFs and cancer, pure chance nevertheless would result in thousands of cases of cancer, including rare childhood cancers, appearing in homes near power lines and substations. Sometimes, the number of cases will seem high (these are called "clusters" by epidemiologists), but chance can be responsible for this as well. For very rare events (such as childhood leukemia, which usually occurs at the rate of one case per 200,000 children), two cases in a single neighborhood can produce a cancer rate that is (depending on the size of the neighborhood) five, ten, and even twenty times higher than the national average. Such a high rate does not mean EMFs causes leukemia unless all other factors are controlled for and the association can be documented by other researchers.

A good writer like Brodeur has no problem finding cases where cancer and other illnesses are *correlated* with exposure to power lines and substations. But hundreds of thousands of such cases will exist *purely by chance*, with no *causation* taking place. Brodeur in fact has never described a single case of human injury scientifically known to have been caused by low-level EMFs. Not even one. All he has given us is case after case of *correlation*, cases any one of us could attribute to brooms and mops in the victims' closets just as well as to the power lines outside their homes.

- The second logical problem with the theory is that the EMF emissions from electric power lines are relatively small compared to the emissions of common household appliances.

For two reasons, our exposure to EMFs from sources inside our homes is greater than what we experience from overhead power lines, transformers, and substations. First, we are physically closer to appliances and the wiring of our homes than we are to power lines; we know that the power of EMFs diminishes rapidly with distance. Second, the strength of a magnetic field is proportional to electrical *current*, not voltage, so a high-voltage power line does not give off a stronger field than do the much smaller lines in our own homes.

As the table on the following page shows, a typical stereo emits an EMF that is between 1.3 and 5 times as strong as that which you are likely to receive standing under a high-voltage wire. The EMF generated by high-voltage power lines is dramatically below the maximum magnetic fields produced by direct contact with various appliances (such as using an electric shaver). But power line emissions appear low even when compared to *typical* emission levels from common household appliances. Computers, stereos, and microwave ovens typically have emissions as high as or higher than overhead power lines.

The table below does not mean you should stop using electric shavers or computers. None of the items in the list is thought to endanger your health. The table is meant only to suggest how EMFs produced by power lines are small compared to everyday appliances, which in turn demonstrates how implausible it is that EMFs could link power lines and cancer. If EMFs are related to cancer, why isn't there any evidence, even anecdotal, linking stereos or clothes dryers to cancer?

Risk and Making Choices

Wertheimer, Leeper, and Brodeur can continue to claim that EMFs

Electromagnetic Field Strengths

Typical and maximum ranges,* in mG

Source	Typical	Maximum
Shaver	50-300	6,875
Blow dryer	1-75	2,175
Computer	1-25	1,875
Microwave oven	3-40	812
Dishwasher	1-15	712
Kitchen stove	1-80	625
Stereo	4-100	500
Electric alarm clock	1-12	450
Refrigerator	1-8	167
Television	1-3	100
Clothes dryer	1-24	93
Overhead power line	**3-20	n.a.

*Maximum exposure is direct contact with the appliance or source. Typical exposure varies based on distance from appliance.

**Measured standing on the ground at the edge of a right-of-way under a 3.6 kV line.

Source: "Power Frequency Magnetic Fields in the Home," *IEEE Transactions on Power Delivery*, Vol. 4, January 1989, pp. 465-478.

might cause cancer or some other disease: It is impossible to prove, once and for all, that they *don't*. This isn't only true of EMFs and cancer: It is true of the association between brooms and cancer, too. In order to counter the claim that EMFs *may* cause cancer, we must contend that EMFs can never, under any circumstances, cause cancer. But since we do not completely understand human life and all the things that influence it, we cannot defend such a universal statement.

Instead of complete certainty, we can only *infer* that our failure to find an association in the past, after rigorous effort, means it is highly unlikely that such an association exists. It is always possible that new evidence, acquired by observing a larger or better sample, will invalidate our original conclusion. For this reason, an element of uncertainty is attached to any generalizations that we make based on inference. This in itself is an important lesson science can teach us: Risk and uncertainty are everywhere and always present. *One hundred percent certainty is never an option.* We should be skeptical of those who say otherwise.

Some risks, such as the risk of dying in a car accident or drowning, are *real* because past deaths attributable to these causes are accurately reported and the cause-and-effect relationship is well understood. Other risks, such as the risk of dying of cancer due to EMFs, are *hypothetical,* and the nature of the association is poorly understood or completely unknown. If people such as Paul Brodeur are correct, then 15 percent of childhood cancer is caused by EMFs. This would amount to a hypothetical added risk of childhood leukemia of about 0.7 per million. As the

Risks of Fatality from Various Causes
(risk in 1989 per one million population, U.S.)

Cause	Risk per million
Real risks	
Car accident	192
Accident at home	90
Drowning	16
Electrocution	3
Lightning strike	.3
Insect stings	.2
Hypothetical risks	
Ingesting pesticide residues (EPA estimate)	3.0
Landfills leak into water supply (EPA estimate)	<1
Toxic emissions from incinerator (EPA estimate)	<1
Exposure to EMFs from power lines (Brodeur's estimate)	<1
Ingesting pesticide residues (FDA estimate)	0.0015

Sources for "real risks": *Statistical Abstract of the United States*, 1992, Table 123, and National Safety Council, *Accident Facts*, 1993. See text for sources for "hypothetical risks."

table on the previous page shows, this risk is nearly 130 times lower than the risk of dying in an accident at home. Since our time and resources are limited, we need to choose which risks we want to pay attention to, and which are just too small to address. The authors consider EMFs to be too small a risk to merit environmentalists' attention at this time.

Conclusion

The EMF cancer scare has caused near-panics in Guilford, Connecticut, Montecito and Fountain Valley, California, and Hewlett, New York. Many people are frightened and demand that elected officials and industry take action to reduce the EMF "threat." Indeed, we *could* spend many millions of dollars moving power lines and designing complicated EMF shields, *just to be sure* EMFs don't expose us or our families to potential harm. But the money we use to combat this extremely unlikely threat would no longer be available to make our highways safer, improve our health care system, or perhaps protect fragile ecosystems and endangered species in Third World countries. Is the trade-off worth it? We simply cannot have it all; we have to make choices.

At this time, the authors believe the best choice is to continue studying the unlikely but possible link between EMF and cancer, but not to invest in "solutions" until we know that a problem exists. There is little evidence now to suggest that EMFs are a problem.

November: Oil Spills

On March 24, 1989, a major oil spill in Prince William Sound, Alaska, turned the world's attention to the long-standing global problem of oil spills. Between 1980 and 1990, approximately 87 million gallons of crude oil were spilled, about two-thirds from vessels and one-third from land-based facilities and drilling platforms.

No one disputes that oil spills hurt wildlife and marine habitat, at least in the short term. But we take issue with those environmental groups that feature oil-soaked birds and other injured marine life in their fundraising solicitations and claim that oil spills are a problem reaching "crisis" proportions. On the contrary, there is good news to report on the oil spill front. In the interest of fairness, we present this side of the story.

Ecological damage by oil spills

The biggest and most destructive oil spill in recent years was the 1989 Exxon Valdez spill in Prince William Sound. How destructive was it? Jack Hilton, a video producer who filmed the impact of the spill in the Sound, gave this report to *The New York Times* in May 1989:

> The [Prince William] Sound is about three times larger than Rhode Island. It contains an estimated 262 trillion gallons of water, into which more than 10 million gallons of crude oil were plunked. That's the equivalent, they say in Valdez, to a teaspoon of fluid in an Olympic-sized swimming pool. The toxicity level rose only momentarily — and microscopically. As they put it in Valdez, there was no appreciable fish kill: Herring spawning is O.K. and the salmon are running. The scenery remains breathtaking. Also pristine. (More than 94 percent of the immense shoreline around the sound was unaffected.)

This report differs considerably from the popular view — formed by television news coverage and the countless newsletters of environmental organizations — of conditions in the Sound soon after the Exxon spill. Why the difference? Hilton's report focused on conditions above water: *What about under water?* In the course of Exxon's massive clean-up effort, scientists from government, academia, and industry studied the water and floor of the Sound. They made three important discoveries:

- *Most of the sea floor of the Sound contained no Exxon Valdez oil at all.* Where oil from the tanker spill was present, it was confined to a few bays close to shore, and even there it represented only a very small increment (no more than a few percent) of the natural petroleum background.

- By far the largest source of oil in the Sound was not tanker spills, but natural seepage from geologic deposits of oil outside the Sound. This seepage, now thought to have taken place for at least 160 years and probably for thousands of years, has created a background level of petroleum that greatly exceeds the amount contributed by the Exxon Valdez and other man-made spills over the years.

- Superimposed on this natural background is a century's worth of

> small spills and leaks from boating operations, fuel tanks, municipal wastewater systems, and other current activities. These deposits, though individually quite small, occur frequently and have a relatively large cumulative effect.

These findings are consistent with research conducted by the National Academy of Sciences, which found that offshore drilling accounts for less than 2 percent of the oil in the world's ocean, with the balance coming from natural seepage. Researchers from Texas A&M University have discovered thriving communities of mussels and tube worms feeding on natural oil and gas seeps on the floor of the Gulf of Mexico, more proof that oil is a natural part of the marine ecosystem.

Returning to Prince William Sound, where did the 10 million gallons of Exxon Valdez oil go? The process of *dilution* is part of the answer: The amount of oil spilled was indeed equal to about "a teaspoon in a swimming pool," and all the water in the Sound is replaced every twenty days by natural circulation. This means oil spilled in the Sound would be difficult to find a few weeks after a spill even if it didn't disappear in other ways. But just as importantly, in the first 48 hours after an accident, almost half (40 percent) of spilled oil *evaporates*, and more evaporates at a slower rate after that time. Finally, between 90 and 95 percent of the oil that remains behind is broken down and eaten by naturally occurring bacteria and other marine life.

Most of the damage caused by an oil spill occurs when waves carry some of the spilled oil to beaches, where it can cover sand and rock and hurt many kinds of marine life. Here, impartial observers have recognized that nature's power to recover, even without human assistance, has been truly impressive. Human assistance, in fact, may be more of a hindrance than a help. Kent Jeffreys, then director of environmental studies for the Competitive Enterprise Institute, wrote in 1991:

> In study after study, it has been confirmed that natural processes take care of spilled oil (which, after all, is a natural, biodegradable substance) whether or not man takes an active role. In fact, vigorous cleaning activities can actually do more harm than good. According to Sylvia Earle, chief scientist for the National Oceanic and Atmospheric Administration, "In terms of the abundance and diversity of life, oiled beaches [in Prince William Sound] that were left untreated are

now similar in most instances to sites where no oil had come ashore. . . . Treated beaches are clearly in the worst shape."

None of this proves that man-made oil spills don't cause ecological damage in the short term. It only shows that the amount of damage falls short of the claims made by some environmental organizations. In April 1993, officials with the National Oceanic and Atmospheric Administration reported that "the Sound has made a remarkable ecological comeback because of human efforts and nature's own cleansing process." One official, however, insisted that "it is perfectly clear that some species remain damaged." This mixed report has the ring of truth.

Economic motives and oil spills

The oil shipping industry has many reasons to want to minimize the amount of oil it spills. Exxon spent $2.5 billion cleaning up the Valdez spill and attempting to repair the damage, plus an additional $3 billion in legal claims from fishermen, canneries, villages, and private landowners. Another 5,000 claims totalling $3.5 billion are pending against the company. On top of this tremendous financial burden, Exxon received a drubbing by the national and international media, permanently staining its reputation among consumers and investors.

Partly in response to the enormous expenses associated with the Valdez spill, oil companies are getting tougher on the companies that carry their oil. Royal Dutch/Shell Group, for example, conducted over 3,500 tanker inspections in 1992 and "flunked" 20 percent of the vessels. Chevron Corp. maintains a computer database of 10,000 vessels and performs its own inspections of a third of the tankers it chooses to carry its oil.

The companies that *insure* tankers also have been prompted to change the way they perform. Because they stand to lose millions of dollars when a major oil spill occurs, the insurers have tightened their inspection of ships and raised premiums for those they judge to be unsafe. Some unsafe tankers are being taken out of service because their owners cannot afford to pay the new, higher insurance premiums, and oil companies refuse to allow them to carry their oil without insurance.

The U.S. oil industry recently created an emergency oil spill response system enabling it to get equipment and manpower to the scene of major spills quickly. The Marine Spill Response Corporation (MSRC), after spending $400 million for vessels and equipment by January 1993, was already the largest oil spill response organization in the world. Another $600 million has since been spent in start-up costs and to operate five regional response centers along U.S. coastlines. The MSRC has an independent, self-perpetuating board of directors who are not affiliated with the petroleum industry.

Finally, the new attention focused on cleaning up oil spills has led to the development of new technologies that promise to accelerate natural processes that break down or allow the efficient removal of spilled oil. Three of these technologies are:

- *Inipol*, a kind of fertilizer for the oil-eating microorganisms that exist naturally in sea water. Five hundred tons of the substance were sprayed on the oil spilled by the Exxon Valdez in 1989. According to EPA and U.S. Congressional Office of Technology studies, the substance made natural biodegradation of oil residues take place at two to three times normal rates.

- *Eco Spheres*, also known as *Heller's beads*, tiny glass beads coated with titanium dioxide. When sprayed over spilled oil, the beads become coated with oil. Sunlight reacts with the titanium dioxide, breaking down the oil into carbon dioxide and water. The residue is a nontoxic, sand-like particle that floats, enabling it to be skimmed and reused or allowed to float to shore and mix with real sand. Heller Environmental, owner of the bead technology, claims it could clean up a spill the size of the Exxon Valdez in just a few weeks.

- *Elastol*, a chemical that congeals oil into a skin that can then be pulled off the water's surface with a device that resembles a spinning drum. The gooey results are then churned like butter in a pumping system, returning the oil to its former state. The manufacturer claims that 97 percent of spilled oil is recoverable with its product.

The private sector has stepped up its efforts to prevent oil spills and to minimize the environmental damage they cause should they occur. Oil producers and shippers realize that oil spills in the 1990s expose them to much larger financial penalties than in the past, and they have responded by improving their safety measures and spill response capabilities. Technological innovations promise to make future oil spill cleanups faster, more economical, and less harmful to marine ecosystems.

New regulations

In addition to the many initiatives taken by the oil shipping industry, federal legislation passed in 1990 will help ensure that fewer oil spills occur and that funds will be available to conduct cleanup activities. The 1990 Oil Pollution Act:

- Raised the financial liability for owners of average-size supertankers operating in U.S. waters to approximately $100 million, up from about $14 million under previous liability requirements.
- Authorized *unlimited* liability if a spill should occur when the ship's captain is intoxicated or when other federal laws are violated.
- Created a 5-cents-a-barrel tax to fund a $1 billion Oil Spill Liability Fund.
- Required new tankers calling at U.S. ports to have double hulls and existing tankers to be retrofitted with double hulls on a phased schedule.
- Made alcohol and drug testing of tanker crews mandatory.

Conclusion

Thanks to all these initiatives and reforms, the number and size of oil spills in U.S. waters since 1990 have been at historically low levels. Outside U.S. waters, progress is occurring at a slower pace because unsafe tankers operate under the flags of nations with lax safety standards, particularly Panama, South Korea, Malta, Cyprus, and St. Vincent. While changes in the international insurance market are being felt by other countries, too, they have been unwilling or unable to match the investment in prevention and cleanup being made by companies based in the U.S. The sources of this problem (including poverty and the instability or corruption of foreign governments) may be beyond the ability of environmentalists in the West to address.

Oil spills should certainly be avoided when possible, but it is wrong to think of them as long-term environmental catastrophes or a problem getting worse over time. Even a spill the size of the 1989 spill in Prince William Sound had few observable effects on wildlife or the region's ecology. The discovery that naturally occurring oil seeps contribute many times the amount of oil as is spilled by man reveals how small a role man-made oil spills actually play in marine ecosystems.

Thanks to industry initiatives, the MSRC, and the Oil Pollution Act, oil spills do not pose an environmental "crisis" in U.S. waters. This is a problem that is well on its way to being solved.

December: Toxic Chemicals

In recent years, exposure to mercury, lead, dioxin, asbestos, some kinds of pesticides, vinyl chloride, polychlorinated biphenyls (PCBs), and other man-made chemicals has been identified as a real or hypothetical threat to wildlife and sometimes to human health. The environmental movement helped to identify these risks and campaigned to have the offending chemicals banned or regulated. This "watchdog" activity is an important role that environmentalists can perform.

Unfortunately, the environmental movement often has shown poor judgment in deciding *what should be done* once it has sounded an alarm. In particular, the movement too often calls for action before sufficient research is available, and for bans on products or evacuations of communities when alternative forms of regulation or inexpensive cleanup measures would produce better results at lower costs. Nowhere are these mistakes more common than in the movement's reaction to toxic chemicals. In fact, as we will show in this discussion, these mistakes have been elevated to the status of deliberate tactics — a "new paradigm" — by Greenpeace and similar organizations that dominate the environmental movement's response to chemical threats.

In the discussion below, we first review the available evidence concerning human exposure to toxic chemicals and the effects of that exposure. We then examine the "new paradigm" claim that traditional rules of scientific research and policy making don't apply to chemical hazards. Finally, we review the environmental movement's response to dioxin and its current campaign against chlorine. These episodes dramatically reveal the errors in reasoning and tactics that often lead the movement to take irrational and counterproductive stands.

The threat to public health

To say that all chemicals may be harmful is to completely miss the real threat posed by some toxic chemicals. The right question to ask is not *"Can chemicals be deadly?"* but rather, *"Do current levels of exposure to toxic substances constitute a public health hazard?"*

Of central importance is the rule of toxicology we have used before: The dose makes the poison. If exposure to a chemical is extremely low, then the likelihood of being harmed by the chemical is also low. This rule has a further implication we have mentioned only briefly: Some substances that are deadly in large doses may be *beneficial* in small doses.

Some minerals, such as iron and potassium, are vitally important parts of our diets, but they would poison us if consumed in large quantities. Similarly, our bodies naturally contain traces of arsenic, cadmium, and chromium, yet these chemicals are thought to be potent carcinogens. Obviously, it is the *amount* of these elements that determines whether they are beneficial or poisonous. Before we can determine whether toxic chemicals endanger our health, we need to know the level of our exposure to them, and the shapes of the dose-response curves involved. (See the sidebar on the following page.)

Our knowledge of actual exposure to toxic chemicals is surprisingly limited. For example, regarding human exposure due to hazardous wastes, Roger Dower of Resources for the Future noted in 1990:

> While the *potential* risks to health from exposure to hazardous wastes may be substantial, little is known about the *actual* risks to the public from past and current disposal practices. Very few studies or formal risk assessments have been conducted in the vicinity of abandoned or currently operating facilities. . . .

Our knowledge of dose-response curves is also limited. A National Academy of Sciences study conducted in 1984 found that no toxicity

Dose and Response: Not Always Linear

The graph below shows three possible relationships between the dose of a substance and cancer incidence. The only evidence a scientist has is in the observed range, in which 10-12 units of dose produce cancer tumors in 10-100 percent of test animals. To estimate the effect of *lower* doses on cancer incidence requires that the scientist *guess* the shape of the dose-response curve.

Line *a* is linear. This is the assumption used in most studies that estimate human risks based on laboratory animal tests. Lines *b* and *c* indicate there is a *threshold* below which the substance no longer increases cancer incidence. For line *b*, the threshold is for doses of 2 units or less. For line *c*, the threshold occurs at 6 units.

By observing only a small interval of the total dose-response curve, a scientist has no way to tell which line — a, b, or c — is the right one.

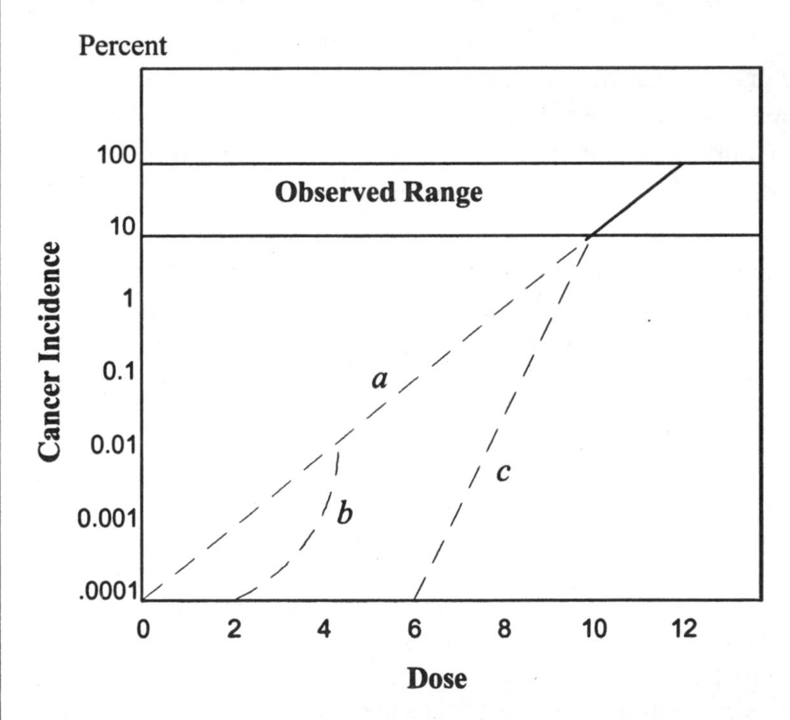

Source: Derived from Jay I. Goodman, "A Rational Approach to Risk Assessment Requires the Use of Biological Information: An Analysis of the National Toxicology Program (NTP), Final Report of the Advisory Review by the NTP Board of Scientific Counselors," *Regulatory Toxicology and Pharmacology* 19 (1994), pp. 51-59.

information was available for three-fourths of the 60,000 chemicals tracked by the EPA. Even when such information is available, it is often of little value; most dose-response information is based on notoriously unreliable maximum tolerable dose (MTD) tests on laboratory mice.

In spite of these gaps in our knowledge, the EPA has attempted to measure the danger to human health posed by toxic chemicals. According to Dower, a "recent study conducted by the EPA's senior managers placed the risks from hazardous waste sites among the lowest the agency has to address." Neither the EPA, nor the National Cancer Institute, nor the Agency for Toxic Substances and Disease Registry has been able to identify a single person whose cancer resulted from exposure to waste site carcinogens.

Using data from 1980, the EPA has estimated the health risks attributable to municipal landfills. According to the EPA, 83 percent of landfills pose less than a one in one million chance of causing cancer or other significant toxic effects. Twelve percent pose a risk less than one in 100,000, while the remaining 5 percent pose a risk of less than one in 10,000. Based on these estimates, the EPA has determined that the operation of all municipal landfills in the U.S. might account for one additional cancer death every 13 years. Current risks from municipal landfills are probably much lower; 14 years have passed since the data supporting the EPA's estimates were collected, and most of the landfills tested have been replaced with new, state-of-the-art facilities.

In Chapter Two we observed that average life expectancy in the U.S. improved from 70.8 years in 1970 to 75.4 years in 1990, and is projected to reach 76.6 years by the year 2000. In Chapter Three, we cited epidemiological evidence that man-made chemicals and pollution of all kinds caused 2 to 3 percent of avoidable cancer deaths in the U.S. in 1970. Given that perhaps a third of all cancer deaths are related to genetics or old age and are not avoidable, and given that human exposure to virtually all forms of pollution has fallen since 1970, we concluded that chemicals and pollution today are probably responsible for less than 1.5 percent of all cancer deaths. We also documented that the overall cancer rate for non-elderly Americans is *falling*. These facts suggest that exposure to toxic chemicals is not a significant cause of cancer or chronic illness in America.

Earlier in the present chapter we described how the cancer risk from exposure to pesticides is believed (by the EPA and the FDA) to be so low as to be indistinguishable from zero, and (according to Dr. Bruce Ames) is thousands of times less than the cancer risk associated with naturally occurring carcinogens in our diets. This finding is particularly relevant to the current discussion of toxic chemicals, because pesticides are the class of chemicals most likely to reveal the carcinogenic effects, if any, of toxic chemicals generally. Unlike any other class of chemicals, pesticides are deliberately released into the environment by widespread spraying on the ground and onto food. Consequently, our exposure to pesticides and their residues is likely to be much greater than our exposure to other chemicals. Some pesticides were persistent and bioaccumulative, and as a result they can still be detected in fish and human fat tissue. Finally, their presence on food gives pesticides a vehicle into the human body that many other chemicals do not have. The absence of evidence linking pesticides to cancer or other forms of illness must be taken as compelling evidence that current levels of exposure to toxic chemicals are not a serious threat to human health.

A NEW PARADIGM?

Some environmentalists appear to have decided that, if scientific research is unable to reveal a threat to public health caused by toxic chemicals, then the rules of scientific research must be changed. These activists have advanced a "new paradigm" for identifying and responding to environmental threats. Descriptions of the new paradigm vary, but four elements consistently appear:

1. *Reverse onus principle:* The burden of proof, now carried by those who claim a substance poses a threat, is shifted to those who claim it does not. According to this principle, a manufacturer should be required to prove that a substance will not threaten human health or the environment *before* receiving permission to release it into the air or water.

2. *Precautionary principle:* Because the causal links between chemicals and effects are often complex and difficult to find, environmentalists may be unable to produce evidence meeting conventional scientific standards of proof. Instead, they should be held to a lower standard of evidence that does not require proof of cause and effect.

3. *Zero discharge principle:* Because ecosystems and the human endocrine and reproductive systems are extremely delicate, no safe level of exposure or emissions exists for some kinds of persistent or highly toxic chemicals. Since controlling emissions *after* they are produced cannot be guaranteed to produce zero discharge, processes that create persistent toxic substances must be phased out, not merely controlled or reduced.

4. *Cost-benefit analysis isn't appropriate:* The threats to the environment and to human health are so grave that conventional cost-benefit analysis is not an appropriate way to determine whether action is necessary. Cost-benefit analysis is usually biased toward chemical manufacturers and against change.

Advocates of the "new paradigm" say it is necessary because traditional methods of scientific investigation and regulation are too slow and "reactive." Several years may pass between the time suspicions about a chemical are first voiced, and when conclusive evidence of a cause-and-effect relationship is finally found. Furthermore, these advocates argue, the newest research suggests that combinations of chemicals act in mysterious ways to produce a "suite of effects" on reproductive, endocrine, and immune systems and *in utero* injury to the unborn. Because such processes are "difficult to detect," environmentalists should be given the benefit of the doubt and allowed to rely on laboratory animal tests, small epidemiologic studies, and observation of the effects of toxic substances on wildlife.

Several objections to the "new paradigm" are worth noting. First, **reversing the burden of proof** gives manufacturers a task that is logically impossible: using inference to prove a universal statement. Chemist Alex Milne, in the June 12, 1993 issue of *New Scientist*, writes that "There can be no absolute proof of 'safety' or 'harmlessness' even if we want there to be one. We have to live with risk."

By requiring this impossible proof, the new paradigm gives environmentalists the power to forbid virtually any human activity. "On this ground," wrote the late Aaron Wildavsky, professor of political science and public policy at the University of California-Berkeley, "many policies and practices that make up the warp and woof of daily life would actually have to be abandoned." Just as importantly, Wildavsky argues, the process of trial and error, which leads to gradual improvements in safety, would grind to a halt. The effect of reversing the burden of proof would therefore be to increase, not reduce, risk. This is the opposite of what proponents of the reverse onus principle claim their principle achieves.

The **precautionary principle**, as interpreted by some environmentalists, has dangerous implications for science, human health, and the environment. Acting with precaution, of course, is often appropriate. In cases involving persistent toxic chemicals, the precautionary principle has a meaningful application: Following its reasoning, chemical manufacturers have largely stopped producing highly persistent and bioaccumulative substances. But new paradigm environmentalists use the precautionary principle to justify relying on research and studies that are unreliable and unlikely to be accurate. This is *not*, as they also claim, what is meant by a "weight of evidence" approach to making public policy.

Under the guise of demonstrating a "weight of evidence," new paradigm environmentalists seek to give a veneer of respectability to flawed and unreliable studies that have been rejected by the scientific community. Once again we are being told that selectively reported experiments involving maximum tolerable dose injections into highly sensitive laboratory animals *might suggest* a danger to human health. Sloppy epidemiologic studies with small sample sizes, questionable data collection methods, and multiple uncontrolled confounders are held up as *suggestive* of a threat to human health. New paradigm environmentalists claim that many bad studies add up to good science, but common sense should tell us otherwise.

Jack Weinberg, a spokesman for Greenpeace, believes the precautionary principle is justified because "what we're debating is not science but public policy. Public policy is informed by many things, including science. One of those things is ethics. What standard of proof do you need to phase out harmful substances?" It is true that we use different standards of proof in different situations. But Greenpeace uses the precautionary principle to justify rummaging through the scientific literature for studies, however flawed, that support its positions. Finding a few, it then claims it has demonstrated a level of scientific support that is "good enough" for making public policy. In fact, this lesser level is definitely not "good enough" to stand in for the views of the entire scientific community, nor is it "good enough" for making public policy decisions affecting the lives and well-being of millions of people.

Ultimately, the debate is indeed about public policy. But first it must be about science. If the science isn't "right," then public policy will go in whatever direction the loudest voices and deepest pockets wish to take it. A *suspicion* that a chemical may be causing harm is not science; extrapolating human carcinogenesis from laboratory animal tests and shoddy epidemiologic research are not science. Nothing in ethics or the public policy process miraculously converts bad research into good science. Public policy decisions that are based on bad science not only fail to protect the public from possible hazards, they expose us to even greater risks.

The **zero discharge principle** also has some plausibility when it is applied to *persistent* toxic chemicals. The ability of chemicals such as PCBs, DDT, and dioxin to accumulate in the environment and in animal fat should be cause for concern. On the other hand, no injury to human health from current concentrations of any of these chemicals has been convincingly documented, and even these low levels are falling. Moreover, most man-made chemical substances (including chlorinated compounds) exist naturally; the background levels of some chemicals are well into detectable ranges even in the absence of man-made emissions. Translating the zero discharge principle into public policy can mean that manufacturers and municipalities must discharge water that is *cleaner* than it was before they used it, and even cleaner than drinking water. Is this sound public policy?

The zero discharge principle appears intended only to ignore the many scientists and policy makers who object to total bans on products that are safely managed or pose virtually no threat to human health. Recasting an extreme goal as a "principle" doesn't respond to the valid concerns raised by these critics. Worse, it stifles informed debate over the pros and cons of bans versus other responses.

The attack on **cost-benefit analysis**, finally, is little more than an admission that draconian product bans are rarely worth the huge costs they impose on consumers and industry. The claim made in one recent report that such analysis contains "an inherent bias toward doing nothing" could hardly be less true: Cost-benefit analysis gives us a very good idea of what can be done with the limited resources on hand, and this information can compel us to radically change our tactics.

Consider, for example, the table below. The cost to avert one death from diphtheria in Gambia is approximately $87. A death due to malaria

Why We Have To Choose Which Risks Are Worth Reducing

Activity	Cost per Death Averted
Third World Countries	
Diphtheria immunization (Gambia)	$87
Malaria prevention (Africa)	440
Measles immunization (Ivory Coast)	850
Improved health care	1,930
Improved water sanitation	4,030
Dietary supplements	5,300
United States, non-environmental	
Improved traffic signs	31,000
Cervical cancer screening	50,000
Improved lighting	80,000
Upgrade guard rails	101,000
Mobile intensive care units	120,000
Breakaway sign supports	125,000
Lung cancer screening	140,000
Breast cancer screening	160,000
United States, environmental regulations	
Asbestos ban	110,700,000
Benzene NESHAP (revised: waste operations)	168,200,000
1,2 dichloropropane drinking water standard	653,000,000
Hazardous waste land disposal ban (1st 3rd)	4,190,400,000
Municipal landfill standards (1988 proposed)	19,107,000,000
Formaldehyde occupational exposure limit #2	86,201,800,000
Atrazine/alachlor drinking water standard	92,069,700,000
Hazardous waste listing for wood-preserving chemicals	5,700,000,000,000

Sources: Bernard L. Cohen, "Perspectives on the Cost Effectiveness of Life Saving," in Jay H. Lehr, *Rational Readings on Environmental Concerns*, pp. 462-465. (Author acknowledges that many of these numbers are only estimates and depend on other factors.) John F. Morrall III, "A Review of the Record," *Regulation* 10 (2) (1986), p. 30. Updated by Morrall, et al. (1990) and printed in *U.S. Chemical Industry Statistical Handbook* 1992, p. 141.

in Africa can be prevented by an expenditure of approximately $440. Switching to the U.S., the cost per death averted by improving traffic signs is $31,000; by increased screening for cervical cancer, $50,000; and by upgrading highway guard rails, $101,000. Now consider the cost of each death averted by the EPA's ban on asbestos, $110.7 million; or the cost per life saved by enforcing limits on atrazine and alachlor in drinking water, $92 billion. *If it were up to you, how would you spend the money?* With results as dramatic as these, is it any wonder that Greenpeace and its followers oppose subjecting their product ban proposals to cost-benefit analysis?

The "new paradigm" is actually not new at all. Its logic led to the decision to ban all uses of DDT in 1972, despite that pesticide's life-saving record in Africa. It was the reason environmentalists ignored the NAPAP report on acid rain and demanded (successfully) that draconian reductions in sulfur dioxide emissions be included in the 1990 Clean Air Act Amendments. The "new paradigm" justified the campaign to ban CFCs, although at the time (and even now) no evidence linked CFCs to increased levels of UV radiation. And today the "new paradigm" justifies spending billions of dollars to avert a single human death by removing the last molecules of chemicals such as atrazine and alachlor, while tolerating much greater threats to human health and welfare.

The "new paradigm" cannot be applied to every environmental problem and still produce meaningful results. Like the laboratory animal tests it often relies on, the "new paradigm" produces too many false alarms. And like many of the environmental regulations it already has spawned, the "new paradigm" will not prioritize environmental hazards and consequently cannot tell us where to spend our limited dollars for the maximum benefit.

"The Greenpeace approach is not anti-science," writes Milne, "although there is a lot of that about. But neither is it science. So what is it? It is moral philosophy at least, and religion probably. All that scientists can say to Greenpeace is: Sorry, your application for membership in the scientific community has been carefully considered — and rejected."

The Dioxin Scares

Many Americans became aware of the "toxic waste crisis" during the late 1970s and early 1980s, when television stations and newspapers gave extensive coverage to the plight of residents of Love Canal, a neighborhood in Niagara Falls, New York. Part of the community, including a school, had been built during the 1950s directly above a hazardous waste dump, operated by Hooker Chemical Co., that had been closed and sealed with clay years earlier. (See the box on the following page.)

The Love Canal "crisis" began with the discovery that possibly toxic chemicals, including dioxin, were leaking into basements and escaping into the air. Lois Gibbs, a resident of Love Canal, blamed her son's epilepsy on the waste and launched a campaign to have government agencies condemn and buy homes in the Love Canal area. At one point, she and fellow residents held two EPA officials hostage, attracting the attention of media and higher government officials.

In 1978, limited evacuations of the site began. In 1980, President Jimmy Carter approved the temporary relocation of 2,500 residents at an eventual cost of some $35 million for relocation and cleanup, and another $20 million in loans and grants.

Around the same time, dioxin was causing a panic in Times Beach, Missouri, where dioxin-contaminated waste oil had been sprayed on streets and fields to control dust. High concentrations of dioxin killed horses kept in an arena near Times Beach, and two children became ill after playing in the area. Fearing that floods in 1982 might carry the dioxin into homes and water supplies, the community was evacuated at a cost of some $33 million. A soil cleanup program is underway with an expected cost of $200 million.

Dioxin was also a contaminant in the herbicide Agent Orange, used in Vietnam from 1965 to 1970. Thousands of military veterans exposed to Agent Orange during combat participated in lawsuits against the U.S. government alleging a wide range of illnesses caused by exposure to dioxin.

The environmental movement jumped on dioxin with both feet. Ralph Nader, Ronald Brownstein, and John Richard, in a Sierra Club book titled *Who's Poisoning America?* claimed that "three ounces of dioxin can kill more than a million people." Samuel Epstein, in two books also published by the Sierra Club (*The Politics of Cancer* and *Hazardous Wastes in America*), and Lewis Regenstein, author of *America the Poisoned*, warned repeatedly that Love Canal was only the tip of a toxic waste iceberg threatening the country.

Searching for Villains At Love Canal

It is widely believed that Hooker Chemical Co. was to blame for allowing homes and a school to be built above a toxic waste dump. Investigative reporting by Eric Zuesse, published in 1981 in *Reason* magazine, paints a much different picture.

The Love Canal school board acquired the toxic waste site in 1953 from Hooker Chemical after threatening to use its powers of eminent domain to condemn and seize the property. The price of the deed: just one dollar. Hooker told the school board that dangerous chemicals lay just four feet beneath the surface, and even had them witness drillings through the landfill's clay cap that exposed the chemical wastes. The title to the property warns explicitly of the presence of hazardous waste.

The school board nevertheless authorized the construction of housing and a school directly above the landfill. During construction of the school, the building's footings and a playground had to be relocated to avoid soft spots caused by buried drums of chemicals. Hooker Chemical publicly opposed the development, even taking out newspaper ads warning the community of potential dangers.

Nearly thirty years passed without incident. Then, a distraught mother searching for the cause of her son's epilepsy and a small-town newspaper reporter hoping to make a name for himself sounded alarms that would eventually lead to the evacuation of 2,500 residents.

Who was the villain of Love Canal? Was it Hooker Chemical, the company that put the chemicals in the ground in the first place, but then went to unusual lengths to discourage development of the site? Was it the school board, which disregarded clear warnings and repeatedly broke through the landfill's cap to allow development of its land? Or was it, finally, a distraught mother looking for an answer to her son's affliction, or a newspaper reporter hoping for a Pulitzer Prize?

The moral of Love Canal is not that one person or another is the villain, but that the search for villains is necessarily fruitless because it directs our attention away from the real issues. Ultimately, the motives of the players in an environmental issue are unimportant compared to the facts, science, and the real level of risk that exists.

Source: Eric Zuesse, "Love Canal: The Truth Seeps Out," *Reason*, February 1981, pp. 17-33.

Into the 1990s, environmentalists stayed close to the dioxin issue, demanding that a zero discharge policy be adopted by the EPA regarding fumes from solid waste incinerators and effluent from paper mills and other factories.

What we know about dioxin

True to the "new paradigm," environmentalists sounded alarms and called for complete bans on dioxin before research established that it endangered human health. Subsequent research has found that dioxin is, at worst, a very weak human carcinogen. Research continues into the effects of dioxin on endocrine and reproductive systems, but these effects also appear to be small or nonexistent. (At the time of this writing, the EPA is preparing a new report on dioxin that is expected to allege adverse effects on human immune systems while calling for further research.)

Studies of the health of Love Canal residents have failed to find any association between chronic illness and exposure to dioxin or other toxic chemicals. A panel named by the Governor of New York and chaired by Dr. Lewis Thomas, chancellor of Memorial Sloan-Kettering Cancer Center, reported, "As a result of this review, the panel has concluded that there has been no demonstration of acute health effects linked to exposure to hazardous wastes in the Love Canal site." The New York State Department of Health reported, "Blood testing, which was designed to screen for liver and kidney abnormalities, leukemia, and other blood diseases, showed no patterns of excess abnormality. . . . None had clinical evidence of liver disease. . . . Cancer incidence was within normal limits." And regarding birth defects, "Efforts to establish a correlation between adverse pregnancy outcomes and evidence of chemical exposure have proven negative."

Studies of the residents of Times Beach, Missouri, also have failed to discover any adverse effects of dioxin on health. Vernon N. Houk, who as director of the National Center for Environmental Health at the Centers for Disease Control had urged the evacuation of Times Beach, said in 1991 that he regretted his decision. "I would not be concerned about the levels of dioxin at Times Beach," he told an international conference on health. If dioxin is a human carcinogen, "it is, in my view, a weak one that is associated only with high-dioxin exposures." The American Medical Association, shortly after the Times Beach buyout, voted to "adopt an active public information campaign . . . to prevent irrational reaction and unjustified public fright and to prevent the dissemination of possibly erroneous information about the health hazards of dioxin."

The health of military veterans exposed to Agent Orange also has been closely studied. Ben Bolch and Harold Lyons report:

> Repeated studies have failed to show a greater incidence of ailments among soldiers who were exposed to [Agent Orange] and who have blood concentrations up to seven times higher than soldiers not exposed to the chemical. . . . Indeed, a series of studies released in 1991 reported "no relationship between Agent Orange-related dioxin and cancer of any kind, liver disease, heart disease, kidney disease, immune system disorders, psychological abnormalities, or nervous system disease."

The National Institute of Occupational Safety and Health has evaluated the health of industrial workers exposed to dioxin levels *fifty times as high* as the exposure received by Vietnam veterans. These workers have shown no increase in cancer risk.

Summarizing this and other research in 1991, Dr. Renate D. Kimbrough, then with the Office of the Administrator of the EPA, wrote: "Thus far, no convincing human evidence exists that suggests a causal positive association between the exposure to PCBs, PCDFs, and PCDDs and a higher incidence of cancer."* In November 1992, Houk updated this summary and foreshadowed EPA's growing interest in dioxin's possible effects on endocrine and reproductive systems:

> High-dose exposure [to dioxin] has some effect on male/female hormone-like activity. There is no evidence that this is associated with any recognized disease in humans. No convincing evidence exists for the association between dioxin exposure in humans with premature mortality, chronic liver disease, immune disease, cardiovascular disease, neurologic disease, adverse reproductive outcomes, or any other

---

*PCDD (polychlorinated dibenzodioxins) is the most toxic member of the dioxin family. PCDF (polychlorinated dibenzofurans) is a less toxic compound often found with, and sharing some of the properties of, dioxin.

> disease, excluding diabetes and cancer. High-dose exposure may be weakly associated with diabetes. This remains to be clarified but does not seem to be a major determinant for the development of diabetes. High-dose exposure, as evidenced by chloracne and very high serum levels (up to 600 times the background level) may result in a small (under 2) increased risk for the category of "all forms of cancer combined" when the population is observed beyond the twentieth year after exposure. Low-dose exposure (absence of chloracne) or lower serum levels of dioxin (up to 60 times background) has not been demonstrated to be associated with increased cancer risk.

The effects of low-level exposure to dioxin on human health have been studied, and no convincing evidence of harm has yet been found. Populations that have been exposed to hundreds of times the amount of dioxin as the average person have had their health carefully monitored for nearly twenty years; no unusual incidence of cancer or other illnesses has been reported. The chemical that many environmentalists consider to be the most deadly of all is not, after all, a serious threat to human health.

Why we were wrong about dioxin

Why were so many environmentalists wrong about dioxin? Lewis Regenstein had claimed in 1983 that "Dioxin can cause severe adverse health effects, and death, at the lowest doses imaginable." This statement was accurate, *but only with regard to guinea pigs*. (See the table on the following page.) Laboratory experiments have found that extremely small amounts of dioxin can kill guinea pigs . . . but hamsters require a dose *1,900 times as high* before suffering the same mortality rate. Other laboratory animals require injections 300 to 500 times as high, and *human* exposure to much higher levels has not been found to have negative effects beyond a temporary skin condition called chloracne. Regenstein and many others made the elementary mistake of *relying on laboratory animal experiments to predict carcinogenesis in humans*.

The opponents of dioxin also relied on poorly conducted epidemiologic studies that *mistook correlation for causation*. For example, a survey of Love Canal residents conducted by Dr. Beverly Paigen, a biologist, was widely reported as showing high levels of association between exposure to toxic chemicals and chronic health problems. But when the Thomas panel examined the Paigen report, they found it to be

> . . . based on largely anecdotal information provided by questionnaires submitted to a narrowly selected group of residents. There are no adequate control groups, [and] the illnesses cited as caused by chemical pollution were not medically validated. . . . The panel finds the Paigen report literally impossible to interpret. It cannot be taken seriously as a piece of sound epidemiological research. . . .

A small number of similarly small-scale, unreplicated, and unreliable epidemiologic studies are cited repeatedly in the literature of Greenpeace and the newsletters and fundraising letters of mainstream environmental organizations. The fact that these studies are too small and too flawed to form the basis of scientific proof is unimportant, according to the rules of "new paradigm" thinking. Together with discredited laboratory animal studies, they constitute a "weight of evidence" that dioxin is a serious threat to human health and must be entirely removed from all air and

How Deadly is Dioxin?

The toxicity of dioxin varies dramatically from one animal to the next. The "Lethal Dose" shown below is the amount required to kill half of the animals in a laboratory test. Doses are measured in micrograms per kilogram of body weight.

Test Animal	**Lethal Dose**
Guinea pig	1
Male rat	22
Female rat	45
Monkey	<70
Mouse	114
Rabbit	115
Dog	<300
Bullfrog	<1,000
Hamster	5,000

Source: Adopted from Michael Fumento, *Science Under Siege*, p. 103. See table for original sources.

water emissions. In the brave new world of radical environmentalism, nothing more is necessary to ban a product.

THE WAR AGAINST CHLORINE

Nowhere is the "new paradigm" more apparent than in the campaign to ban chlorine. The case for a ban is presented in two publications of the International Joint Commission (IJC), a once-obscure agency of government that has been used by Greenpeace activists as an effective platform for their views. Since the IJC's reasoning is pure "new paradigm," the four elements of the paradigm can serve to organize our discussion of its anti-chlorine campaign.

■ Reverse onus principle

". . . [T]he burden of proof [must] be shifted," says the IJC, "so that those promoting the use of industrial chemicals must prove there is no reason to believe that those chemicals will threaten human and ecosystem health, *before* their use and discharge is permitted."

Since many of the most persistent and toxic substances in the Great Lakes (including PCBs, DDT, dioxin, and dieldrin) are highly chlorinated compounds, the assumption must be that all chlorinated compounds threaten human health and the ecology. To meet their burden of proof, says the IJC, chlorine manufacturers must prove, beyond a reasonable doubt, that their products and wastes pose no threat.

Chlorine manufacturers, of course, haven't met the reverse burden of proof . . . because *it cannot be met.* Yesterday's research showing no adverse effects of chlorinated products could be contradicted by tomorrow's research, making it impossible to say with absolute certainty that no risk exists. But the same is true of any other substance, natural as well as man-made. Risk and uncertainty are unavoidable. Consequently, the burden of proof must remain with those who imagine that chlorine endangers human health or the environment.

Claims that chlorine is a uniquely dangerous or unstable substance are rebuttable. Not all chlorinated substances are either highly persistent or extremely toxic. For example, less than 1 percent of the chlorinated compounds associated with paper manufacturing would meet such a definition. Furthermore, chlorine and chlorinated compounds exist naturally. According to Dr. Gordon W. Gribble, professor of chemistry at Dartmouth College, over 1,500 naturally occurring chlorinated compounds have been identified. Natural emissions are huge: Between five and 28 million metric tons of chloromethane and two million tons of carbon tetrachloride are produced every year by natural processes. Dioxin occurs naturally whenever wood or other vegetable matter is burned, and even PCBs are found on lake beds without man's intervention. Chlorine exists naturally inside our bodies, where it helps us digest food and keeps our blood pH-balanced.

Chlorine *is* highly reactive (which makes it an ideal building block for modern chemistry), but so too are many other common elements: sodium, phosphorus, potassium, calcium, iodine, and hydrogen, for example. Each of these elements is an important part of the human diet and exists in small amounts in our bodies. Should we, following the reverse onus principle, assume that each of these substances is a threat to human health and ought to be banned unless proven safe?

■ The precautionary principle

". . . [A]ll persistent toxic substances are dangerous to the environment, deleterious to the human condition, and can no longer be tolerated in the ecosystem, whether or not unassailable scientific proof of acute or chronic damage is universally accepted. [C]onventional scientific concepts of dose-response and acceptable 'risk'," says the IJC, "can no longer be defined as 'good' scientific and management bases for defining acceptable levels of pollution. . . ."

According to the IJC, scientific research has documented injury to wildlife in the Great Lakes caused by toxic substances, many of which are chlorinated compounds. Limited laboratory and epidemiologic studies suggest that humans may suffer similar harms through a complex and difficult-to-find effect on the human endocrine and reproductive systems. While not yet conclusive, the IJC believes this evidence meets a "weight of evidence" test.

The IJC is using the precautionary principle to justify its reliance on irrelevant and poor-quality research. To begin with, injury to wildlife in the Great Lakes today is largely the result of persistent traces of *past* pollutants, including PCBs, DDT, and dieldrin. Reports of such injuries are largely irrelevant to the issue of whether chlorinated substances *now in use* and at *current rates of emission* are causing harm. Available data suggest they are not.

Tests cited by the IJC showing injury to laboratory animals provide very little useful information about the effects of chlorinated compounds on *human* health. We already know that laboratory animals react very differently than do humans to such highly chlorinated compounds as dioxin and PCBs. The IJC relies heavily on a single peer-reviewed epidemiologic study by J.L. Jacobson and others. This study alleged to have found an association between toxic chemicals in the Great Lakes and low birth weights and developmental deficits among infants born in 1980 and 1981. The small sample size (fewer than 200 mothers of newborns) and the manner in which subjects were selected severely compromise the study. Other methodological problems include:

- To determine their level of exposure to toxic chemicals, subjects were asked to recall how many fish meals and what kinds of fish they consumed during the six years preceding their pregnancies. These recollections formed the most important data in the study, yet they are likely to have been very inaccurate. For example, a meal of lake trout was assumed to contain five times the dose of toxic chemicals as did a meal of brook trout. Can *you* accurately recall how many meals of fish you've had during the past six years, and how many of them were lake trout as opposed to brook trout?

- Mothers who recalled eating the most fish also tended to weigh less before pregnancy, were three times as likely to use alcohol during pregnancy, and were more likely to use cold medicines and consume caffeine during pregnancy. The number of twins born to women selected for the study was three times the number that would be expected to appear in a random sample. All of these factors are known to be associated with low birth weights and developmental deficits among newborns.

- Even if the study's results were reliable, they show only a very weak relationship between an infant's health and a mother's recollection of having eaten fish during the preceding six years. The results show no statistically significant relationship at all between an infant's health and umbilical cord blood levels of PCBs. This measurement is considered to be the most accurate indicator of a fetus' *in utero* exposure to PCBs and, presumably, to other toxic chemicals.

- Subsequent epidemiologic surveys done in Wisconsin and North Carolina failed to confirm the associations thought to have been found by the Jacobson researchers.

For reliability and accuracy, the Jacobson study must rank with the Wertheimer and Leeper study of EMFs and the Paigen survey of Love Canal "victims." It is not sufficient evidence to assert that humans were harmed by toxic chemicals in the Great Lakes in 1980 and 1981, and certainly not that a harm continues to exist today after over a decade of steadily falling toxic chemical concentrations in lake water and fish.

The IJC has no estimate of how many people are exposed to life- or health-threatening levels of toxic chemicals in Great Lakes water, how severely these persons were harmed, where such harms took place or when, or what chemicals caused the alleged injuries. In the entire IJC report and its voluminous appendices, injured *victims* of toxic chemicals are conspicuously absent. The IJC admits that its evidence of injury to human health falls short of proof:

> Unfortunately, we are simply not in a position to provide the most convincing scientific evidence for showing that persistent toxic substances are injuring humans — that is, published data derived from human studies with the power to detect the many possible small risks of injuries that can do a lot of damage, and cost society a lot of money and grief because of the large numbers of people exposed. There are many confounding influences that are difficult, if not impossible to unravel.

But if the effect of toxic chemicals on human health is significant, then careful science and epidemiologic studies *can* discover the association. Scientists have the tools to "unravel" the cause-and-effect relationships, if they exist. So far, there is no evidence that such relationships exist. In a remarkable display of Orwellian newspeak, the IJC declares that the "absence of evidence is not evidence of absence," and that the threat to human health they cannot prove must, nonetheless, exist.

■ Zero discharge principle

"Within the environment's carrying capacity for human activity," says the IJC, "there is no space for human loadings of persistent toxic substances. Hence, there can be no acceptable loading of chemicals that accumulate for overly long periods, except that which nature itself generates." Consequently, emissions of chlorine-based substances into the Great Lakes Ecosystem must be stopped. Since the goal of zero discharge cannot be reached if chlorine continues to be used in the manufacture of other products, chlorine must be completely banned from production and all uses.

The goal of zero discharge is, as we have pointed out, a long-standing part of the "new paradigm." The case for a complete ban on chlorine, then, does not derive from anything Greenpeace or the IJC have discovered about chlorine or its presence in the Great Lakes; rather, it was Greenpeace's preconceived and ready-made solution for the chlorine "problem" from the very beginning. Application of the zero discharge principle to chlorine, however, is unjustified.

The chlorinated compounds being discussed are neither highly persistent nor extremely toxic. Virtually all truly persistent substances are already controlled, and as a result are found in the Great Lakes Ecosystem in declining concentrations. End-of-the-pipe emission controls and changes in production processes have been so successful in reducing dioxin emissions that three-quarters of paper mills in the Great Lakes region have emissions below the lowest detectible levels. There is no evidence that emissions this low endanger human health or wildlife.

Existing restrictions on factory emissions have been so effective that point sources now account for just 10 percent of water pollution into the Great Lakes. Consequently, imposing a zero discharge standard on point sources amounts to making a huge investment to achieve small gains in water quality. The zero discharge standard would require factories to make their emissions cleaner than the water they start with, cleaner even than drinking water, and probably cleaner than Great Lakes water was even in its completely natural state.

Science, of course, cannot justify this kind of silliness. But according to Greenpeace and the IJC, anything less than zero discharge is "ethically and morally unacceptable."

■ Cost-benefit analysis isn't appropriate

"It is the conviction of the International Joint Commission," reads the IJC report, "that the risk of such damage [to human health] exists, and that virtually any level of risk of this type should be considered too high to accept. Our society cannot afford to take this risk and should reduce it." Later, the IJC says "The efficiency calculations contained in benefit-cost analyses are not objective and value-free but, in fact, reflect the values of the status quo and are inherently biased towards it. Thus there is an inherent bias toward doing nothing."

Contrary to the opinion of the IJC, it is both possible *and necessary* to place a price on the benefits that would come from banning chlorine. The ban would have an imperceptible effect on Great Lakes water quality and wildlife, and consequently would produce few if any benefits. A claim that banning chlorine would reduce health care spending by $100 to $200 billion — made by the IJC without documentation or support of any kind and now frequently cited in Greenpeace literature — is ludicrous. Even the highest estimates of all health care costs related to pollution of all kinds come to just a fraction of these figures. Most researchers believe that ending the use of chlorine to disinfect drinking water would dramatically *increase* the incidence of illness and death due to water-borne pathogens, thereby driving health care costs *up*, not down. According to the EPA, the lack of disinfected water in other parts of the world results in over 9 million deaths every year.

Phasing out chlorine has been estimated by industry sources to cost $90 billion a year — $1,440 a year for a family of four — and the loss of 1.3 million jobs. These figures may be exaggerated, as Greenpeace claims. But it seems just as likely that they *underestimate* the true cost. Chlorine is used in tens of thousands of manufacturing processes in the U.S. and around the world. Not unlike the CFC phase-out, removing chlorine and its thousands of related products from manufacturing processes and consumer products would be hugely expensive. At the same time, it would create new and yet-unmeasured threats to human health.

The authors believe it is no exaggeration to say that the campaign against chlorine provides a case study of everything that is wrong with environmentalism today. The campaign is backward-looking, based more on the effects of PCBs, DDT, and other discontinued products than on the real threat, if any, of products currently being used. It shows environmentalists desperately endorsing every study, no matter how flawed, that supports prejudices and superstitions. The campaign is focused on a goal — zero discharge — that is both arbitrary and unnecessary. And once again, the campaign against chlorine shows environmentalists ignoring the social and economic costs of their proposals and refusing to admit that the benefits of victory may well be negligible.

Conclusion

What evidence we have — and it is admittedly incomplete — suggests that toxic chemicals pose a very small and diminishing threat to human health and the environment. There is no evidence that *anyone* ever died from exposure to hazardous waste in the U.S. The odds of injury from municipal landfills are about one in a million. Cancer rates are falling and life expectancies increasing, facts that suggest that the expanding use of chemicals during recent decades has not increased cancer or chronic illness rates. The fact that pesticides have not been shown to cause any human injury signals that toxic chemicals as a class pose little threat to human health.

Dioxin, once thought to be the most deadly chemical threat to human health, has been shown to be a minor threat at worst. While research continues into the possibility that it may have subtle effects on the human endocrine and reproductive systems, the evidence available now shows little basis for believing this to be the case.

The campaign against chlorine demonstrates how the mistaken reasoning and tactics embodied in the "new paradigm" undermine support for the environmental movement and waste its resources. The IJC report may represent the most consistent and thorough application to date of this new ideological framework. The results are disappointing, to say the least. Its misreading of the scientific record and Orwellian use of language signal the rise in the environmental movement of doctrine and myth and the decline of science and common sense. In the long run, this cannot be good for either the movement or the environment.

Whether the environmental movement changes its view of chemicals will determine its future credibility. Billions of dollars are being squandered responding to a "toxic waste crisis" that is not a crisis at all. We believe the environmental movement's indiscriminate campaign against chemicals must come to an end, the sooner the better.

Which problems are real?

In this lengthy Chapter 4, we have discussed twelve "environmental crises" that aren't, on closer inspection, crises at all. Most are *problems* that can be addressed with further research, rational thought, and careful planning. Some are just theories that haven't panned out. Environmentalists can breathe a sigh of relief. The sky isn't falling after all!

To each of the "crises" we discussed, the leaders of the environmental movement responded with panic, exaggeration, and emotion. The very use of the word "crisis" over and over again in the literature of the movement suggests that the concept has come to represent standard operating procedure, not the exceptional or infrequent need to respond rapidly. Concerned environmentalists responded to those calls for immediate action many times, only to be told afterwards (usually by someone outside the movement) that there was no crisis to begin with. No apologies or retractions have been issued by the environmental organizations that sounded the alarms. Worse still, these groups show no sign of realizing that they *have* been wrong so many times.

The cost of this "eco-insanity" has been steep. Lives have been lost, whole communities evacuated, and jobs destroyed when demagogues calling themselves environmentalists have exploited public fears of radiation, electromagnetic fields, pesticides, and chemicals. Every day, millions of people unnecessarily inconvenience themselves and think they are doing something "good for the environment," when in fact their actions make no difference or may even make some environmental problems worse. Billions of dollars have been squandered trying to avoid hypothetical risks, such as acid rain and ozone depletion, that turned out not to have posed a real risk after all.

The people who have been hurt by false alarms — and they now number in the tens of millions — are people just like us. We're the ones who pay with our jobs when unnecessary environmental regulations are passed. We pay with our money for unnecessary emission controls on our cars, and sometimes we pay with our lives for the lightweighting and downsizing that were done to meet unnecessarily high CAFE standards. We pay for replacing the CFCs in our cars and appliances, and we pay for "clean gas." We pay to have power lines moved or buried because of some people's fear of EMFs. We pay for the unnecessary smokestack "scrubbers" installed by coal-burning utilities to fight "acid rain." *We just pay and pay and pay.*

So who benefits from the "crisis of the month club"? The winners aren't difficult to find. They include the leaders of environmental organizations like Greenpeace USA (annual budget, $18 million), the Sierra Club (annual budget, $50 million), and Natural Resources Defense Council (annual budget, $18 million). The publishers of *The New Yorker* and the women's magazines that featured the EMF scare probably made some money by exaggerating that "crisis." And the politicians? They seem to stay in office more by talking about problems than solving them, so environmental "crises" benefit them, too.

It is difficult to devote careful thought and serious attention to real environmental problems when everything is portrayed as a crisis. We wonder how much longer the environmental movement will be able to cry wolf and expect its members to respond. We ponder how much good could be achieved if the resources now devoted to the "crisis of the month" were devoted instead to solving real environmental problems.

The authors recognize that real environmental *problems* exist. Population growth and deforestation plague some Third World countries. Forestry practices in the U.S. could be improved. The residues of persistent pesticides continue to injure wildlife and slow the recovery of some species of birds and mammals. Further progress should be made in many

Not Crises, and Sometimes Not Even Problems		
Disproven theories, never were problems	Acid rain	Plastic
Unproven theories, not problems today	Global warming Ozone depletion	Electromagnetic fields
Past problems, now nearly solved	Automobiles Nuclear power	Oil spills
Persistent but manageable problems	Pesticides	Toxic chemicals
Problems mainly in Third World countries	Deforestation	Resource depletion

areas, including protecting the air and water and cleaning up hazardous waste sites. We encourage action in these and other areas, and in Chapter Eight we will describe more specifically the actions that should be taken.

Clear thinking about many environmental "crises" reveals only solvable problems. This confirms our earlier finding: *The world is getting cleaner, not dirtier.* Despite all the rhetoric and calls to action, there are fewer environmental problems today than there were thirty years ago. The odds of being hurt by something in the environment are lower today than they were at any time in recorded human history. That's something environmentalists can take some credit for.

5. Prosperity and the environment

CAN WE HAVE prosperity and still protect the environment? Are a high and rising standard of living, job creation, and technological advancement compatible with preserving wilderness areas and keeping our air and water clean?

Some environmentalists answer "no" to these questions. In fact, the notion that economic growth necessarily hurts the environment underlies many of the "crises" discussed in the last chapter. Lester Brown's Worldwatch Institute can be relied on to supply grist for this mill, as this passage from the Institute's 1992 *State of the World* report suggests:

> Eliminating these [environmental] threats to our future . . . demands reduced consumption of resources by the rich to make room for higher living standards for the poor. And with current notions of economic growth at the root of so much of the earth's ecological deterioration, it calls for a rethinking of our basic values and vision of progress.

If you picture the environmental movement as a popular song you might hear on the radio, then this anti-progress, anti-growth theme would be a drum beat pounding ominously in the background while the lead singer describes global warming, ozone depletion, or dioxin poisoning. Nearly all the major environmental organizations march to the beat of this drummer.

At first glance, the notion that prosperity leads to pollution seems self-evident. Prosperity means people live in bigger houses that require more energy to heat and cool. It means they can afford to travel more, generating more air pollution and again consuming more energy. The wealthier people are, the more meat they eat, which means more grain must be fed to cattle rather than people. This can lead to deforestation when forests are cut down to make way for cattle ranges. Prosperity means natural resources are consumed at a faster pace, moving up the time when these resources are depleted. And wealth generates waste, burdening the world with ever-growing mountains of garbage.

A more careful examination of the impact of prosperity on the environment, however, reveals three reasons why the *pro*-environmental effects of economic growth offset its *anti*-environmental effects.

1. Higher income and environmental protection

In poor societies, the concern that comes before all others is *survival.* If survival requires that wooded areas be cleared for firewood or grain fields, then forests will be cleared regardless of the consequences for wildlife. In poor countries such as China and the former Soviet Union, coal is often burned with little or no emissions control, because the sophisticated "scrubbers" used in America are too expensive to obtain and use. Similarly, raw sewage is dumped into many of the rivers and streams of poor countries (and even wealthier countries such as Italy) because treatment of these wastes must come second to producing much-needed food, clothing, and shelter.

Wealthy societies have the *luxury* of investing in environmental protection, and they do. The United States, for example, has invested over $1 trillion in pollution abatement since the first Earth Day in 1970, and annual spending is now estimated to be $150 billion. In 1985, public and private spending on pollution abatement in the U.S., measured as a percent of our gross national product, was as high or higher than any other country in the world (see the table below), no doubt made possible by the fact that the U.S. is one of the richest nations in the world.

Public and Private Spending on Pollution Abatement

Country	Percent of GDP in 1985
United States	1.5
West Germany	1.5
United Kingdom	1.3
Netherlands	1.3
France	.9
Norway	.8

Source: Frances Cairncross, *Costing the Earth*, p. 24, citing OECD statistics. Only countries for which both public and private expenditures were available are included in this table.

A 1993 report, prepared by the EOP Group, Inc. for the Global Climate Coaltion, estimates that:

> [T]he U.S. is allocating a substantially greater share of its GDP to environmental protection than the European Community — 1.7 percent vs. 1.2 percent — a difference of 40 percent. U.S. environmental expenditures as a percent of GDP are projected to grow to at least 2.7 percent by the year 2000. This estimate does not include the full cost for implementation of the Clean Air Act Amendments of 1990 and does not include the costs for any major new climate change mitigation program.

This level of spending on pollution abatement would be impossible if the economy of the U.S. were not growing. Frances Cairncross explains the relationship like this:

> Clean technology is easier to introduce in new and fast-growing industries. Indeed, because new technology is almost always cleaner than the old sort, a country with low levels of capital investment (such

> as Poland and Britain) will tend to be relatively dirty. Fast-growing industries have the opportunity and flexibility to build in new technology. But with the important exception of chemicals, the fast-growing industries are often those, such as office machinery or electronics equipment, that are only moderately polluting.

Even the "important exception of chemicals" may be a problem solved by technological advancement: Between 1987 and 1990, EPA statistics show that the U.S. chemical industry reduced its toxic emissions by 41 percent even as it expanded output by 10 percent.

The table on the previous page reports only pollution abatement expenses, not additional spending on parks and nature preserves or the countless unreported conservation projects taking place on private property. Much of this activity, too, would be impossible if our affluence did not allow us to meet our basic needs of food, clothing, and shelter, and still have money left to spend preserving the environment.

2. Economic efficiency and the environment

The same process that fuels economic growth also fuels reductions in pollution, making the one a natural partner of the other. This process is the gradual improvement in the efficiency of resource use: getting more use out of fewer resources, resulting in less pollution-causing waste. We discussed this process briefly when we discussed energy supplies and resource depletion. Let's look at it more closely here.

Imagine you are the president of a big telecommunications company. To serve your customers, you use telephone lines made of copper. The copper is expensive, and paying for the lines is a considerable part of your budget. If you could reduce that expense, you could earn higher profits or, by lowering your prices, raise profits by winning customers away from your competitors. So you have an incentive to study ways to find a less-expensive substitute for copper.

You soon discover *fiber optics*, a material made out of glass (which, in turn, is made out of common sand). A fiber optic cable can carry thousands of times as many messages as a copper cable, making its cost-per-message lower. Your desire for higher profits and your need to compete with other companies (which also have discovered fiber optics) drive you to replace your copper cables with fiber optic cables as quickly as is economical. Since the copper in the used cables is valuable for other uses, you sell it to a company that specializes in stripping away the insulation and selling the copper to other manufacturers.

By switching from copper to fiber optics, you have helped *conserve* scarce copper and energy resources for other uses in the future. (The energy was needed to mine, refine, and manufacture the copper wire.) Your decision wasn't based on any deliberate intent to conserve scarce natural resources, yet this was one of the results.

As you are installing fiber optic cables, your competition suddenly switches to *satellite transmission* and *cellular phone* technologies, which don't require cables at all. They are now poised to undercut your prices and take away your customers! In order to compete, you enter the satellite and cellular arena, too. By making this switch, you are *conserving* the energy and even the common sand that would have been used to manufacture fiber optic cables. But once again, conservation wasn't your goal: making a profit was.

This story is actually a realistic account of changes in the telecommunications industry in just the past decade. Hundreds of thousands of tons of copper that *would have been* used to manufacture telephone cables are no longer needed, thanks to technological progress and an incentive system that rewards efficiency. Here is a compelling example of how efficiency contributes to our prosperity (by making communication less expensive and higher quality) *and* conserves natural resources.

The Council on Environmental Quality has identified several other real-world examples of corporate initiatives that benefit both the environment and the corporate bottom line. Among these examples:

- AT&T's Columbus, Ohio, plant saved $210,000 by implementing changes in processes that eliminated emissions of perchloroethylene.

- Chevron saved $10 million in waste disposal costs and reduced hazardous waste by 60 percent in thc first three years of its Save Money and Reduce Toxics (SMART) program.

- A Ford assembly plant in Lorain, Ohio, cut its paint sludge volume by 30 percent and its annual disposal costs by $56,000 in one year.

- The International Paper Company expects to save $100 million in disposal expenses between 1988 and 1995 by recycling and reusing manufacturing wastes.

- The 3M Pollution Prevention Pays program has resulted in cumulative worldwide savings from 1975 to 1990 of $537 million ($450 million from 3M's U.S. operations).

People in industry are coming to understand the connection between efficiency and pollution. "Most waste happens because something is not being used properly," says Chris Hampson, board director of ICI, a chemical manufacturer based in Britain. "Waste may happen because a plant is only 90 percent efficient in its use of raw materials. The rest is going out in waste. A lot of pollution is associated with inefficiency." The drive to improve efficiency is also a drive to reduce pollution.

Consider one more example: *forest industries*. When natural stands of timber were very large compared to the demand for wood products, paper and lumber companies had no need to *economize* on their use of this resource. As a result, branches, bark, and other leftovers from a lumbering project were often left behind or burned without energy recovery. Clear-cutting was common and replanting was rare, since there was little point in planting what was already available in abundance.

Soon, competing demands for the forests began to emerge and the supply of unharvested natural forests relative to demand began to shrink. Lumber companies soon found that they could enhance their profits by using the leftovers from lumbering to make paper pulp and to generate steam for paper mills. They discovered that the application of forest management techniques — such as fire prevention, spraying for certain highly destructive pests, and quickly replanting harvested areas — paid off in higher yields of usable wood per acre.

These investments increased profits and improved efficiency, as they were intended to do, but they also led to the practice of sustainable yield forestry. The benefits to wildlife from this evolution have been tremendous, yet this was not the primary consideration that led to these innovations . . . making this another example of how the quest for economic efficiency leads to environmental protection.

To summarize, the process of increasing economic efficiency produces both economic growth *and* a cleaner environment. This means prosperity, rather than being the enemy of a clean environment, is actually its logical and even necessary partner. Efforts to slow down or stop technological change or economic growth could have the unexpected result of harming, rather than protecting, the environment.

3. Imagination and the Environment

Underlying the Worldwatch Institute's view that "the rich" must reduce their consumption of resources "to make room for higher living standards for the poor" is a flawed premise that every environmentalist should recognize and reject. This assumption is that the physical amount of a resource in the ground matters more than the power of human ideas. This assumption leads us to believe that progress of any kind — whether it is progress in improving our environment, raising our standards of living, or improving our health — relies more on *things* than on *ideas.* Until this notion is rejected, we are trapped in a mindset that denies the most promising sources of progress while giving support to policies that may actually harm rather than protect the environment.

How do we know that ideas or *brain power* are more important than things or *natural resources* stored in the ground? Max Singer, in his remarkable book *Passage to a Human World*, explains it like this:

> Resources, people, and ideas are all that exist; so some combination of them must be the source of wealth. At least one of them must change if we are to get more wealth. Which of these has been changing to increase our wealth? Not the original resources; they are fixed. Not the people; their fundamental characteristics are largely what they have been for forty thousand years. . . . The big change is ideas. Since wealth is multiplying and the only potential source of wealth that is changing is ideas, it must be *the ideas* that are responsible for the increase in average wealth. New ideas are being created all the time and useful old ideas are spreading. More and more people are learning how to create wealth.

"The point that most wealth comes from ideas not from things needs to be belabored," according to Singer, "because it is so absolutely fundamental, and because the opposite idea is so insidiously natural and common." We agree, so let's belabor the point for a moment.

Some environmentalists view the world as if it were a *baked pie* ready to be served. If "the rich" get a big slice, then there is less available for "the poor." But this image would have us all sitting around the pie with forks at the ready, and none of us able or willing to step into the kitchen to make more pies. This hardly reflects the real world, wherein nature's bounty must be continuously discovered, refined, and brought to market. Humans are not antelope, which simply eat whatever nature chooses to offer; humans delve below the Earth's surface and above its clouds to find new ways to fulfill their needs.

Better than the baked pie image is a picture of mankind working in the kitchen of a busy restaurant. Rather than sitting around a table hoping to be served, we are rushing around trying to fill the stream of orders coming in from our hungry customers. We are always looking for new and less expensive ingredients for our pies or ways to waste less flour, shortening, and fillings. If we can discover a way to produce more pies at a lower cost, then *everyone* can get bigger slices of pie.

Won't even the most creative pie maker eventually run out of flour? Not if we can offer to pay more to get it, because land and other resources now used for other things will be put to work producing flour. If even this avenue is exhausted, we could stretch our supply of wheat flour by using fillers and substitutes (soy flour, for example). If even this avenue is eventually exhausted, we may switch from making pies to making soup, which is nutritious but doesn't require flour at all.

The point of this extended metaphor is that so long as we have imagination, our rising prosperity will not cause us to run out of natural resources. Our success at filling wants is virtually never limited by the quantity of *things* available. It is limited only by our ability to apply *ideas* to the puzzle of how to produce things of higher value from things of lower value.

Markets and pollution

Which economic system is most able to produce the prosperity that enables us to invest in environmental protection? Which system rewards the efficiency gains that produce both prosperity and a clean environment? Which system expands the pool of natural resources by placing its highest values on ideas rather than things?

The empirical data on each of these questions, as we will show, are very clear: Market systems — also called free enterprise or capitalism —

outperform socialism, communism, and "mixed-economies" (half market and half socialism) on all three scores.

Per-capita gross domestic product (the value of all the goods and services produced in a country divided by its population) in countries with market economies greatly exceeds the levels in socialist countries. (See table on the following page.) Dr. Gerald W. Scully, professor of economics at the University of Texas at Dallas, examined per-capita growth rates and efficiency measures over the period 1960 to 1980 for 115 economies. In particular, he asked whether these variables were influenced by the degree of political, civil, and economic liberties enjoyed by their citizens. Here is how he summarized his findings:

> It was found that the choice of the institutional framework has profound consequences on the efficiency and growth of economies. Politically open societies, which bind themselves to the rule of law, to private property, and to the market allocation of resources, grow at three times (2.73 to 0.91 percent annually) the rate and are two and one-half times as efficient as societies in which these freedoms are circumscribed or proscribed.

"On average," wrote Scully, "societies that subscribe to private property rights and a market allocation of resources grew at a 2.76 percent rate compared to a 1.10 rate in nations in which private property rights are circumscribed and the state intervenes in resource allocation." Trends since 1980 — including the economic collapse of communist countries and the growth of the U.S. economy compared to the mixed economies of Western Europe — suggest that market economies have become even better at producing prosperity and efficiency in recent years.

This prosperity has meant better stewardship of the environment. While air pollution levels in the capitalist nations of the West fell between 1970 and 1985 (as documented in Chapter 2), environmental conditions under communism deteriorated sharply during this period. For example:

- Chemical plants in the Soviet Union for many years emitted large amounts of a potent pollutant, fluorine, into the atmosphere. Despite numerous studies by engineers that showed that the fluorine could be recovered at a profit and sold to other enterprises, the plant managers

Comparing the Wealth of Capitalist and Socialist Nations

		Per-capita gross domestic product, 1989
Capitalist Nations		
Japan		$22,900
United States		20,910
Canada		20,240
France		17,000
Britain		14,580
Socialist Nations		
Soviet Union		9,226
Czechoslovakia		7,876
Romania		4,896
Poland		4,625
Yugoslavia		2,474
Side-by-Side Comparisons		
Capitalist	South Korea	4,920
Socialist	North Korea	1,427
Capitalist	Taiwan (ROC)	7,390
Socialist	China (Mainland)	547
Capitalist	West Germany	19,520
Socialist	East Germany	9,669

Source: *Statistical Abstract of the U.S.*, 1992, Table 1371.

found it *easier* to continue to pollute, and so nothing was done to control emissions.

- Children from the Upper Silesia area of Poland were found to have five times more lead in their blood than children from Western European cities. Half of the children in that area suffered from pollution-related illnesses.

- Romania had no air pollution controls and in some areas horses were only allowed to stay for two or three years. "They have to be taken away, or else they will die," says Dr. Alexandru Balin, a physician in the Romanian town of Copsa Mica.

- In Leuna, in what was formerly East Germany, at any given time 60 percent of the population suffered from respiratory ailments. Four out of five children in Espenhain developed chronic bronchitis or heart ailments by age seven. In Telpice, a town in northwest Czechoslovakia, air pollution kept children inside for about a third of the winter.

- Drinking water in Hungary was seriously contaminated with arsenic. Sewage treatment was nonexistent or very primitive in many large cities.

- The Soviet government dammed the two rivers feeding the Aral Sea, located between Uzbek and Kazakhstan Republics, reducing the sea's area by nearly half. The exposure of its enormous salt bottoms has resulted in devastating salt storms, local climate changes, and the eradication of some twenty of the 24 fish species native to the Aral Sea. Some 60,000 people who worked in the fishing industry lost their jobs.

Trends in per-capita energy use provide further evidence that market economies have better environmental records than socialist economies. The graph on the next page shows how per-capita energy consumption in capitalist countries initially rises as income increases, but then falls as improving efficiency gradually outpaces prosperity-driven increases in energy demand. For socialist nations, the rise is much more steep, and it is broken only when economic growth stops and per-capita income is forced to fall. This graph is a vivid portrayal of how markets, by rewarding efficiency and innovation, enable us to move past an energy-intensive stage of economic development and become increasingly energy-efficient, whereas socialist nations remain trapped in a world with both low standards of living *and* high levels of energy consumption.

To summarize, the free enterprise system's record for producing wealth and efficiency is superior to that of socialism and communism.

This has led to a level of environmental protection and energy efficiency in capitalist countries that is much superior to that of socialist and communist countries.

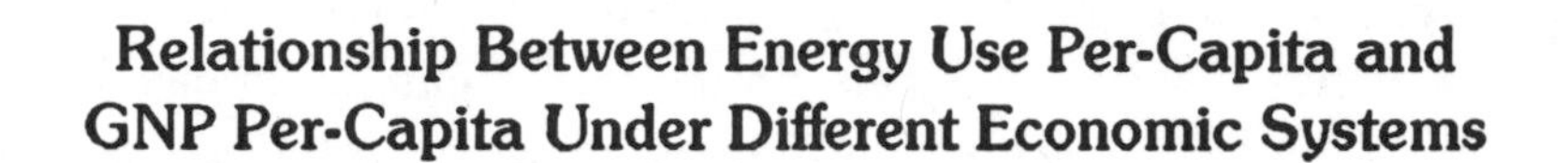

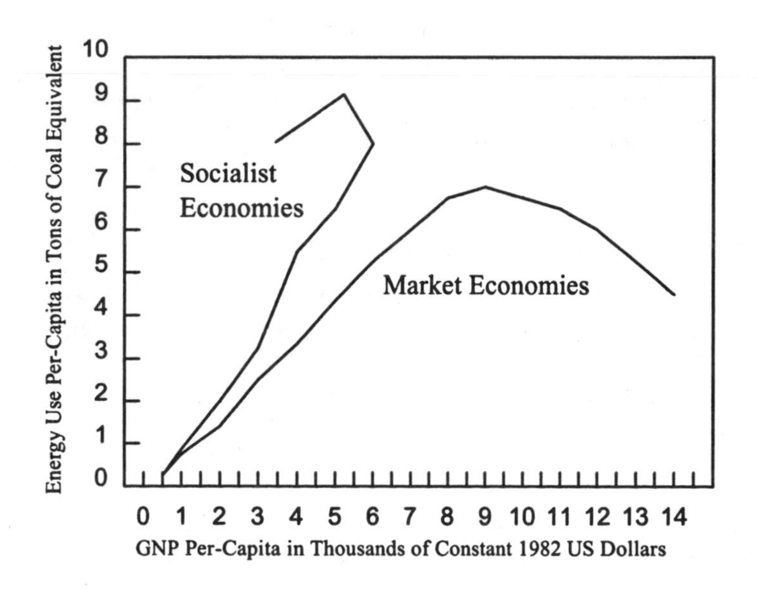

Source: Mikhail S. Bernstam, *The Wealth of Nations and the Environment*, 1991, p. 55.

Why markets protect the environment

The superior economic and environmental performance of capitalism is probably not what many environmentally conscious readers expected. The images that have stayed with us from grade school or college classes are of the industrial revolution's smoky factories, sweatshops, violent strikes, child labor, and colonialism. A system that would allow such atrocities, we feel almost instinctively, cannot be trusted to protect the rights of workers or a fragile environment. Even a professional writer on economics, the aforementioned Frances Cairncross, writes:

> For it is only government that can decide how much society should value the environment, and how that value should be inserted into economic transactions. The market, that mechanism that so marvelously directs human activity to supply human needs, often has no way of putting a proper price on environmental resources.

It is time to update our attitudes toward capitalism, and particularly our understanding of how it puts "a proper price on environmental resources." Capitalism is based on a system of markets and private property rights. When rights are correctly defined and enforced, capitalism will protect the environment for four reasons:

- ✔ It creates incentives to do the right things;
- ✔ It generates and distributes needed information;
- ✔ It enables people to trade things or rights in order to solve problems that otherwise can't be solved; and
- ✔ It enables property rights to evolve over time.

The free-enterprise system creates wealth, rewards efficiency, and protects the environment better than any other system yet devised by man. The tireless campaign against this system by some quarters of the environmental movement is wrong-headed and counterproductive.

Incentive structures

A market system uses transferable property rights to create incentives to do the right things. Property rights, in turn, consist of having control over the use of a resource. The owner of a resource stands to benefit if the resource is put to its best use. Conversely, the owner will suffer a loss if the resource is misused or squandered. And if the property right is transferable, then owners must consider not only the value *they* place on a resource, but also the values that *others* may place on it.

To see how these incentives can change the fate of animals, consider the following examples:

- One hundred years ago, there were three billion passenger pigeons. They were hunted to extinction; the last remaining passenger pigeon died in 1914. Two hundred years ago, great herds of buffalo roamed the American plains, but they too were nearly made extinct. (Although today they can be found in growing numbers in national parks and on private ranches and farms.) Because they were migratory and owned by no one, neither passenger pigeons nor the buffalo were protected by people willing to invest in their conservation.

- Similarly, in African countries where elephants are owned in common, they are being hunted to the edge of extinction, the victims of poachers in search of ivory. But in countries such as Zimbabwe, Botswana, Malawi, Namibia, and South Africa, where individuals and communities are allowed to own elephants and profit from their sale, elephant populations are voluntarily protected and *growing* at the rate of 5 percent per year.

Without private ownership, it is difficult to protect wildlife, forests, or other environmental resources, because no one directly benefits when the resource is conserved or suffers a loss if the resource is mismanaged. When natural resources are owned collectively (or "by the government"), each of us may use or manage the resource very negligently, because we aren't affected much by our careless behavior. As a result, public ownership often leaves the environment dependent on people's charity or "good instincts." These qualities are admirable, to be sure. But as the passenger pigeon, buffalo, and African elephant show, we can't rely on admirable qualities alone to protect rare or endangered animals.

Private property rights are also a way of ensuring that those who control resources take account of the effect of present actions on *future* resource values. The price of a resource today reflects the value of the future income that could be earned by using or selling the resource. Therefore, owners have every reason to take account of the future effects of their actions. However, under a system of central planning and state ownership, asset values take a back seat to short-term objectives, such as meeting the goals of a "five-year plan." Government resource managers tend to be short-sighted; because they do not *own* the resources they manage, they are not likely to be penalized when their mismanagement reduces the value of the resources under their control.

Examples of the impact of poorly defined rights can be seen in air and water pollution. Individuals or organizations that pollute usually are not faced with the full consequences of what they have done; the costs associated with polluted air and water are borne by everyone, not just the polluters.

Another good example of the poor incentive structures that result from poorly defined property rights was found under communism in the Soviet Union and Eastern Europe. In those countries resource managers were rarely rewarded for taking actions that preserved the environment, and there was little penalty for over-exploitation. Consequently, tremendous environmental degradation occurred.

Creation and use of information

How does a farmer know whether to plant wheat or corn in the spring? How does a manufacturer know how many and what kind of products to make? How does an investor know with which business or bank to entrust his money? The answer in each case is *prices*.

Prices represent a remarkably efficient network for consolidating the information that resides in the minds of millions of individual consumers and thousands of producers of goods and services. The farmer produces wheat because wheat prices are higher this year and corn prices are down. He doesn't need to interview a hundred people to determine which they like more, wheat or corn. He has only to check the prices at the wholesale market to find the answer to his question.

Prices in a market economy provide a two-way information system linking consumers and producers. The better the price system works, the less waste is likely to be created. Such an information flow depends critically upon private property rights, because prices represent offers to take actions with regard to property. Only when the person making the offer pays the true cost or reaps the entire benefit of his or her actions do prices convey accurate information.

With central planning and state ownership of property, prices that accurately reflect reality are the exception, not the rule. Prices in a centrally planned economy represent the values of a small number of political leaders, not the desires of real buyers and sellers. Also, there is no feedback mechanism by which prices are adjusted so they become more accurate with time. In the face of such an *information blackout*, it is not surprising that environmentally unsound decisions dominate.

For example, government ownership of our National Forests means those responsible for managing and making appropriate trade-offs between logging and recreation find it difficult to gather adequate information about the values that society places on those two uses. Because logging interests can point to an existing price for their resource, they have often gained more consideration than people who want to use the areas for recreation. A system of private property rights that allows recreational users to bid against people who want to put a resource to a consumptive use would generate superior information.

Creating exchange solutions

A market system allows disagreements over the value of natural resources to be resolved through the exchange of money or rights. For example, if a small wilderness area is about to be cleared and turned into a cornfield, environmentalists can approach the owner and offer to pay him the amount he might otherwise expect to make by planting corn on the land. The farmer gets what he wants — income off land he owns — and the environmentalists get what they want — preserved wilderness. Such exchanges to protect the environment have saved the lives and habitat of elephants, geese, and other wildlife in places around the world. (See the box on the following page.) They can be agreed to quickly, without committees or voting, and they do not require the use of force or the violation of property rights.

Many times there are legal barriers to exchange that prevent the effective use of resources and attention to environmental quality. In 1987 there was a severe drought in Montana and irrigation demands removed most of the water from many streams. Irrigators took enough water from the Ruby River, a prime trout stream in southwestern Montana, to cause a major fish kill. The amount of flow that would have been necessary to prevent the kill was relatively small, and the value to people who wanted to maintain the fish stock was clearly greater than it was to irrigators. An organization, Trout Unlimited, stood ready to purchase water — just enough to keep fish alive — from farmers who had the right to irrigate. But such an exchange was impossible, because Montana law did not recognize any defensible property right to instream flows of water.

How Exchanges Are Protecting the Environment

Elephants in Africa

"When rural Africans can benefit from elephant hunts and from selling elephant products, they have an economic stake in elephant conservation. That stake can be sizable: $25,000 is the price of an average Zimbabwe hunt where elephant is the main trophy. Further income is generated for rural communities when animals that destroy property are killed by National Park personnel and the ivory and hide are given to the community. Income from hunting and ivory also helps finance enforcement of anti-poaching measures.

"One Zimbabwean subsistence community recently curtailed poaching in Gona-re-Zhao National Park and villagers agreed to devote some of their land to wildlife in exchange for hunting permits for elephants and buffalo that overflowed from the park. The permits were sold to a safari operator. Part of the proceeds was used to develop community facilities and the rest distributed directly to community members who lost crops to animal damage."

Source: Randy Simmons and Urs Kreuter, "Save an Elephant — Buy Ivory," *The Washington Post*, October 1, 1989.

Geese and Armadillo in Louisiana

"The Audubon Society, a group opposed to oil and gas development in most wilderness settings, acted differently when it owned the land and mineral rights. The Rainey [Wildlife Sanctuary, ten miles south of Intercoastal City, Louisiana] is home for deer, armadillo, muskrat, otter, mink, thousands of geese, and many other birds, and it would seem unlikely that Audubon would allow natural gas production there. But since the 1960s there have been oil wells in Rainey. . . . In return for allowing Consolidated Oil and Gas to produce on the sanctuary, Audubon receives royalties. Because the Society cares about the environment, they impose strict contractual restrictions on how the gas can be extracted; and because those restrictions cost the oil company more, Audubon receives lower royalties. That is the price they pay for caring for the environment."

Source: Terry L. Anderson and Donald R. Leal, *Free Market Environmentalism*, p. 90.

Evolution of property rights

Efficient markets, as we noted earlier, require that property rights be defined, enforced, and made transferable. Historically, these tasks have been performed by the common law (sometimes called the civil justice) system, which allows the victims of property rights violations to seek compensation from their transgressors in a court of law. While the operation of the common law system has been considerably compromised in the twentieth century by the intrusion of statutory law, the common law remains an important part of the market system and, as we explain in the next chapter, could be an important part of future efforts to expand protection of the environment.

Under the common law system, precedents set by past court decisions form a body of law that largely determines how subsequent cases are decided. Since each new lawsuit brings with it small differences in facts and in the values of the parties involved, it is an opportunity to test whether past decisions, based on older technologies and values, are still applicable or whether adjustments may need to be made. This process of continuous refinement and revision gives the common law system its unique ability to *evolve* over time.

Rising efficiency and prosperity clearly have led to greater public concern for things that once were regarded as unimportant or unaffordable: clean air, clean water, and preservation of wilderness areas, among them. The common law system allows the rising value of environmental protection to be translated into action by gradually hiking the amount of damages awarded to the victims of pollution. This process would be especially successful if private property rights to clean air and clean water were better defined and enforced than historically has been the case — a shortcoming that perhaps could have been solved had the common law strategy not been interrupted earlier in this century.

Conclusion

Let's briefly summarize what we have found.

- Prosperity is not incompatible with a clean environment. In fact, prosperity is *necessary* for making the large investments needed to keep our air and water clean and to protect wilderness areas.

- Innovation — the use of ideas to solve problems — is more important than the finite supply of things in determining how prosperous a people will be. There is little danger that we will run out of ideas.

- Property rights are the critical link between actions and accountability. A well-functioning property rights system creates appropriate incentives, generates useful information, and allows exchanges to move resources to the places where they are most highly valued.

- As values and technology change, a market system is able to change, too, developing well-defined, transferable rights to resources that have become more valuable over time.

Focusing on property rights, or systems of accountability, helps us understand why environmental problems exist. It also helps us find solutions that will succeed. In the following chapters we will use this understanding of property rights to develop policy recommendations for solving environmental problems.

Contrary to the anti-growth and anti-free enterprise rhetoric of some environmentalists, growth and free enterprise have proven to be compatible with and even essential to a clean environment. Our comparison of the actual records of market and socialist countries shows that the environment is protected better by markets than by centralized government planning.

6. Why can't the government protect the environment?

DURING THE THREE decades since publication of *Silent Spring*, much of the environmental movement has relied on government to stop pollution, safeguard human health, and protect wildlife. So heavy is this reliance that many environmentalists measure the movement's progress by the strictness of government-enforced air and water pollution standards, the amount of land placed under government control, and the number of plants and animals given protected status under the government-enforced Endangered Species Act. Getting the government to protect the environment is the sole objective of some of the largest environmental organizations in the U.S.

In the discussion that follows, we examine how well the government has performed this role. We find the record to be a poor one, particularly in light of the immense resources that have been spent complying with government's environmental regulations. We then re-examine the rationale for relying on government rather than private efforts and the courts to protect the environment. We sketch an alternative strategy that relies on property rights, markets, and the courts to hold polluters accountable to their victims.

We realize that most people take for granted that government must play a major role in protecting the environment. We hardly expect our brief discussion here to change many minds, and actually that is not our purpose. The property rights approach that we present in this chapter offers some genuine insights into *why* environmental problems exist and, consequently, *how best to solve them*. Even people committed to relying on government should find this discussion illuminating.

Government's record

Government in the U.S. has performed its role as protector of the environment in two principal ways: First, by owning and managing some 720 million acres of land (about 32 percent of the entire country); and second, by establishing and enforcing regulations that prohibit certain levels of pollution and the destruction of certain plants and animals. The discussion below is not an exhaustive review of government programs in these areas, since such programs are numerous and sometimes very complex. Instead, we focus on several specific activities that serve to demonstrate how government programs often lead to unexpected and disappointing results. News of such *government failures* does not spread very far or very fast, giving many environmentalists a one-sided and mistaken view of government's record.

Government as landlord

The territory given over to the federal government to manage and protect has grown considerably during the past thirty years. (See chart on the following page.) The National Park System, for example, more than tripled in size between 1960 and 1992. The National Wildlife Refuges System increased by a factor of five, and the National Wilderness Preservation System grew by a factor of ten since 1964. Only the National Forest Service did not see significant growth during this period.

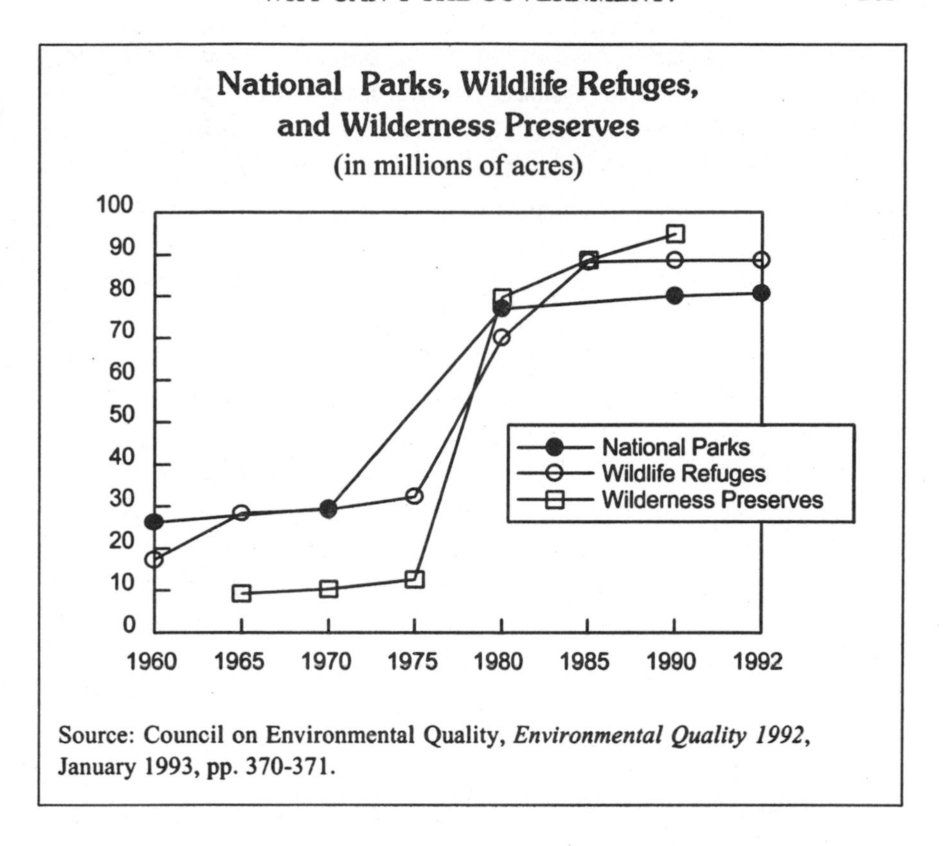

Source: Council on Environmental Quality, *Environmental Quality 1992*, January 1993, pp. 370-371.

Of great concern to environmentalists is the manner in which the federal government oversees logging in the National Forests. The record here is not a good one. The federal government systematically subsidizes logging on public lands where, in the absence of subsidies, it is almost certain no logging would take place. Part of the subsidy is in the form of publicly financed roads for the logging industry — some 342,000 miles snaking through every part of the nation's forests. According to Dr. Richard Stroup, senior associate of the Political Economy Research Center:

> These roads, primarily designed to facilitate logging, extend into the ecologically fragile backcountry of the Rocky Mountains and Alaska, where they are causing massive soil erosion, damaging trout and salmon fisheries and causing other environmental harm. In many cases, the costs of these logging activities far exceed any commercial benefit from the timber acquired; so this environmental destruction would not have occurred in the absence of government subsidies.

During a six-year period in the 1980s, the federal government lost nearly $3 billion on timber sales. These losses are the second form of subsidy for environmental destruction: In effect, taxpayers are paying the lumber industry to log environmentally and recreationally valuable areas. Many of these areas are so dry, cold, or steep that nature may never be able to restore the forests once they are removed.

Subsidized logging is not, unfortunately, the only way government encourages environmental damage. The National Park Service has allowed elk and bison populations in Yellowstone Park to greatly exceed the habitat's carrying capacity: The number of elk in 1988 was estimated at 16,000, versus just 3,100 in 1968. Overgrazing has killed willows and aspen to the point where the beaver, dependent on this vegetation, has nearly disappeared from Yellowstone. Hungry elk and bison wander out of the park in search of food, threatening to infect cattle with brucellosis, a bacterial disease that causes cattle to abort their fetuses. After the 1989 fires in Yellowstone, park managers did nothing to keep elk and bison in the park or to lure them back. Only when state officials asked hunters to start shooting the bison did park officials attempt to lure the animals back into the park and take responsibility for feeding them.

The federal government mismanages land under its control in other ways. Ranchers are permitted to graze their herds on public lands at fees well below the prices paid for private grazing land. Since the cost is low and the ranchers have no guarantee that their cheap grazing licenses will be renewed in subsequent years, they overgraze the land and seldom replant grazed areas. The result is unnecessary erosion and the destruction of habitat for native species of wildlife.

Through its farm programs, the federal government also encourages environmental mismanagement of *privately* owned land. With one hand, the federal government supports the prices of some crops, encouraging over-production. With its other hand, the government pays farmers to idle some of their land. In an effort to take advantage of both subsidies, farmers seek to grow more crops on fewer acres, resulting in an over-intensive agriculture. More fertilizers and pesticides are applied, more irrigation water is used, and the land is worked harder than it otherwise would be. As a result, more fertilizers and pesticides run off into local water supplies, and soil is more likely to erode. The federal government's agricultural disaster relief programs have similarly negative consequences by encouraging farming of marginal land in flood plains.

The environment also suffers because the federal government subsidizes the wasteful use of water to irrigate crops that are already in surplus or which have low value (such as hay and alfalfa). The farmers who benefit from these subsidies value the water they use so little that they refuse to spend even a *penny per ton* to keep it from leaking out of pipes and canals. Frances Cairncross writes:

> Virtually everywhere, the costs of installing, operating, and maintaining irrigation systems are carried largely by the taxpayer. . . . [I]n the 1980s farmers enjoyed an implied subsidy of $1 billion a year. In California's Central Valley, farmers pay less than 10 percent of the average supply cost of irrigation water. . . . [A]pproximately 40 percent of the subsidized water is used to irrigate crops that are already in surplus . . . [and] 30 percent of the area irrigated with federal water was planted with low-value crops such as hay, alfalfa, and other pasture.

Max Singer says "the true shortage is . . . not water for drinking. It is not water for farming. *It is water to allow farmers and others to save money for themselves by using water-wasteful irrigation methods.* They can do this because taxpayers pay most of the real cost of the water which is wasted."

Government subsidies for farm irrigation can cause serious environmental damage. They can lead to falling water tables, which can alter lake levels and river flows, drain wetlands, or lead to invasion of underground lakes (called aquifers) by salt water. Heavy irrigation can cause a build-up of salts and heavy metals in the soil, making it infertile. Excessive irrigation can cause trace elements (such as selenium) to leach from the soil into streams and lakes, where it kills fish and water birds. And the construction of dams and diversion of rivers can harm fish and wildlife.

All of these harms to the environment, and more, are paid for by taxpaying environmentalists. This is not the record that most environmentalists hoped for when they entrusted their environment to the government. What went wrong?

The bureaucrats who manage government-owned land and water rights are honest and hard-working individuals. But they do not benefit personally if the resources placed under their care are put to the best use or managed for long-term sustainability. Instead, their self-interest is best served by responding to political pressure from loggers, ranchers, and farmers. These interest groups seek to maximize the short-term production of specific outputs (lumber, beef, and alfalfa) almost regardless of the long-term environmental impact. Forestry expert Randal O'Toole recently described the incentives facing the Forest Service like this:

> Resources are priced [by the Forest Service] at less than fair market value, leading users to demand greater quantities than can be produced efficiently. With the support of user groups, the Forest Service requests increased budgets from Congress to prevent supposed resource "shortages." These budgets allow the agency to provide resources below cost which, in turn, increases the quantities demanded and provides support for further budget increases. This pattern is made worse by the fact that managers receive positive feedback from timber and grazing in the form of funds retained out of fees. These funds give managers an even greater incentive to sell below cost and even negatively value resources to increase their budgets, which, in turn, increases quantities demanded and leads managers to claim that shortages are imminent if further budget increases are not provided.

In addition, the Forest Service doesn't keep the recreation fees it collects; instead, these monies go to the Treasury or to state and county governments. By contrast, the Forest Service gets to keep 25 percent of revenues from timber sales. It is no surprise, then, that the Forest Service is more likely to listen to lumber companies than to environmentalists, a situation not likely to change until environmentalists start to pay their own way.

Once we understand the incentives facing the Forest Service and the interest groups who use public lands, the difficulty of ending the government's degradation of the environment becomes apparent. The logging roads, unprofitable timber sales, and excessive grazing are not accidents that could be corrected by better bureaucrats or a new Administration. They are part of the very nature of government ownership of public lands. The situation will not improve next year or the year after . . . or ever. It is the natural and expected result when government becomes a landlord.

GOVERNMENT AS REGULATOR

Besides trusting the government to own and manage 32 percent of the land area of the U.S., the environmental movement has asked government to establish and enforce standards for air and water quality. How well has government performed this task?

The bulk of current environmental policy relies on regulations that set rigid standards and require specific behavior, an approach economists call *command-and-control* regulation. These regulations typically order companies to roll back their emissions by certain amounts or to a certain standard. In the case of Superfund, which focuses on cleaning up the results of past pollution, these laws assign financial responsibility to those companies and industries deemed best able to pay.

For many reasons, the command-and-control approach to regulation is very costly and often ineffective. For example:

- Command-and-control regulations usually fail to acknowledge that some polluters can reduce their emissions very inexpensively, while others can do so only at great cost. Rather than achieve the maximum reduction for the least possible cost, command-and-control regulations often require equal or proportional reductions in waste by all sources, resulting in much higher costs per unit of reduction achieved.

This point has been amply documented by T.H. Tietenberg, a leading environmental economist and professor of economics at Colby College. Tietenberg surveyed eleven empirical studies comparing the cost of complying with command-and-control regulations to the least-costly methods of achieving the same level of pollution reduction. All eleven found that the cost of complying with regulations exceeded least-cost, ranging from a regulation/least-cost ratio of 1.07 (for reducing sulfates in Los Angeles) to 22.0 (for reducing particulates in the Lower Delaware Valley). The mean average ratio was 6; the median average was about 4. That is, complying with federal regulations typically cost between four and six times as much as the least-costly means of reducing emissions by the same amount.

- The persons who write and enforce command-and-control regulations lack detailed knowledge of procedures, opportunities, and costs — knowledge that the managers of factories and owners of resources have. Consequently, regulations often mandate equipment and procedures that achieve less emissions reduction than could be obtained in other, less-expensive, ways.

In 1992, Amoco Oil Company and the EPA completed a study of an Amoco refinery in Yorktown, Virginia to document this problem. Researchers compiled a comprehensive inventory of the facility's wastes, options for waste reduction, and the environmental regulations it was required to follow. They found that the best pollution reduction options for the plant "did not coincide with existing regulatory requirements," and that "equivalent levels of protection could have been achieved at 25 percent of the cost of current regulatory programs." In other words, allowing the plant's managers to apply their own ingenuity to the problem of reducing waste from the refinery would have cost just one-fourth as much as complying with the regulations, yet would have achieved the same level of emission reductions.

- Enforcing command-and-control standards is easiest when the source of pollution is a relatively large facility whose emissions are readily monitored. But this kind of monitoring is expensive and often impossible when the problem involves *nonpoint* sources of pollution.

According to Michael Levin, former director of EPA's regulatory innovations staff, pollution today does not arise mainly from "large sources of visible emissions susceptible to standard engineering solutions that you can slap on by centralized rule making." Nonpoint sources of pollution, he says, "are not the kinds of problems that people were trying to deal with in 1970, after Earth Day." Daniel Dudek, senior economist for the Environmental Defense Fund, agrees: "Pollution from small or extremely dispersed sources . . . is beyond the reach of conventional regulation."

- Command-and-control regulations proliferate as bureaucrats attempt to compel compliance and businesses and municipalities demand to know what is expected of them.

In a June 1993 editorial in *Science*, Philip Abelson reported that local governments are now required to comply with 419 "essential" environmental regulations and to monitor more than 130 chemicals in their water supplies. "Not only do the local governments not have the money to carry out environmental mandates," wrote Abelson, "they frequently do not know what it is they are supposed to implement." He further reports instances where municipal costs of complying with environmental regulations "exceeded EPA estimates by a factor of 20 or more."

Small businesses feel besieged, too. Sid Marder, head of an Illinois business group devoted to monitoring environmental regulations, says such regulations "come out by the bushel-full," with the result that "even the state EPA is unable to interpret or understand them all." He can reel off anecdote after anecdote of bureaucratic delays, expensive litigation, and laws whose interpretations vary from bureaucrat to bureaucrat and from day to day. "It's not that business is good and is always doing it right," Marder says, "It's that the programs are so wrong. We're wasting so much money that real environmental hazards are not being addressed."

- Businesses often correctly fear that if they find a way to reduce emissions at one facility below the level required by current laws, regulations mandating the use of "best available technology" will require that they implement the new procedures at every facility, regardless of cost considerations.

By discouraging companies from doing any better than the government standards, command-and-control regulations actually stand in the way of pollution reductions that might otherwise occur. Such regulations discourage innovation in pollution reduction technologies, since no one wants to demonstrate the feasibility of expensive new technology that will become the basis for tomorrow's rule-making. Jessica Mathews, then vice president of World Resources Institute, summarized the effects of command-and-control regulation on innovation like this:

> Regulations are . . . inherently static. Even rules that specify the use of "best available" technologies cramp innovation. Such regulations do spur the use of what is at the cutting edge when they are written, but an entrepreneur with a better product a few years later faces a market wedded to whatever the rule specified.

Due to these many limitations, command-and-control regulations have taken us as far as they can. Proof of this is found in the dramatic costs and very modest benefits predicted for the latest generation of such regulations. The 1990 Clean Air Act Amendments, according to Dr. Robert W. Hahn, an adjunct research fellow at Harvard's Kennedy School and a resident scholar at the American Enterprise Institute, will carry a price tag that exceeds whatever benefits it produces by about $16 billion each year — more than $300 per household. Resources for the Future places the excess cost of the same legislation at between $15 and $25 billion a year.

Why do the EPA and other federal agencies rely so heavily on command-and-control regulation when so many serious problems follow from this strategy? Part of the blame must fall on Congress, which has increasingly taken to dictating detailed instructions and even emission standards to the enforcement agencies. Part of the problem may also be that federal agencies want to justify their own existence and annual increases in their budgets; command-and-control regulations clearly require large staffs and enforcement budgets. Finally, environmentalists and their representatives must bear some responsibility, too, since they often have called for rigorous enforcement of inflexible emission standards and technology mandates.

Superfund: a case study

Federal regulations regarding hazardous waste were put in place in 1976 by the Resource Conservation and Recovery Act (RCRA). In 1980, amid the widespread publicity generated by the Love Canal scare, Congress passed the Comprehensive Environmental Response, Liability, and Compensation Act (CERCLA, or Superfund), governing the cleanup of existing hazardous waste sites. In 1984, RCRA was amended to include detailed and highly restrictive regulations; it was amended again in 1986 by the Superfund Amendments and Reauthorization Act (SARA).

To implement these laws, the federal government has directed much of its attention, and between 25 and 50 percent of its annual budget for protecting the environment, to addressing hazardous waste. (Recall that EPA senior managers place hazardous waste at the *bottom* of their lists of priorities.) In addition, complying with RCRA and Superfund is costing private industry an estimated $9 billion to $13 billion a year.

What have been the results of this massive investment? "Superfund has been a disaster," said President Clinton on May 10, 1993. Superfund "has become a behemoth, towering over American environmental policy, gobbling vast quantities of public and private cash and management time," wrote Frances Cairncross in *Costing the Earth*. Dr. Marc K. Landy, associate professor of political science at Boston College, and his co-author Mary Hague described Superfund in 1992 like this:

> Superfund has produced an enormous legal morass that constitutes a substantial drain on public and private resources; yet it has yielded very little in the way of environmental improvement. While estimates of sites in need of cleanup have risen to thousands, fewer than 70 have been fully cleaned.

Why has the federal government's toxic waste cleanup program been such an expensive failure? Analysts have pointed to many problems with the laws. First, Superfund uses the courts to enforce "strict and retroactive liability" and "joint and several liability" on companies that once produced the waste dumped on the sites. Strict and retroactive liability means parties are held responsible for helping to pay for the cleanup even if their dumping practices were legal at the time and even if they were operating under orders and licenses from government agencies. Joint and several liability means any single waste producer can be held liable for most or all of the cost of a cleanup if other polluters cannot be found or made to contribute to the cleanup cost. *These policies are a logical consequence of the "reverse onus principle"* discussed in Chapter 4.

Second, RCRA and Superfund "[treat] all wastes and all waste facilities as posing the same relatively high risks," writes Roger Dower of Resources for the Future. "Variations in the health or environment risks posed by regulated substances and activities are presumed to be minimal, or at least of little economic significance. The potential for misusing scarce resources is therefore tremendous." *Note that disregard for actual risk is consistent with the "precautionary principle."*

A third problem is that the 1986 amendments to Superfund require that waste sites be cleaned up to "background conditions," a level of cleanliness that may far exceed genuine human safety requirements or even environmental conditions that prevailed before contamination occurred. For example, the water underneath a contaminated site must be made clean enough to drink, and the dirt must be so clean that a person could eat half a teaspoon of dirt from the site every month for 76 years and not get cancer. These standards — called "drinkable leachate" and "edible dirt" by their critics — often require the removal of tons of minutely contaminated dirt to specially lined toxic waste landfills, an unnecessary and often environmentally destructive process. *Note, again, that these standards are what one would expect from an application of the "zero discharge principle."*

Superfund has given rise to enormous amounts of litigation. As a result, an estimated one-third to one-half of all Superfund spending goes to lawyers, not actual site cleanup. One study for the insurance industry estimated that litigation would add $8 billion to the cost of cleaning up 1,800 sites. Litigation has driven the average cleanup cost per site to a staggering $22 million.

The risk of litigation arising from Superfund is now so great that many companies are abandoning properties or refusing to purchase sites that hold any risk of having been contaminated by previous owners. The result is a loss of jobs in metropolitan areas and a construction boom in suburban and rural areas. From an environmental perspective, this is a bad trade-off, since development is being encouraged in previously wooded or agricultural areas. Moreover, suburban development may generate more air pollution due to longer commutes and less use of urban mass transit systems. Defenders of Superfund, once again in keeping with the "new paradigm," believe that *"cost-benefit analysis is inappropriate."*

Clearly, the federal government's attempt to regulate toxic chemicals and hazardous wastes has been an expensive failure. Superfund has squandered billions of dollars while making barely a start on cleaning up the nation's hazardous waste sites. Its failure illustrates how far off target a government program can go when the principles of the "new paradigm" are put into practice.

Government and wildlife

In addition to protecting forests and regulating pollution, the government is trusted to protect endangered plants and animals. Over 1,000 species and subspecies are listed as endangered or threatened under the Endangered Species Act (ESA), and another 3,500 are candidates for listing. The ESA has been used by defenders of wildlife to negotiate thousands of changes to or restrictions on land use during the two decades since the law's enactment. There is little doubt that these changes have protected many populations of plants and animals that otherwise would have been injured or killed.

What is much less clear is whether the ESA's *net effect* on wildlife

Endangered Species Act: Yes, But Does It Work?

In the twenty years since it was enacted, just 16 species have been removed from the Endangered Species Act (ESA) list. Of these, ten were removed from the list due to extinction or original data error. Even the remaining six hardly constitute success stories.

Three species of birds native to the island of Palau, in the Pacific Ocean, were removed from the endangered list when additional populations of the bird were found, *not* because the originally identified populations were protected. The same pattern was true of the Rydberg milk-vetch and the American alligator. (The National Wildlife Federation admits that the alligator "never should have been placed on the Endangered Species list.")

In the sixth case, that of the California gray whale, recovery of the whale was due more to the Mexican government's actions to protect the whale's calving and wintering grounds in Baja California than anything done by the Fish and Wildlife Service.

Of course, removing a species from the endangered list is not the only definition of success. Some truly endangered species have benefited from the ESA but remain endangered. Still, the Act itself explicitly defines success in terms of eventual delisting of species, and by this measurement it has been a disappointment.

Source: See Ike Sugg, "Specious claims of species statute?" *The Washington Times*, April 5, 1993.

has been significantly positive. Just 16 species have been removed from the endangered list since the law took effect, and most of these were delisted for reasons other than protection or preservation of habitat. (See the sidebar above.) If the ESA is working as advertised, we should be able to point to many more successes than this.

The ESA may unintentionally cause the injury and death of almost as many endangered creatures as it saves. At first glance, the law may seem wholly appropriate to the task of protecting wildlife. But in fact, it creates a set of perverse incentives that leads to less, not more, voluntary effort to protect wildlife. Richard Stroup describes the incentives as follows:

> **Under the Endangered Species Act, the owner must sacrifice any use of the property that federal agents believe might impair the habitat of the species — at the owner's expense. Furthermore, if the owner either harms the species or impairs its habitat, severe penalties are imposed. The perverse incentives created by the law may well lead an owner to surreptitiously destroy that animal or plant — or any habitat that might attract it.**

In the past, a property owner might have taken satisfaction in knowing that his land was home to an eagle or spotted owl. Being conservation-minded, he would probably report the sighting to the local forester or newspaper, thereby helping to establish the rare animal's population and location. He also may have invested in protecting the bird by erecting a fence or minimizing commercial activities in the area around the nest.

The provisions of the ESA create a very different set of incentives, and consequently a different kind of conduct. Today, the report of an eagle or spotted owl nesting on private land means a forest can no longer be logged, or a house cannot be built, or part of a golf course or campground must be closed. To avoid losing use of a valuable asset, a landowner might be tempted to destroy a nest or even kill the endangered animal. Alternatively, the owner might allow critical habitat to be destroyed by logging or development as quickly as possible, before anyone else can see and report the protected animal. Obviously, each of these outcomes is much less beneficial to wildlife than the pre-ESA responses.

The problem with the ESA has nothing to do with the intentions of its authors or advocates, and everything to do with the unintended consequences of environmental regulation. The rules meant to protect wildlife have instead made acts of private stewardship illegal or extremely costly. The good will of landowners is simply not enough to counterbalance the real legal and economic dilemma the law sometimes creates. The result over the past twenty years has probably been millions of small unreported acts of violence against protected plants and animals. Just as importantly, millions of small actions that *would have* encouraged and benefited wildlife probably did *not* take place during this period because the ESA made such activities too risky.

The extent of the backlash against protected species caused by the ESA is necessarily unknown, though there is anecdotal evidence that it is substantial. We cannot, of course, know whether these unseen and unreported activities entirely offset the seen and reported cases where wildlife was saved by the ESA. But the lack of overall progress in removing species from the endangered list, and the compelling logic of the backlash against wildlife, persuade us that government's efforts to protect endangered wildlife have been largely unsuccessful.

Government's record: good enough?

No environmentalist can be pleased with the government's record over the past thirty years. Its management of public lands often has been deplorable. To subsidize logging in ecologically sensitive areas is truly a betrayal of the movement's trust. Subsidies for irrigation, grazing, and farming all degrade the environment, not protect it. The government's reliance on command-and-control regulations has stifled innovation, imposed huge and unnecessary costs on businesses, and left us unprepared to cope with nonpoint sources of air and water pollution. And contrary to the claims of those who defend it, the Endangered Species Act may be responsible for as much injury to as protection of wildlife.

If, as the research seems to indicate, compliance with environmental regulations costs between four and six times as much as the least-expensive way to accomplish the same level of emissions reduction, then $3 of every $4 spent on pollution abatement in recent years has simply been wasted. With pollution abatement costs now running at $150 billion a year, the waste could be over $100 billion a year. The mind reels at the thought of what could be achieved with a more efficient investment of this money. Isn't there a better way?

The environment and "market failure"

In the previous chapter, we demonstrated that markets create incentives and opportunities to protect the environment so long as property rights are well defined and enforced. But we also acknowledged that rights are difficult to establish and enforce in some areas. Three areas in particular have stubbornly resisted the application of property rights: air, water, and wildlife. Efforts in the past were stymied by three factors:

- All three resources once were thought to be available in virtually unlimited supplies, so very few people saw the value of protecting or conserving them.

- All three resources migrate across traditional property borders, thus making traditional definitions of ownership (such as capture, improvement, and sustained use) inappropriate.

- All three resources are used or valued by millions of people. Consequently, getting agreement on rights is a costly and cumbersome process.

It can hardly be a coincidence that virtually every serious environmental problem, historically and today, occurred or occurs in those areas where well-defined systems of property rights are lacking. Indeed, upon further reflection it becomes clear that this is the essence of pollution and wildlife problems: *No one owns the resources involved, and consequently no one protects them.* For example, while some species of wildlife have been hunted to extinction, no farm animal ever has suffered the same fate. Similarly, no one deliberately pollutes the air and water *inside* their home, yet they may pollute the "public" air by driving a car that is not properly tuned, or pollute the "public" water by allowing pesticides and fertilizers to run off their lawn or field.

Clearly, those things that have private owners are protected from extinction and pollution, while those things that have no specific owners are subject to abuse. Because of their problematic natures, air, water, and wildlife have been left unprotected.

The failure to protect natural resources is commonly blamed on the free enterprise system. Since markets fail, the argument goes, we must rely on a non-market mechanism: government intervention. But this reasoning misses the essential point: It is not *markets* that have failed, but the *judicial system* that defines and enforces rights. In the discussion that follows we ask whether a system of rights to clean air, clean water, and wildlife could be established and enforced within the context of a free enterprise system.

Wildlife and property rights

While the attention of many environmentalists has been on activities related to the Endangered Species Act, an even more significant movement to protect endangered animals has been growing in the U.S. and around the world. We can describe this movement somewhat loosely as the *privatization* of wildlife protection.

As ecological awareness spreads and prosperity rises, more land is being set aside for conservation and more resources are being invested in wildlife protection. As some kinds of wildlife become more rare, hunters, tourists, and environmentalists are willing to pay higher prices to hunt, see, or preserve them, creating a growing source of revenue for those who can meet this demand. Most wildlife species are still unowned migratory resources, but property owners have used their rights to create private safe havens for a growing number of endangered or threatened species. Four specific privatization tactics have emerged.

- *Buy the most ecologically vulnerable sites and protect them.* Several nonprofit organizations, including The Nature Conservancy, Ducks Unlimited, and Trout Unlimited, are buying or leasing large tracts of land in the U.S., and increasingly around the world, to preserve wildlife habitat. Ducks Unlimited, in existence since 1937, has probably done more to preserve and increase duck populations than any other organization, public or private, in the world. The Nature Conservancy, with a 1992 budget of $275 million, owns millions of acres of land throughout the U.S., which it manages strictly for conservation. Typical of its holdings is the 12,000-acre Pine Butte Preserve in northern Montana, which contains essential habitat for grizzly bears.

- *If others own it, teach them to be good stewards.* Since the largest share of wildlife habitat is found on private land, instructing private landowners on how to manage their property for wildlife conservation as well as other uses is an effective way to privatize the protection of habitat. A growing number of organizations, including the Sand County Foundation, Forest Trust, and Cascade Holistic Economic Consultants, now specialize in this activity. Thanks to their efforts, an increasing share of forests in the U.S. are managed for wildlife habitat as well as timber, and farms and ranches around the country are being turned into private wildlife refuges.

- *If they don't like wildlife, pay them to tolerate it.* A third strategy is to pay private property owners to protect the wildlife that occupies their land. Defenders of Wildlife, an environmental group, pays for any loss of livestock due to wolves. The group also awards private landowners up to $5,000 if they can show that a litter of wolf pups has been successfully reared on their property. According to Hank Fischer, Northern Rockies representative for Defenders of Wildlife, the group has raised $100,000 for its compensation fund; since 1987, $12,000 has been paid to ten different ranchers. "Defenders' compensation program has played a key role in reducing the hostility toward wolves that typically results when livestock losses occur and ranchers aren't compensated," writes Fischer. "Consequently, the wolf population in northwestern Montana has continued to increase steadily, and opposition from the livestock industry has been minimal. Instead of waiting for the government to act, we're pressing forward and attempting to solve problems on our own."

- *If necessary, raise them yourself.* The past thirty years have witnessed a rapid growth in the number of wildlife and hunting reserves and captive breeding programs. Such programs are responsible for the remarkable recoveries of alligators in Florida, bighorn sheep in Wyoming, and elephants in five African countries. Stephen M. Weaver, a biologist studying African habitats, says game ranching "has resulted in the annual transformation of tens of thousands of acres of agricultural holdings back into native wildlife habitat. Species which will never be hunted, for sport or for meal, are enjoying a tremendous piggyback benefit. Habitats that are optimal for a trophy bull kudu also support the badger-like ratel, the baboon, the Cape turtle dove, and numerous other species." The Exotic Wildlife Association, an international game ranching organization, has 450 members who own 200,000 head of some 125 species; over 19,000 of these animals belong to species that are threatened or endangered in the wild.

The privatization trend is taking place in both wealthy developed countries and Third World countries. Weaver reports flying over Zimbabwe and observing how private game ranches have dramatically changed that country's landscape, rescuing hundreds of thousands of acres from overgrazing by cattle. In many cases, conservation organizations based in the West are making investments in Africa, Asia, and South America to establish private game reserves in the most threatened areas.

The economic logic behind the privatization trend is very strong: Ownership creates a motive that does not otherwise exist to protect and preserve wildlife. By pooling their resources and supporting organizations such as Ducks Unlimited or The Nature Conservancy, environmentalists are buying critical ecosystems in the U.S. and around the world to ensure wildlife protection. Their efforts, combined with those of many landowners and game ranchers, are gradually overcoming the problems associated with establishing property rights to migrating wildlife. Continuation of this trend will ensure that wildlife in the next century will be better protected than ever before.

POLLUTION AND PROPERTY RIGHTS

Prior to the end of the nineteenth century, common law frequently served to protect clean water and privately owned habitat by compelling polluters to compensate other property owners. This process is still used around the world and in the U.S. — for example, the many lawsuits filed against Exxon for damages caused by its 1989 spill in Valdez, Alaska — but it is increasingly compromised by immunities to civil liability granted by statutory laws. Could an expanded reliance on common law remedies, achieved by selectively repealing statutory laws that protect polluters from civil liability, provide an alternative to government intervention? The authors believe that it could.

Thanks to the efforts of environmentalists over the years, the first barrier to establishing property rights to air and water — the perception that supplies of clean air and clean water were limitless — already has been cleared. There is widespread acceptance of the notion that these resources are in short supply and need protection. The ability of common law to evolve over time to accommodate changing public values means civil proceedings today will give more credence to claims of environmental injury, and produce larger awards when guilt is determined, than they would have in the past.

The second barrier, concerning the migratory nature of air and water, can be overcome. Pollution of air and water eventually makes its presence known by injuring wildlife, vegetation, or human health. (This injury is, in fact, implicit in the definition of pollution.) Even in the absence of a widespread environmental consciousness, the common law system creates an incentive for private parties to monitor the effects of pollution on their land, businesses, and health and to sue polluters to recover whatever damage can be proven. Thus, an expanded system of common law remedies to pollution would create a system to monitor environmental problems. Such a system, because it would rely on the self-interest of those doing the monitoring, would likely be more efficient and accurate than today's necessarily sporadic inspections by the EPA and other government agencies.

New technologies allow us to add inexpensive and inert chemical tracers or radioactive isotopes to pesticides, fertilizers, smokestack emissions, and other sources of pollution, thereby allowing us to trace pollution back to its source. This has been tested by the Winter Hazes Intensive Tracer Experiment in Canyon Lands Park, Utah. Chemical tracers were introduced into the stack of a coal-fired generating plant several hundred miles from the park. Through the use of monitoring stations, the degree of pollution caused by the generating plant was determined. In the same way, effective monitoring could be introduced for all major industrial pollutants, giving victims of pollution the evidence they need to finger polluters in civil court proceedings. In a similar way, the Stedman mobile auto exhaust testing device could provide evidence of pollution from mobile sources, enabling victims of air pollution from automobiles (such as those in the Los Angeles basin) to name specific drivers in a suit for damages.

What of the third barrier — the large number of people affected by pollution and therefore the huge cost of negotiating and enforcing a system of rights? The class action suit is a cost-effective way to mobilize large numbers of victims and represent them in court. Increasingly sophisticated statistical models of exposure and risk assessment could provide sufficient data to define a class of victims and their extent of injury. (If the best available research can't prove a harm exists, then we can only conclude that no problem exists to be solved.) The ability of modern computers to "crunch" huge amounts of data quickly might reduce to a manageable size the challenge of processing millions of claims and entitlements. The "information superhighway" may provide the inexpensive, high-speed, and simultaneous communication vehicle needed to enforce such a thing as a right to clean air.

While all this is speculative, it directs our attention to the fundamental issues involving pollution. Our reliance on government intervention to control pollution has led us to overlook the emergence of technologies that allow us, for the first time, to trace pollutants to their source, accurately assess their harm, and organize class action suits for damages. These technologies may mean that a common law solution to pollution has become (or is about to become) a viable alternative to relying on government.

Property rights versus government intervention

In recent years, property rights have been used to protect many species of wildlife, with growing effectiveness. As a result, we are witnessing the gradual privatization of wildlife and wilderness protection efforts around the world. By creating incentives to protect wildlife, rather than the perverse incentives created by the ESA to destroy it, privatization appears to be a superior alternative to relying on government.

Some of the same trends that have made the privatization of wildlife possible also are making a property rights solution to pollution more plausible. Unfortunately, in many cases statutory laws prevent the evolution of a property rights approach to pollution abatement. These statutory provisions rely on command-and-control regulation by a centralized agency that sets permissible levels of pollution.

The manner in which the common law system discovers the appropriate size of awards for damages makes the common law approach a promising tool in the battle against pollution. The judicial process is essentially an adversarial one in which the alleged victims of pollution present the strongest possible case for their victimhood, while the alleged polluters put forth the strongest case denying their guilt. The final decisions of guilt or innocence and the size of the awards, if any, are made by independent judges and juries. This process measures, more accurately than any political process could, the true extent of injuries and the value society places on such injuries.

A common law approach to air and water pollution, then, would have two dramatic advantages over continued reliance on government intervention. First, it would be *more efficient* because it would accurately measure the extent of injury that is occurring, and then call forth expenditures up to that amount to compensate victims or prevent continued pollution. Second, it would be *more just* than government intervention because it would penalize actual polluters (not innocent taxpayers) and compensate actual victims of pollution (not bureaucracies or lawyers.)

The common law strategy, in conclusion, appears to be superior to government intervention via regulation in many ways. The decision to rely on the government to protect the environment, it now seems clear, was only a "second-best" strategy adopted because the necessary technology had not yet been developed to implement a property rights solution. Today, the technology exists — but the consequences of government intervention stand in the way of its implementation.

Conclusion

Ever since 1962, it seems, the environmental movement has been saying "Let the government do it." Environmentalists have leaned heavily on the government to protect the nation's forests, allowing it to manage 32 percent of the entire country's land area. We relied on government to protect endangered plants and animals, and now have thousands of such creatures "listed." We surrendered our right to sue polluters in court in exchange for command-and-control regulations on pollution levels, and then spent $1 trillion in thirty years trying to reduce emissions.

Having shown earlier in this book that environmental conditions today are better than they were thirty years ago, we will not contend here that government has always and everywhere failed to protect the environment. It is unlikely, for example, that reductions in air and water pollution would have occurred as quickly in the absence of government regulations, or that landfill safety would have improved at the speed it did in the past decade. But these victories often came at much too high a price: billions wasted on litigation, footdragging, and focusing on the wrong problems. Behind these victories, too, were some conspicuous failures: below-cost logging sales, farm and ranching subsidies, Superfund, and the apparent failure of the Endangered Species Act. This mixed record may not lead us to *abandon* government intervention as a strategy in the future, but it should lead us to be alert to the existence of alternative strategies that offer hope of better results.

A property rights and market strategy may be just the alternative that environmentalists have been searching for. Private ownership overcomes the perverse incentive structures that afflict government agencies and seem to confound many government regulations and programs. Markets offer a way to determine the true cost of pollution, allowing us to move beyond a reliance on politics that often has failed to deliver good results at a reasonable cost. Environmentalists owe it to themselves to study this alternative closely and to apply it widely to environmental problems.

7. Rules for eco-sanity

THE BIGGEST BARRIER to further improvements in environmental quality is not a lack of money. Spending on environmental protection in the U.S. is greater, both in dollar terms and as a percentage of gross domestic product, than it ever has been, and also considerably higher than spending in other countries.

Is the biggest problem that the wrong people are in the White House, the Forest Service, or the EPA? No. Government's management of the National Forests and enforcement of pollution standards have been relatively unaffected by which political party happens to hold office. (Contrary to the claims of both major parties.) Below-cost timber sales and subsidies to agriculture, for example, have taken place under the administrations of Presidents Carter, Reagan, Bush, and Clinton. As Randal O'Toole and others have pointed out, the people who serve in the U.S. Forest Service and other agencies are honest, talented, and committed.

What, then, is the biggest barrier to improving environmental protection? *We believe it is the environmental movement itself.* More specifically, we believe the lack of understanding and critical thinking on the part of most environmentalists has compromised the movement's ability to be an effective force for environmental protection. Many environmentalists don't think clearly about the issues, relying instead on environmental organizations to do their thinking for them. This trust has been rewarded with campaigns against "crises" that don't exist and support for policies that are clumsy, expensive, and sometimes counterproductive. Similarly, environmentalists have said *let the government do it . . .* and then they failed to pay attention to what the government actually did. A closer look quickly reveals that government's record on the environment is a poor one, and that government often suffers from perverse incentive structures and information blackouts that render it an unreliable ally of the movement.

We aren't saying that environmentalists should abandon environmental organizations or the government. Both have important roles to play in protecting the environment. But environmentalists need to be better informed about environmental problems. The popular wisdom on issue after issue bears little resemblance to what objective scientists have to say. This "disconnect" means many environmentalists are wasting their energy — and the dollars of consumers, businesses, and taxpayers — fighting nonexistent problems or problems that already are being solved, while bigger problems go unnoticed. Environmentalists also need to improve their critical thinking skills so they can see through the deception and exaggeration that has characterized the promotions of some environmental organizations and the popular media's coverage of environmental issues.

In this chapter we summarize facts, rules, and principles environmentalists can use to recognize real environmental threats and see past scare tactics. Equipped with these "rules for eco-sanity," the reader should be able to separate myth from reality, rhetoric from science, and unproven theories from real risks. He or she also should be able to evaluate proposed solutions to see how close they come to addressing the real sources of environmental problems, and how likely they are to be effective. In the chapter following this one, we put these tools to work building a "common-sense agenda" for protecting the environment.

Rules for Eco-Sanity

Facts to Remember

The environment is cleaner than at any time in the past half-century.
The environment is safer than at any time in recorded history.
Life expectancy has never been longer.
Cancer rates are falling, not rising.
Predictions of impending global ecological disasters are untrue.
Most environmental problems have been or are being solved.
Ideas are more important than things.
Prosperity is good for the environment.

Rules of Critical Thinking

Correlation is not causation.
Not everything can be explained.
Trends can't predict the future.
Facts count for more than opinions.
Don't forget the past.
We can never avoid risk completely.
We have to make choices.

Lessons from Science

It is impossible to prove that something does not exist.
The dose makes the poison.
The dose-response relationship is often not linear.
Mice are not little men.
Epidemiologic studies can be unreliable.
Risks can be measured and ranked.
Science is not immune to politics.

Rules for Eco-Sanity

(continued from previous page)

Principles of Political Economy

Pollution problems occur where rights are not defined and enforced.
Rights to air, water, and wildlife can be defined and enforced.
Ownership leads to better stewardship.
Incentives are better than commands.
Exchanges can help solve environmental problems.
Government programs suffer from incentive problems.
Government programs suffer from knowledge problems.
Government subsidies cause waste.
Greater efficiency leads to less pollution.

Lessons from False Alarms

The alarmists can no longer be trusted.
Some environmental groups profit from false alarms.
The media gives false alarms extensive publicity.
Beware of stories with innocent victims and terrible villains.
Don't react out of fear.

Facts to remember

1. The environment is cleaner than at any time in the past half-century. The average American in 1994 is exposed to fewer potentially harmful pollutants than at any time since the 1930s. Air and water pollution, which had risen during the 1940s and 1950s, have fallen consistently and considerably since that time. Today, pollution of all kinds is responsible for less than 1 percent of cancer deaths.

2. The environment is safer than at any time in recorded history. The probability that a substance or natural process will cause human injury is the lowest it has ever been. The threat of naturally occurring poisons and pathogens in our water and food is the lowest it has been in recorded history. Similarly, our risk of accidental exposure to hazardous substances while at work or from waste sites in our communities has never been lower. There is no longer any reason to be afraid of the environment.

3. Life expectancy has never been longer. The average life expectancy of Americans has steadily increased since the time such records were first kept. Most medical experts believe this trend will continue. These are important facts because they contradict claims that man-made chemicals and pollution are making the world a less healthy place to live. Longer lifespans mean that, as a people, we are becoming *healthier* over time, not more sickly. This would not be true if we were "poisoning the environment."

4. Cancer rates are falling, not rising. We've lived with pesticides, automobiles, and electromagnetic fields for nearly a century. During this period, overall cancer rates among the nonelderly population went *down*, not up. Cancer rates among the elderly appear to have increased, but this is due partly to better diagnosis and partly to the rapid decline of other causes of death. There are no "invisible killers" in the air, water, or food that are causing cancer. There is certainly no "cancer epidemic."

5. Predictions of impending global ecological disasters are untrue. There is no scientific validity to claims that acid rain, global warming, deforestation, or ozone depletion will cause global environmental disasters at any time in the future. The theory that acid rain posed a significant threat was disproved by the NAPAP report. A small amount of global warming may occur in the future, but it poses no harm to (and may actually benefit) life on the planet. There is no evidence that ozone depletion caused by man-made CFCs is resulting in higher levels of UV radiation on the Earth's surface, nor would the degree of increase that some predict have any adverse effects on human, animal, or plant life.

6. Most environmental problems have been or are being solved. Automobile emissions, for example, have been reduced by 90 to 97 percent during the past twenty years. The threats of deforestation and resource depletion have been eliminated from the developed countries of the world, and remain problems only in Third World countries torn by civil war and acute poverty. Oil spills are less common and cause less ecological harm than in the past. Landfill technology has advanced "by light-years" in the past decade. Those environmentalists who remain focused on these problems are keeping the rest of us from moving forward on opportunities to protect the environment in new ways.

7. Ideas are more important than things. Human knowledge, says economist Julian Simon, is "the ultimate resource" because it is able to find uses for things that are apparently useless. Innovation and the use of reason to solve problems make us wealthier than our grandparents, not any change in human nature or in the amount of natural resources. The "gloom and doom" school of thought within the environmental movement systematically overlooks the role of ideas in finding new resources, managing waste, and protecting human health and the environment. Their zero-sum solutions are unnecessary and often don't work.

8. Prosperity is good for the environment. The fear that prosperity leads to environmental destruction saturates the literature of the environmental movement. But prosperity has made it possible for us to invest in parks and wildlife preserves, clean our air and water, and treat or store our wastes. The same process that fuels our economic growth — growing efficiency in our use of natural resources — also leads to less waste and pollution. The record here in the U.S., as well as in countries around the world, is perfectly clear on this point: Prosperity is not only *compatible* with a clean environment, it is environmental protection's necessary precondition.

Rules of critical thinking

1. Correlation is not causation. "Correlation" means that two things tend to happen at the same time; "causation" means that one thing is known to cause another thing. Just because two things happen at the same time doesn't mean one is *causing* the other. We need proof, including a reasonable theory showing the path by which one thing causes another to occur. Most environmental scares — including global warming, electromagnetic fields, and dioxin — resulted when the correlation of two things was mistaken for causation. To avoid future errors, we need to challenge people who rely on correlations to *prove* that one thing is actually causing another thing to happen.

2. Not everything can be explained. The truth, in 1994, is that the causes of most specific cases of cancer, miscarriage, and child deformity in the U.S. are unexplained. We simply don't know whether a specific case of brain cancer, for example, is due to a genetic condition, nutrition, alcohol or drug abuse, a fall in early childhood, or a combination of all of these factors. While we should sympathize with the victims of these afflictions, we should not confuse them with experts on the causes of their illnesses. A victim's guess is no more reliable, and may be less reliable, than the guesses of any other nonexpert. Some day, the work of toxicologists, epidemiologists, and other scientists may produce the answers we seek, but that day has not yet arrived.

3. Trends can't predict the future. During the 1970s, global temperatures fell several years in a row and "experts" like Dr. Stephen Schneider predicted a new ice age. During the 1980s, temperatures rose several years in a row and the "experts," including Schneider, predicted catastrophic global warming. The cold winter of 1993-94 prompted *Time* magazine and some scientists to warn of an approaching *ice age.* These predictions, along with predictions of a "population explosion" and eventual resource depletion, were wrong because they were based on projections of past trends.

4. Facts count for more than opinions. The person with the loudest voice or most controversial opinion often gets the most attention. This is certainly true in the environmental movement, where claims of impend-

How Much Will Arnold Schwarzenegger Earn in the Year 2000?

The problem with relying on trends is that even long-term trends will fail to predict the future if the underlying mechanisms that produce the observed effects are not understood or are changing. To illustrate this, *The Economist* tried to project actor Arnold Schwarzenegger's earnings in the year 2000 based on his actual earnings between 1986 and 1991.

Depending on which year is used as a starting point, Mr. Schwarzenegger's earnings in 2000 could be as high as $360 million or as low as *minus* $140 million. Which prediction is the most accurate? There is no way of knowing *based on past trends.*

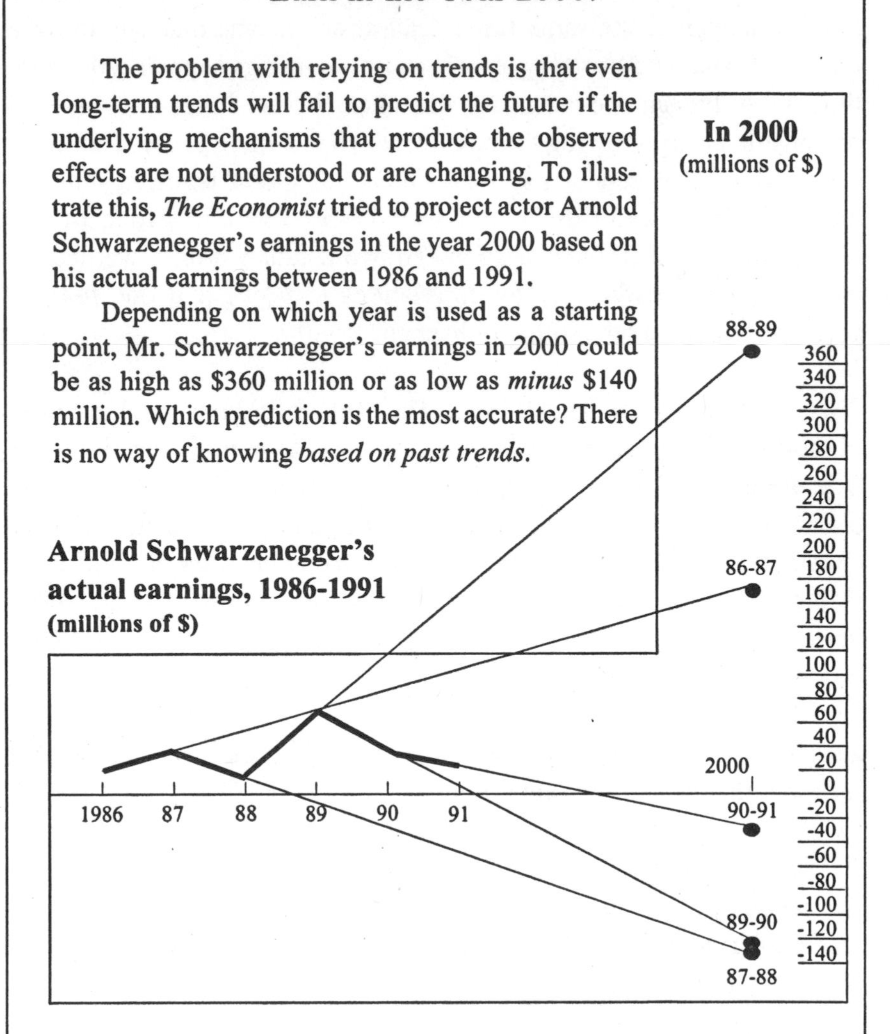

ing disaster get extensive play. To avoid being misled by "experts" who may represent a minority view within the scientific community, try to obtain the relevant *facts* and then make up your own mind. On many environmental issues, a few *numbers* tell us more than a thousand *pictures*. For example, the destruction of the world's rainforests changes from a "crisis" to a manageable problem once we recognize that rainforests are being diminished at a rate of well under 1 percent per year. Similarly, plastic containers move to the bottom of our agenda when we learn that they constitute less than 1.5 percent of the solid waste in a typical landfill.

5. *Don't forget the past.* During the 1970s, many prominent environmentalists predicted an "energy crisis" and a "population explosion." Some twenty years later, oil reserves have grown and population growth is slowing. Ronald Bailey, commenting on Paul Ehrlich and Lester Brown, says "One reason such apocalypse abusers thrive is that the public has no long-term memory. People are unlikely to remember that a doomster made dire predictions twenty years ago that have since been proved wrong." Bailey is right. We need to remember yesterday's false alarms and who sounded them if we are to respond correctly to future calls to action.

6. *We can never avoid risk completely.* Everything we do carries with it some risk, even common activities such as taking a bath (drowning) or crossing the street (being hit by a car). Seemingly harmless things (like balloons and tooth picks) sometimes kill people. There is *no such thing* as a product, decision, or action that carries *no* risk whatsoever. So when someone tells us "there may be a risk" that a chemical, nuclear power plant, or landfill will endanger our health, we should not be frightened. Instead, we should calmly ask, "How much risk is there?" If the risk is unknown, we should wait until reliable evidence is available for us to estimate the risk. If the risk is one in a million (the level of risk often found for things like incinerator fumes and pesticides), it may not be worth attempting to reduce it any further. Keep in mind that the risk of drowning (16 in a million), or dying in an accident at home (90 in a million), or dying in an automobile accident (192 in a million) greatly exceed the alleged environmental risks being decried by some organizations.

7. *We have to make choices.* We can't buy two items at the grocery store with the same money; we have to choose one or the other. The same is

true of how we clean the environment: We have to choose among different ways to do it. We can't *do everything, all at once*, because trying to do so would be extremely wasteful, unnecessarily injure many people, and probably produce unintended consequences that harm the environment. Instead, we must apply the same prudence that we apply to other important parts of our lives. Because of the law of diminishing returns, a "zero discharge" policy will cost huge sums of money and produce very little benefit. We must *prioritize* threats to the environment and find *efficient* ways to address them. The more carefully we do these things, the more threats we will be able to successfully address. The importance of environmental issues doesn't somehow exempt them from this discipline. In fact, their importance makes careful planning and efficiency all the more necessary.

Lessons from science

1. It is impossible to prove that something does not exist. Some environmental groups insist that unless a substance or action can be "proven to be harmless" to human health or the environment, it should be restricted or banned. This is an impossible standard to meet. As Elizabeth Whelan says, "One cannot prove that a link doesn't exist, as it is impossible to prove a negative. All that can be said in these cases is that there is no evidence that such a link is based on fact." This is why good scientists never say "there is no risk of harm" or "this chemical does not cause cancer." It is impossible for scientific research to prove, beyond doubt, the truth of such universal statements. Insisting otherwise is at the root of Greenpeace's "reverse onus principle." While this principle may be a clever rhetorical device, it is neither scientific nor helpful to those seeking to identify real risks.

2. The dose makes the poison. Some chemicals can be highly toxic, so it is natural for us to be concerned about their possible effects on human health and the environment. But the *real*, as opposed to hypothetical, threat posed by a substance depends on our exposure to the substance, or its *dose*. Many toxic substances, both man-made and natural, are present in the air, water, and our food, but they are present in such small amounts that only recently have we invented the tools needed to discover their presence. There is no evidence that these substances pose any threat to human health at current levels of exposure. There is good reason to suppose that they are harmless, since many substances that are deadly in large quantities are harmless or even beneficial in small quantities. So when someone tells us a chemical is "highly toxic" or can be found "in measurable amounts" in the food we eat, we should ask, "How much of it are we exposed to?" and "What proof is there that *this dose* poses any harm?"

3. The dose-response relationship is often not linear. Much research regarding the effects of chemicals on human health is based on an assumption: If large doses of a chemical have a certain effect on laboratory animals, then smaller doses will have proportionately smaller effects on humans. Unfortunately, we don't know for sure whether this is true. If the relationship between dose and effect is not linear, then small doses may have little or no effect on health. When confronted with claims that even a small dose of a chemical may be harmful to human health, we should ask: "Does this study assume a linear relationship between dose and effect?" If it does, we should be skeptical of its accuracy.

4. Mice are not little men. Experiments on laboratory animals are valuable ways of measuring a chemical's toxicity or its likely effects on wildlife. But such experiments fail to accurately assess human cancer risks for many reasons. The enormous doses fed to laboratory animals cause tissue damage and stress, which can lead to tumors even if the substance being tested is not carcinogenic at normal doses. (See "Of Mice and Men" on the following page.) Animal tests assume a linear relationship between dose and response, whereas the body's ability to repair cell damage probably creates thresholds below which no permanent cell damage occurs. Animal tests also assume that mice and humans respond the same way to chemicals, even though mice sometimes respond to chemicals very differently than rats and guinea pigs. Consequently, we can't assume that substances that cause cancer in laboratory animals are also human carcinogens.

5. Epidemiologic studies can be unreliable. Like laboratory experiments, epidemiologic studies can be valuable guides to discovering harmful substances, but they too are frequently misused in the debate over how to

Of Mice and Men

To test whether decaffeinated coffee might cause cancer in humans, scientists fed laboratory animals the equivalent of *12 million cups of coffee a day*. Based on the number of animals that developed cancerous tumors, and assuming a linear relationship between the dose and the effect, the scientists estimated how many cases of cancer might develop in humans consuming three or four cups of coffee a day. Incredibly, studies like these form the basis of much of the modern concern over cancer-causing chemicals in our food, air, and water.

Source: See Richard Stroup et al., *Progressive Environmentalism*, National Center for Policy Analysis, April 1991, p. 49.

protect human health and the environment. If a report claims to have found an association between a food or chemical and human health, ask the following questions: How many subjects were in the study, and how were they selected? Did the survey rely on the memories of victims and their relatives, or on more objective published data? How carefully chosen and monitored was the "control group" that was not exposed to the food or chemical? And what was the range of the study's possible conclusions (its "margin of error")? Are the lower estimates near zero or even negative? A sound epidemiologic study can survive scrutiny of this sort and give us reliable information. Many of the studies we hear and read about, however, fall short.

6. Risks can be measured and ranked. Researchers can measure and compare the risks associated with different courses of action. Assuming their estimates are based on sound assumptions (not simplistic extrapolations from laboratory animal tests, for example), we can use them to *rank* environmental problems according to how much risk they pose to the environment or our health. This, in turn, helps us prioritize problems and decide where our limited resources would be best spent. While a particular risk has an objective, or real, value, each of us places a *subjective* value on it. Some people fear even small risks and are willing to do things differently to avoid them. Others tend to discount risks and routinely engage in activities known to be quite risky. Scientists can help us by assigning objective values to each risk, but they can't tell us how *risk-averse* or *risk-tolerant* we as individuals should choose to be.

7. Science is not immune to politics. Most scientific research taking place in American universities is subsidized by the government, which means it is influenced by politics. Some scientists have political beliefs or loyalties that influence their views, especially on subjects outside their area of technical training. To know when science is being politicized, we should ask the following questions:

- Is a report being issued by an independent scientist or by a government agency? The first is less likely to be politicized than the second.

- Is a scientist addressing an issue outside his or her discipline? For example, Dr. Helen Caldicott, head of the Union of Concerned Scientists, is a pediatrician, not a nuclear scientist; Dr. Paul Ehrlich is a butterfly specialist, not a demographer; and Ralph Nader is a lawyer, not a scientist. When they comment on issues outside their areas of specialty, look for facts and independent research that support their opinions.

- Has the study been reviewed by the author's peers? Unless a report is published in a peer-reviewed scientific journal, it has not been scrutinized by members of the scientific community. If a report is called "preliminary" it probably has been rushed to the media without peer review.

- Is there experimental evidence that supports the theory, and has the experiment been replicated? Chance will result in experiments that appear to find a correlation between two things even if a real cause-and-effect relationship doesn't exist. The only way to know for sure that the relationship is real is for other researchers to replicate the experiment and attain the same results. Be wary of the solitary study; by itself, it may prove nothing.

Principles of political economy

1. Pollution problems occur where rights are not defined and enforced. When things are privately owned, the civil justice system keeps us from invading or damaging them. But when they are owned in common — like air, rivers and lakes, wildlife, and in some cases public lands — we are often driven by competition with others to exploit them quickly and with little regard for their future value. The result is often pollution, unsustainable rates of development, and endangerment of wildlife.

2. Rights to air, water, and wildlife can be defined and enforced. Historically, property rights held polluters accountable for the damage they caused. The peculiar nature of air, water, and wildlife, however, led to the adoption of statutory laws that pre-empted common law solutions in most situations. Rising prosperity, greater awareness of environmental issues, and technological innovations may be making a return to the property rights strategy possible. Ducks Unlimited, The Nature Conservancy, Defenders of Wildlife, and similar groups are showing that the property rights solution can work to protect wildlife.

3. Ownership leads to better stewardship. We tend to take better care of things we own than of things we only rent or borrow. Ownership brings together the *right to use* something and the *responsibility* for changes in the value of the resource. Natural resources are no different from houses in this regard: If we fail to repair a leak in the roof of a house we own, we suffer a financial loss as the house's re-sale value falls. If, on the other hand, we *rent* the house, then the lost money comes out of the landlord's pocket, and so we have little incentive to make the necessary repairs. A good landlord sometimes can get his tenants to act with as much responsibility as is shown by some homeowners, but we have seen already that government is generally a poor landlord. Natural resources, therefore, are better cared for if they are owned by the people who use them.

4. Incentives are better than commands. There are two ways to make people do what we want them to do: pass laws compelling them to act a certain way, or give people incentives to act the way we want. The first way requires detailed information about how people must act, a way to monitor their behavior, and an apparatus to punish those who attempt to evade the commands. Creating the right incentives, by contrast, takes advantage of the detailed information that already exists in each person's mind, requires little enforcement or monitoring, and is unlikely to produce evasive actions. A property rights strategy works through incentives; government intervention relies on commands. Consequently, the property rights strategy is likely to produce better results, and fewer unintended consequences, than government intervention.

5. *Exchanges can help solve environmental problems.* What if the person who owns a natural resource doesn't place a high value on it, and therefore fails to manage it well? Transferable property rights enable those who value a resource most highly to bid it away from those who value it less. Potential buyers — for example, nonprofit organizations and clubs devoted to conservation — can use their property rights to purchase or lease land, reward good stewardship, or purchase covenants that restrict allowable uses of land. Such exchanges reveal the true cost of protecting the environment and ensure that this cost is shared by those who value the environment most. The almost endless variety of property rights exchanges gives this strategy great flexibility in responding to environmental problems.

6. *Government programs suffer from incentive problems.* Government officials seek to expand their budgets and authority by delivering short-term benefits to special interest groups. Because they do not own the resources they manage, these officials are unlikely to manage them for maximum asset value. The special interest groups who stand to benefit most from changes in government policy are the *renters* of natural resources or people who are getting free use of unowned resources such as air and water. They lobby *for* short-term subsidies and continued free use and *against* investments in long-term asset management and determining property rights. Too often, they get what they want.

7. *Government programs suffer from knowledge problems.* Government agencies often suffer from an information blackout due to the absence of prices and competitive markets. When attempting to plan the use of the national forests, for example, the government faces the impossible task of balancing the public's interests in wood products, recreation, and conservation without knowing how much people are willing to pay for

each kind of use. Similarly, when it formulates laws limiting the emissions of factories, government operates without knowledge of what new technologies are about to appear, what trade-offs each factory faces, or how much people living near each factory value cleaner air versus (for example) more jobs or higher pay. When government attempts to perform tasks (such as garbage collection or hazardous waste cleanups) itself, its monopoly status means it does not compare its own efficiency to that of competing organizations. As a result, government agents cannot know how good a job they are doing — or how much harm they are causing.

8. Government subsidies cause waste. The federal government tries to help farmers by selling them water at artificially low prices. But this subsidy quickly leads to waste, since it makes buying more water less expensive than conserving water. The lower the price of water, the less is spent preventing its waste. Over time, subsidies are transformed into *entitlements*, and their beneficiaries lobby against any attempts to reduce them. The result is that the cost of providing the subsidies is much greater than the actual benefit received by the farmers, yet it is politically impossible to reduce or end the subsidies. The same relationship between subsidies and waste exists in a wide range of areas, including grazing and logging. Subsidies may *appear* to produce the intended benefits at first, but over time they invariably cause changes in behavior that cancel out whatever good they may otherwise produce.

9. Greater efficiency leads to less pollution. Efficiency means producing the most output with the least input. Since pollution often results from the incomplete use of an input (raw materials), improving efficiency often leads to less pollution. Over time, a system that rewards efficiency will also tend to produce less pollution than one that tolerates inefficiency. Countries with market economies have proven to be more efficient and to produce lower rates of pollution than socialist countries. From this we can conclude that environmental protection policies that encourage efficiency are likely to lead, in the long term, to less pollution.

Lessons from false alarms

1. The alarmists can no longer be trusted. Alarmists within the environmental movement have sometimes called our attention to real environmental problems, and by doing so they have helped lead to faster adoption of solutions. Increasingly, though, they issue false alarms, often one immediately following another, without ever setting the record straight. They were wrong, for example, when they predicted a "cancer epidemic," a "population explosion" that could end only with worldwide famine, and depletion of many of the world's natural resources. Their predictions regarding global warming, ozone depletion, and acid rain are being proven wrong as well. This poor record compels us to doubt their credibility and to ask, "Since you've been wrong so many times before, why should we believe you now?"

2. Some environmental groups profit from false alarms. Some environmental groups use the "crisis-of-the-month" approach because it's a proven money-maker. In 1992, the top twelve environmental groups in the U.S. raised $638 million by using such appeals. Greenpeace alone cranked out a staggering *43 million* fundraising letters in 1990. Environmentalism is now big business, complete with six-figure salaries, Washington D.C. offices, and lots of lawyers and lobbyists. "Crises keep donations flowing to environmental advocacy groups," writes Ronald Bailey. "Without them, how could advocacy groups justify their pleas for donations?"

3. The media gives false alarms extensive publicity. Time magazine put NASA's "ozone hole" news conference on its front cover, but buried the report that it was a false alarm in a small article deep inside the magazine. Global warming has generated thousands of newspaper and magazine articles and scores of television reports and documentaries, but reports of *falling global temperatures* in 1991, 1992, and 1993 were seldom seen (outside of academic journals). In light of the media's dismal record, we should be cautious — not cynical, but skeptical — of the accounts of environmental issues that appear on television and in newspapers and popular magazines.

4. Beware of stories with innocent victims and terrible villains. Labeling people "victims" and "villains" makes for good newspaper copy and fundraising letters, but it often obscures the truth and leads us to false conclusions about what needs to be done. We are quick to believe that big companies are *villains* who care only about profits, not public safety or the environment. We forget that everyone — including environmental organizations and authors — has an agenda and may derive profits, directly or indirectly, from environmental issues.

5. *Don't react out of fear.* Always demand facts before you form an opinion. The environmental movement has produced some writers who are truly expert at using fear to make us suspend our usual powers of judgment and common sense. Elizabeth Whelan says of this tactic: "The sense of urgency and the resulting panic are enhanced by the introduction of fear of the unknown; we might not have data now that indicate that it causes cancer, but just in case . . . We are left paralyzed by anxiety, because the unknown is actually scarier than the real thing, given the ability of our imagination to run wild." The scare tactic is built into such concepts as the "reverse onus principle" and "the precautionary principle." We should react to such rhetoric with patience and caution, not fear. We should demand sufficient facts and supporting evidence to reach an informed opinion. We should not allow fear to determine the positions we take *or* the donations we make to environmental groups.

8. A common-sense agenda

THE "RULES FOR ECO-SANITY" give us the tools we need to build a new agenda for the environmental movement: 40 specific recommendations for policy changes or new initiatives to protect the environment. Every recommendation on the following pages meets our common-sense test of addressing a *real* problem in an *efficient* way.

Not everyone agrees with the common-sense approach. Al Gore, for example, calls for "embarking on an all-out effort to use every policy and program, every law and institution, every treaty and alliance, every tactic and strategy, every plan and course of action — to use, in short, every means to halt the destruction of the environment and to preserve and nurture our ecological system." Robert Hahn quite accurately labels this the "kitchen sink" theory of environmental policy design: Do everything, all at once, regardless of cost or necessity.

We believe that the kitchen sink approach serves taxpayers, consum-

A Common-Sense Agenda

Cleaner air

1. Trace air pollution to its source.
2. Reduce auto emissions by using congestion fees and fines.
3. Give plant owners and managers flexibility to meet emission goals.
4. Allow companies to reach reduction goals by helping other companies reduce their emissions.
5. Reform tradeable emission permit systems.
6. Begin re-establishing common law remedies to air pollution.
7. Remove regulatory barriers to the construction of nuclear power plants.
8. Policies to avoid: Carbon taxes or a cap on carbon dioxide emissions; Stricter auto emission standards or other command-and-control regulations; bans or moratoria on incineration.

Cleaner Water

1. Identify the sources of water pollution.
2. Replace command and control regulations with market-based solutions.
3. Create water markets.
4. Phase out federal construction subsidies for municipal waste treatment.

5. Phase out water subsidies for farmers.
6. Begin re-establishing common law remedies to water pollution.
7. Policies to avoid: New controls on point sources; noisy campaigns against dioxin and chlorine.

Managing Toxic Chemicals

1. Stop relying on maximum tolerable dose (MTD) tests on laboratory animals to predict human cancer risks.
2. Drop the assumption of a linear dose-response relationship.
3. Focus policy on real-life exposure, not laboratory measures of toxicity.
4. Use cost-benefit analysis.
5. Reform Superfund.
6. Policies to avoid: Laws that ban or mandate reduced use of specific chemicals; zero discharge standards.

Protecting Public Lands and Wildlife

1. Stop subsidizing logging on public lands.
2. Manage public lands for multiple benefits.
3. Stop subsidizing cattle grazing on public land.
4. Give ownership to those who now use public lands.
5. Increase user fees.
6. Reform the Endangered Species Act.
7. Support continued privatization of wildlife.

(continued on following page)

A Common-Sense Agenda

(continued from previous page)

8. Policies to avoid: Expansion of land under government control; not charging recreational users full cost; "strengthening" the Endangered Species Act.

Solid Waste Solutions

1. Change our personal habits.
2. Support an integrated approach to solid waste management.
3. Stop subsidizing garbage disposal.
4. Continue to phase in new landfill technologies.
5. Support recycling, but only when it pays for itself.
6. Policies to avoid: Bans on certain kinds of packaging; "Dates and rates" legislation; minimum recycled content laws; the German "Green Dot" system.

What Concerned Environmentalists Should Do

1. Ignore "crisis of the month" prophecies.
2. Start speaking for yourself.
3. Stop supporting organizations that exaggerate environmental problems.
4. Don't automatically join every local campaign.
5. Support environmental organizations that exercise eco-sanity.

ers, *and the environment* very poorly. Rather than representing a new plan or strategy, the Gore approach represents the same old indulgent, crisis-driven, and often-irresponsible tactics of the past. After 32 years of this approach, it is fair to suggest moving on to a new and more responsible strategy. We've all matured as individuals. Is it asking too much that the environmental movement mature as well?

The reader will note that the Common-Sense Agenda is not more "moderate" than the Gore plan, in the sense that we do not settle for a lower level of environmental protection and safety. Our disagreement with Gore and those like him is almost entirely one of strategy. In place of the tactics of fear, loud demands, bad science, and command-and-control regulations, we favor reason, good science, respect for the rights of others, and incentive-based solutions. We are convinced that action along the lines we suggest would lead to a *cleaner* environment, *sooner*, and at a dramatically *lower cost* than would action along the lines suggested by Gore.

Cleaner air

1. Trace air pollution to its source. New technologies allow factory and power plant emissions to be traced to their sources and the exhausts of moving automobiles to be accurately and inexpensively measured. This technology should immediately be put to use so we can more accurately identify the sources of air pollution and their degree of responsibility for poor air quality. Without this essential information, we cannot fight an effective battle against air pollution.

2. Reduce auto emissions by using congestion fees and fines. Due to the dramatic progress already made in reducing the emission levels of new cars, efforts must shift to addressing the one car in ten that still pollutes and the problem of auto congestion in major cities. The Stedman testing device makes it possible to efficiently and conveniently identify polluting autos and issue tickets to their owners. Charging a higher price to use congested routes during rush hours could substantially reduce congestion-related pollution. Both strategies promise to deliver reductions in overall auto emissions at a fraction of the cost that would be required by continued tightening of new car emission standards.

3. *Give plant owners and managers flexibility to meet emission goals.* Research by Resources for the Future and the Amoco/EPA team has demonstrated that emission goals could be reached at just one-sixth to one-fourth the cost of complying with government regulations. Allowing plant owners and managers to use their own judgment to reach federally determined emission goals would take advantage of their detailed knowledge of local conditions, require less spending on monitoring and enforcement, and encourage innovation. The EPA has allowed limited experiments along these lines since 1979; the concept should replace smokestack controls as the preferred way of regulating air pollution in the future.

4. *Allow companies to reach emission goals by reducing pollution from existing sources.* Since 1976, federal law has allowed new firms to locate in cities not meeting the federal air quality standards provided they *offset* their added pollution by reducing an even larger amount of pollution from existing sources. Achieving reductions beyond the amount required by law earns a company an emissions reduction credit, which is a tradeable currency. Most offset trades occur within firms, but many have taken place between firms. This arrangement allows private investments in pollution abatement to concentrate on where the cost of abatement is lowest, thereby producing the maximum reduction per dollar spent. Just as importantly, it rewards innovation and "beating the standards." As environmentalists, we care more about *how much* reduction takes place than *who does it*, so we should favor expansion of the offset concept. Unfortunately, the current trend in federal law seems to be toward imposing new regulations on the use of offsets.

5. *Reform tradeable emission permit systems.* The 1990 Clean Air Act and the Regional Clean Air Incentives Market (RECLAIM) in southern California create trading systems that allow pollution sources with high abatement costs to buy reductions from sources that have lower costs. These systems are similar to the offset system described above, and for this reason they show promise as a way to achieve large emission reductions efficiently. However, both tradeable emission systems as they are now designed fail to provide the degree of legal predictability and protection of rights that would prompt most firms to use the permits; instead, most firms will choose to rely on private market-based alterna-

tives. (See the sidebar on the following pages.) The solution is to genuinely protect the property rights of all parties in the trading process and, where possible, rely on *existing market institutions* rather than attempt to create artificial markets.

6. Begin re-establishing common law remedies to air pollution. As it becomes available, state and federal governments should make public the information, produced by Recommendation #1, on the sources of local air pollution. Government, industry, environmental groups, and community and civic organizations should begin a dialogue over how and when statutory laws against air pollution should be replaced with re-established civil law remedies. Since state and federal laws precluding recovery of damages by victims are numerous, the process of repealing these laws must be undertaken in a coordinated fashion by various government agencies. But even slow movement in this direction is certain to prompt many polluters to reduce their emissions voluntarily in order to avoid future legal claims.

7. Remove regulatory barriers to the construction of nuclear power plants. Increased reliance on nuclear power to generate electricity would lead to cleaner air, but several public policies now interfere with the siting and building of nuclear power plants. One is antitrust laws that prevent the nuclear power industry from agreeing to a single standard design for nuclear facilities, which in turn means each design must be separately certified before construction can begin. Another is the blatant politicization of the approval process that has led to costly and crippling delays in construction. Other countries, such as France, have shown that the nuclear power industry can be safely and inexpensively expanded by adopting policies that avoid these unnecessary expenses and delays. The U.S. should follow their lead.

8. Policies to avoid. Environmentalists should withdraw their support for the following policies:

- *Carbon taxes or a cap on carbon dioxide emissions.* The evidence supporting the theory of catastrophic global warming is much too weak to support either a cap on total carbon dioxide emissions or devices, such as a carbon tax, intended to reduce such emissions. The

Shortcomings of Government-created Markets for Emission Trading

Title IV of the 1990 Clean Air Act (CAA) allows utilities to trade sulfur dioxide emissions credits, and the Regional Clean Air Incentives Market (RECLAIM), recently approved for improving air quality in southern California, contains a similar market-based trading system that also would apply to non-utility sources and nitrogen oxide emissions. For these systems to work, the ground rules and property rights guarantees must be as stable and predictable as those operating in alternative private markets. Unfortunately that is not the case for either the Clean Air Act or the RECLAIM system.

In both cases, allowances and credits are denied property right status. Specifically, the government agencies involved say that they do not intend to be held responsible for alterations or even elimination of the emissions trading system. In other words, the government does not want to be inconvenienced by the prohibition, in the Fifth Amendment of the Constitution, on takings without compensation. The implication of this mistake for the Clean Air Act is that the electric utilities will simply average their emissions within their respective corporate bounds and not deal with other utilities except through power pools. (In power pools, the thing being traded is electricity, for which property rights are clearly defined.)

Another reason electric utilities will avoid the artificial market in the CAA is the nature of state regulation of electric utilities. Utilities will simply invest in abatement equipment or switch fuels, since such costs are almost always allowed by regulators to be passed on to the ratepayer. On the other hand, a utility that gambles on the stability of the allowance market will have to answer, in prudency review hearings, why it ignored the warnings contained in the Act that the federal government would not be responsible for legislative or regulatory changes that adversely affect the value of allowances.

In the South Coast Air Basin (SCAB) where most of the emission sources are not utilities, similar accommodations will nevertheless take the place of credit trading. Firms that face moderate to high costs of reducing emissions will shut down or relocate outside of the SCAB. In most cases, relocation by these firms will be less costly than

(continued on the following page)

investment in abatement measures. The assets of these departing firms, including the emission reductions, will then be purchased by firms that intend to stay in the SCAB. Thus, the trading of emission reductions will largely be internalized within the well-defined legal structure of the firm. There is also the possibility that some trading will take place within joint venture arrangements among emission sources, and through bundling of emission charges in utility bills. All of these alternative institutions have property rights guarantees that are superior to the RECLAIM credits.

The lesson that will most likely be learned from these two experiments is that existing market institutions (that is, those with well-defined property rights) will dominate those concocted by government.

Sources: James L. Johnston, "A Market Without Rights: Sulfur Dioxide Emissions Trading," *Regulation*, Fall 1991, pp. 24-29: and James L. Johnston, "How Market Oriented is the RECLAIM System?" presentation at the WEA International Pacific Rim Conference, Hong Kong, January 11, 1994, author's manuscript.

U.N. global warming treaty does not commit the U.S. or other nations to specific reductions, and other countries are already retreating from their pledges to make specific reductions by the year 2000.

- *Tighter emission standards for new cars and other command-and-control regulations on air emissions.* Command-and-control regulation is an outdated instrument of public policy that already has achieved virtually all that can be achieved. Environmentalists should oppose more restrictive auto exhaust standards, "zero discharge" standards, and laws mandating the use of "best available technology."

- *Bans or moratoria on incineration.* Incineration is a safe and cost-effective means of waste disposal, particularly in those parts of the country where geography makes landfills expensive to site or a threat to groundwater supplies. New EPA regulations governing incinerator fumes have reduced emissions to below the levels set for factories and power plants. Incinerators have been estimated to pose a risk to health of less than one in a million.

Cleaner water

1. Identify the sources of water pollution. Emissions from point sources, such as factories, are now a small fraction of the total pollution entering most lakes and streams in the U.S. (See illustration below.) Nonpoint sources, such as runoff from farmland, lawns, and construction sites, dumping by commercial and recreational boaters, and (in the case of lakes) deposition from the air, are now the largest problems in need of control. The same technologies that allow us to trace air pollutants to their sources enable us to track, for example, pesticides back to farmers who are using them improperly. Once again, accurate databases of local sources of pollution are essential if efficient pollution abatement plans are to be designed.

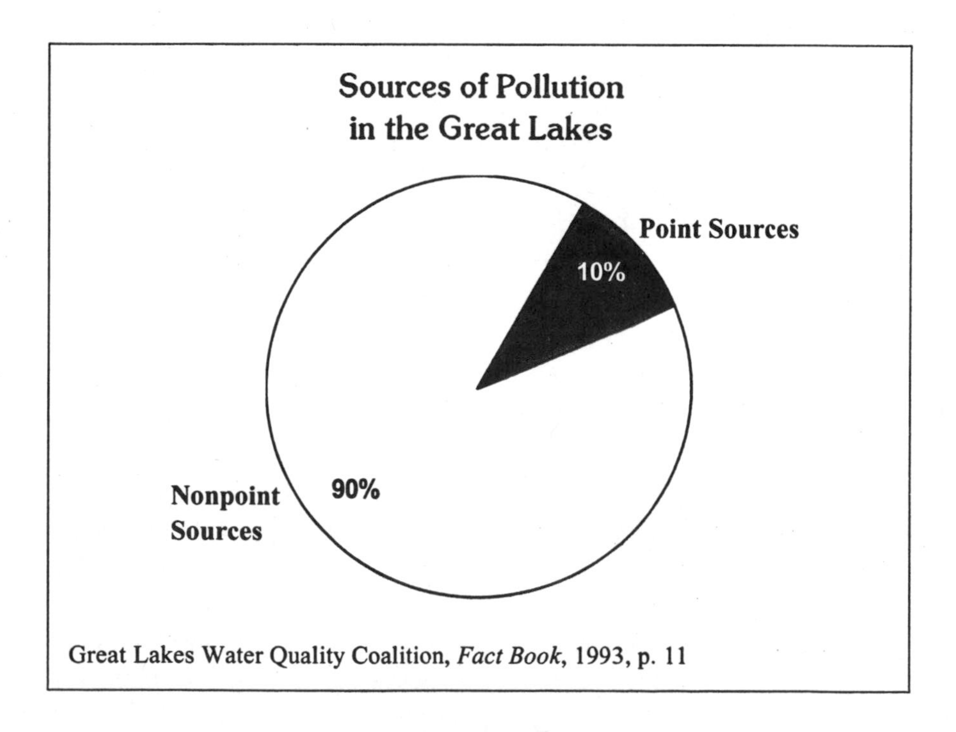

Great Lakes Water Quality Coalition, *Fact Book*, 1993, p. 11

2. *Replace command-and-control regulations with market-based solutions.* The Clean Water Act imposes uniform effluent standards on all point sources of water pollution, regardless of the large differences that often exist among factories in the costs of emission abatement, and regardless of actual water quality in the river or lake into which the effluent is being placed. Such an approach forces some companies to spend millions of dollars squeezing out small amounts of waste while encouraging others, who could reduce their emissions less expensively, to continue polluting at regulated levels. The concepts of offsets, used effectively to combat air pollution, should be applied to water pollution. Experiments in tradeable allowances and credits could further contribute to more cost-effective water pollution abatement.

3. *Create water markets.* Where several groups compete to use the same supply of water, governments should help define and enforce tradeable water rights to promote the most efficient use of the limited supply. Progress in this direction already has been made in California, where values have been assigned to different uses of water, including wildlife preservation in San Francisco Bay. In southern California, the water market concept enabled Los Angeles to spend $230 million to modernize the irrigation system serving area farmers. In exchange for its investment, the city receives the right to use the water that otherwise would have been wasted. This investment in conservation would not have taken place without the creation of a market for water rights.

4. *Phase out federal construction subsidies for municipal waste treatment.* The $75 billion in federal subsidies invested in the design and construction of municipal waste treatment facilities has helped reduce water pollution from this source, but there is ample documentation that this effort (like all arrangements based on subsidies) was wasteful and inefficient. Some communities built larger and more expensive facilities than they needed, and most communities overlooked alternatives involving source reduction and low-cost treatment systems. (See the sidebar on the next page.) Ending the federal subsidy will force local communities to consider all of their options without the distorting influence of "free" federal dollars earmarked for one kind of approach. Given an undistorted choice, more communities would embrace less-expensive and more environment-friendly ways of treating liquid waste.

5. *Phase out water subsidies for farmers.* The same rationale for phasing out grants for municipal waste treatment applies to federal water subsidies for farmers. Below-market pricing of water to farmers, particularly in the western U.S., is responsible for tremendous amounts of wasted water, damage to soil and wildlife, and very little social benefit. Such subsidies should be phased out as quickly as possible.

6. *Begin re-establishing common law remedies to water pollution.* The same process recommended for restoring a property rights solution to air pollution should be started with regard to water pollution. Statutory laws against water pollution should be amended or repealed as the ability of injured parties to document damages is established and the right to sue polluters in civil court is restored. Once again, moving to restore this property rights approach will prompt polluters to reduce their emissions in anticipation of future liability.

A Better Way to Treat Liquid Wastes

Land-based, or circular, waste treatment systems have a long history in the U.S. and other countries. New, high-tech designs allow hundreds of communities throughout the U.S. to avoid the expense and environmental damage of constructing capital-intensive and chemical-based linear treatment systems.

A typical land-based system involves pumping liquid waste into the bottom of man-made ponds, where solids separate from water and are broken down by biological action. The upper layers of water in the ponds prevent odors from escaping during this biological process. Partially treated water is removed from the ponds and sprayed over lawns or crops, allowing plants and bacteria in the soil to complete the cleaning process as the water filters down to replenish the aquifer from which it was originally drawn.

Land-based systems are already working in Muskegon County, Michigan; Northglenn, Colorado; Lubbock, Texas; Itasca, Illinois; Stephens City, Virginia; and Chandler, Arizona.

Source: See Jack Scheaffer, *Managing Water Resources: A Better Way* (Chicago, IL: The Heartland Institute, 1987).

7. *Policies to avoid.* Extreme new restrictions on emissions into lakes and waterways are not necessary and may be counterproductive. What is needed instead is a better tailoring of existing restrictions to efficiently solve real water quality problems. The federal government is ill-equipped to accomplish this tailoring, especially when it uses command-and-control regulations. Environmentalists should not join the noisy campaign against chlorine, chlorinated compounds, or dioxin emissions from paper mills and other point sources. Concentrations of these substances are well below levels thought to endanger human health, and dramatic progress has been made in recent years. The "zero discharge" standard set by some environmental groups would impose unacceptably high and completely unnecessary costs on manufacturers and municipalities.

Managing toxic chemicals

1. *Stop relying on maximum tolerable dose (MTD) tests on laboratory animals to predict human cancer risks.* There is now widespread agreement in the scientific community that MTD tests on laboratory animals are unreliable indicators of human cancer risks. Until the EPA and other federal agencies stop using such studies as the basis for their rule making, there will continue to be panics, unnecessary product bans, and unnecessary evacuations of entire communities.

2. *Drop the assumption of a linear dose-response relationship.* Along with ending reliance on MTD laboratory tests, environmentalists should drop the false assumption that the relationship between a chemical's dose and its effect on human health is always linear. There are too many cases where the relationship is not linear to justify blindly applying this standard to every substance. Assuming a linear relationship almost certainly overestimates the threat of very low doses of many chemicals.

3. *Focus public policy on real-life exposure, not laboratory measures of toxicity.* Measures of toxicity alone are meaningless unless accompanied by evidence of human exposure. The deadliest substance in the world is harmless if no one is exposed to it; conversely, seemingly benign products are deadly in excessive amounts. Federal and state policies should be based on real exposure to chemicals, not hypothetical

risks deduced from laboratory toxicity measurements. Where industry is doing a good job protecting its workforce and the general public from a toxic chemical, no public interest is served by further restricting industry's manufacture and use of the substance.

4. *Use cost-benefit analysis.* Past efforts by the EPA to regulate toxic chemicals have produced enormous costs per death averted (see the table on page 162), producing clear evidence that the nation's resources are not being used efficiently to address real environmental hazards. Congress should require that cost-benefit analyses be conducted on all current and proposed environmental regulations. Rules that fail to meet some threshold of cost effectiveness should be repealed or set aside. There is no doubt that such a review would lead to a redirection of funds away from small and hypothetical risks and toward larger and real hazards.

5. *Reform Superfund.* Superfund has been a hugely expensive failure. Charged with cleaning up existing hazardous waste sites, it has squandered billions of dollars and cleaned only a handful of sites around the country. The most important changes that should be made are these:

- Require the EPA to set a specific cancer risk level that it defines as an unacceptable risk.

- Factor real exposure levels into decisions to list sites for cleanup.

- Draw up a priority list for cleanup of Superfund sites based on the site characteristics developed by the EPA, the exposure classification, and the estimated remediation costs.

- Change Superfund's inequitable methods for determining liability by removing joint and several liability, limiting retroactive liability, and specifying mitigating circumstances.

- Give states leeway to relax cleanup and liability standards. (A number of states, including Ohio, New Jersey, Michigan, and Wisconsin, already are moving in this direction.)

- Experiment with auctioning "orphan" hazardous waste sites (that is, sites where responsible parties able to pay for the cleanup have not been found) to private businesses. Where the cleanup cost is relatively low and the property is valuable, such sites could be sold and cleaned without any public dollars being used. Where cleanup costs exceed the market value of the site, it should be sold to the company that requires the smallest *subsidy* to take ownership. In this way, a competitive market for cleanup services will emerge.

6. *Policies to avoid.* Several bills being considered by state legislatures and the U.S. Congress seek to reduce hazardous waste generation by categorizing more chemicals as "toxic" and mandating reductions or outright bans on their use. Such an approach has serious flaws, the most important being the familiar confusion between dose and exposure. The use of very poisonous substances during manufacturing processes poses a threat neither to human health nor to the environment provided these substances are managed properly. Critics have not demonstrated that industry is failing in this regard, and a regulatory apparatus already exists to ensure that hazardous waste is disposed of safely. Banning or forcing reductions in the use of basic elements that form the building blocks of modern chemistry would have a devastating effect on the production of thousands of "downstream" products, including computer chips, automobile components, and pharmaceuticals. The enormous costs of chemical bans are not nearly balanced by the imperceptible benefits in air and water quality that might result.

Protecting public lands and wildlife

1. *Stop subsidizing logging on public lands.* With one hand, the government limits logging by declaring large areas to be off limits to logging and by using the Endangered Species Act to prohibit logging even on private lands. But with its other hand, government subsidizes logging on ecologically frail hillsides and in arid climates to the tune of hundreds of millions of dollars a year. The Clinton Administration has indicated an interest in doing the right thing: It announced plans to end below-cost timber sales within four years. Environmentalists should help the President meet that deadline.

2. *Manage public lands for multiple benefits.* The Forest Service's original mandate was to manage public lands for multiple use, but pressure from powerful mining and lumber companies in the past often led to second-class status for recreation and conservation goals. Now, some environmental groups seem to believe it is "their turn" and are demanding that conservation be elevated above all other uses. The temptation is understandable, but the consequences are not good. The tactic turns public lands into a political football, to be protected or debased depending on who is elected or what deals are struck on issues completely unrelated to environmental protection. Policies prohibiting even the exploration for oil and minerals on some public lands squander the tremendous value that may lie beneath the ground, value that could be tapped in order to produce revenues to purchase and protect rare and endangered habitat.

3. *Stop subsidizing cattle grazing on public lands.* Subsidized grazing contributes to soil erosion and displacement of native species in the West. The Clinton Administration has announced its support for higher grazing fees, but even its proposal would leave fees well below private rates. If the President and Congress lack the courage to end these subsidies outright, then they should pursue the sale of grazing land to the ranchers, an option we've discussed earlier and propose again below.

4. *Give ownership to groups that now use public lands.* Even if their use of public lands is unsubsidized, the various classes of users will have only weak incentives to manage public lands for their long-term sustainability. Rather than making investments to preserve the future value of the assets they use, these renters would press for *more* current use at *lower* prices. We agree with Richard Stroup and John Baden when they write:

> Privatizing the national forests should end many of the obstacles to good management. Not only would decision makers be given larger amounts of validated and continuously updated information, but political obstacles to efficient management would largely disappear. Perhaps just as important, environmentalists, timber producers, miners, recreationists, and others who make demands on the Forest Service would quickly move away from their carping and fault-finding toward positive and constructive accommodation.

5. *Increase user fees.* If public lands are not sold to their users, then at least users should pay full price for the use they receive. We've already discussed the subsidies received by ranchers and lumber companies, but persons who use forests for recreation or who support conservation also have been undercharged. User fees are well below the costs of maintaining national parks and public waterways, and are dramatically below the income that *could* be generated if development were allowed. By paying fees, proponents of recreation and conservation could raise their standing before the Forest Service and other government agencies that now tend to listen more closely to lumber, ranching, and farming interests.

6. *Reform the Endangered Species Act.* While the idea behind the Endangered Species Act (ESA) is noble, its accomplishments have been few. Like other environmental protection regulations, the ESA makes no distinction between high risks and low risks, requiring the Fish and Wildlife Service to protect every species it determines to be endangered "without reference to possible economic or other impacts." Its prohibitions against ownership of endangered species makes their conservation by voluntary initiatives less likely, and the sweeping powers given to the government to restrict the use of private land where endangered animals are found have created a strong incentive for private landowners to destroy habitat and even kill endangered animals when they are found. The ESA needs revision to prioritize risks, re-introduce cost-benefit analysis, and restore incentives for private landowners to protect rather than destroy habitat and animals.

7. *Support continued privatization of wildlife.* Programs such as the wolf compensation plan operated by Defenders of Wildlife show great promise as a way to protect endangered species. So too does private land acquisition by Ducks Unlimited and The Nature Conservancy; consulting for good stewardship by organizations such as EcoTrust and Cascade Holistic Environmental Consultants; and private gaming and reserve management. Such activities work because they *get the incentives right.* If even a small percentage of the billions of dollars now wasted on other environmental campaigns were invested instead in private wildlife conservation, more progress could be made in this area in one or two years than the ESA has made possible in twenty years.

8. Policies to avoid. Environmentalists should be skeptical of those who call for constant expansion of the national parks and wilderness areas despite increasing evidence that the government mismanages the land for which it already has responsibility. Demands that recreational users of public lands should not have to pay the full costs of their use are irresponsible and unfair to other users. In the long run, refusing to pay their own way is why environmentalists often get defeated in their confrontations with logging, ranching, and agricultural interests. Proposals to "strengthen" the Endangered Species Act would lead to less, not more, protection of wildlife by imposing greater restrictions and penalties on the owners of private land that is host to an endangered species.

Solid waste solutions

1. Change our personal habits. More important than the enactment of any law concerning solid waste is changing the way we buy, use, and discard objects. "Reducing waste can mean one of only a few things," writes Frances Cairncross: "Buying products that use less raw material to serve their function; buying products that can be recycled or reused; buying products that last longer; or simply buying less." All of us need to keep these options in mind when we're at home, at work, and on vacation. Industry is responding to the growing environmental awareness of consumers by reducing packaging and reformulating products to make them less hazardous or persistent in the environment: It is up to each of us to put our money behind our convictions and purchase such products.

2. Support an integrated approach to solid waste management. Because nothing can be endlessly recycled or reused, environmentalists should support an integrated approach to solid waste management that includes source reduction, recycling, waste-to-energy plants, and landfills. All four strategies have their place in an environmentally sound and efficient waste management strategy, which is why the EPA and many solid waste experts endorse this balanced approach. Technological advances have made incinerators and landfills safer than ever before. Opposition to landfilling based on fear that we are running out of room to store waste is näive: All the garbage produced in the U.S. during the next 500 years would fit in a single landfill just twenty miles to a side.

Opposition by some elements of the environmental movement to any disposal method other than recycling is unrealistic and unnecessary.

3. *Stop subsidizing garbage disposal.* The best way to encourage recycling and source reduction is to stop subsidizing the disposal of garbage. Most communities don't charge *by the bag* for garbage, but instead charge each household a flat fee. Many communities don't even break out garbage collection as a separate item on their residents' tax bills. These practices discourage source reduction and recycling. If your community doesn't charge by the bag for garbage collection, see what can be done to change the policy. Communities that have made the switch report reductions of between 25 and 45 percent in the amount of waste sent to landfills. This as much or more reduction as can be achieved by a very aggressive community recycling program.

4. *Continue to phase in new landfill technologies.* Older landfills around the country should be closed or retrofitted with new technologies, such as groundwater monitoring, leachate collection, and water-shedding caps. During the next ten years, thousands of small and less safe landfills will close while a smaller number of much larger, high-tech landfills will open to take their place. Communities need to stay involved in the planning and operation of community landfills, but activists should observe that the original reasons for opposing landfills are no longer compelling. In fact, opposing a new landfill today probably means requiring that an older, less-safe landfill remain in operation somewhere else. Environmentalists should avoid being recruited into NIMBY ("Not In My Backyard") campaigns against landfills unless there is clear evidence that a site is unsuited for a landfill.

5. *Support recycling, but only when it pays for itself.* Recycling is not necessary to avoid a shortage of landfill space. Nevertheless, recycling makes sense when the cost of the recycled product is lower than the cost of producing it from virgin materials (e.g., aluminum cans) or when the material being recycled is a major presence in the waste stream and consequently contributes to the cost of solid waste disposal (e.g., paper). Some things, however, probably just aren't worth recycling. The high cost of sorting and cleaning most used plastic containers (PET soft drink bottles being a conspicuous exception) makes recycled plastic more

expensive and lower quality than virgin plastic, while plastic's small presence in the waste stream (just 4.1 percent in the case of plastic containers and packaging) means it contributes very little to total disposal costs. So when does recycling genuinely help the environment? Most likely when all the expenses required to recycle a product add up to less than the market value of the recycled product. When this isn't the case, it means more energy and other scarce resources were consumed in the recycling process than were saved by it. This, finally, produces our rule of thumb: Support recycling, but only when it pays for itself.

6. Policies to avoid. Misguided solid waste policies are still being debated or are already on the books in many states, a legacy of the "solid waste crisis" scare of the 1980s. Legislators and environmentalists should save their energy for more important battles than whether to ban plastic cups. In particular, there is no reason to support these policies:

- *Bans on certain kinds of packaging.* These bans result in virtually no reduction in solid waste volume since their targets usually constitute a tiny fraction of a percent of total solid waste and because the substitutes for them are just as bulky and unlikely to be recycled. Product bans are another obsolete tactic from the past; they don't work, and we don't need them.

- *"Dates and rates" legislation.* These laws mandate that certain percentages of a product (often types of plastic packaging) must be recycled by a certain date or else fines, mandatory return policies, or even bans are imposed. Now that the "crisis" is over, there is no point keeping these laws on the books. This is particularly true of laws regarding plastic packaging, which ranks all the way down with old shoes and discarded linens as a fraction of the solid waste stream. These laws are dinosaurs that don't deserve our support.

- *Minimum recycled content laws.* These laws require that newspapers and paper purchased by government agencies contain no less than a specified percentage of recycled paper fibers. The intent was to "create a market" for the paper collected (unnecessarily) through mandatory community recycling programs around the country. Once again, we ask: If recycling paper is worth doing, why should we need a law forcing people to do it? It ought to pay for itself.

■ *The German Green Dot system.* In 1991, Germany enacted an "Ordinance on the Avoidance of Packaging Wastes" requiring manufacturers and distributors to eventually take back, process, and recycle all their packaging. Popularly called the "Green Dot" system, this program is hailed as a model for the U.S. by some environmentalists. Clear thinking, however, shows it to be absurd.

The cost of solid waste management would skyrocket since every type of packaging must be recycled regardless of how ill-suited it might be to the recycling process. Indeed, the collecting and processing of packaging in Germany now costs *twice* as much as does other household garbage, and the cost will rise further as recycling quotas are phased in. Also, some especially difficult-to-recycle packaging — such as transparent multi-layer plastic — produces major cost-savings for consumers by preserving foods and making spoilage detectable. Such packaging will be replaced by coated paper and other materials that are more easily recycled but provide less protection from spoilage and are not transparent. The amount of food wasted as a result of this trade-off will be many times greater than the amount of packaging that is not now being recycled.

Finally, the Green Dot system leaves unanswered a crucial question: Where is the market for all of this used material? If manufacturers produce packaging with 50 percent or even 75 percent recycled content, who buys the other 50 percent or 25 percent? Germany's answer at first was to export the excess material to other countries, resulting in the flooding and destruction of markets for used materials in those countries. International outrage against the practice forced a decision to halt such exports. More recently, German officials announced they will allow incineration and landfilling of excess recyclable material . . . material, we note, that was collected and processed at considerable expense, only to be burned or buried with other garbage.

So Germany is back to a system where some packaging is recycled and some is not. Only now, the system costs twice as much to operate (and the cost is steadily rising), valuable packaging materials have been removed from the market, and decisions about what to do with excess used materials are being based, not on what is best for consumers, but on what is negotiated among government officials, bureaucrats, and manufacturers. This, clearly, is no model for the U.S.

What concerned environmentalists should do

1. Ignore "crisis-of-the-month" prophecies. Your mailbox will continue to be crammed with fundraising appeals and newsletters claiming some new and urgent crisis has been discovered. Television specials and the evening news will frequently claim global warming, ozone depletion, and toxic chemicals are environmental catastrophes "just around the corner." (They will *always* be "just around the corner.") Our best advice to the reader is to ignore this crisis-of-the-month rhetoric and appeals that use it. Focus instead on real, not imaginary, environmental problems. This doesn't mean you are less committed than other environmentalists: It only means you're smarter. Use the Rules for Eco-Sanity to measure and test the claims you hear. Starting today, pledge that you won't fall for yet another trumped-up scare.

2. Start speaking for yourself. When the leaders of many environmental organizations express their alarmist views, the media and many policy makers believe they are speaking for you, the average environmentally concerned American. They don't know that you might disagree with these spokesmen on some issues. If you don't take the trouble to speak for yourself, they will never know. The easiest way to speak out is to write letters to elected officials and to the editor of your local newspaper. Writing once a month is not too often. An even better way to spread the word is to talk seriously to your friends, relatives, and the people you work with. Best of all is to confront other members and the leaders of the environmental organizations you belong to. Tell them what's on your mind, and if necessary challenge the message they are delivering.

3. Stop supporting organizations that exaggerate environmental problems. Some environmental groups just plain don't deserve your support, no matter how big they are or how slick their magazines look. These are the organizations that exploited the dioxin scares and are riding the global warming and chlorine scares for every nickel they can raise. Says

Keith Schneider of *The New York Times*, ". . . these groups are in danger of becoming the green equivalent of the military lobby, more interested in sowing fear and protecting wasteful programs than in devising a new course." Try writing to them to ask that they change their tune, though we know from personal experience that this doesn't work very often. *Stop giving them money.* This gets their attention *and* frees up your donation budget to support organizations that are more reliable and focus on real problems.

4. Don't automatically join every local campaign. Your community may be next in line for a dioxin, pesticide, or electromagnetic fields scare. Should this happen, our advice is: Don't step forward until you see real evidence that an environmental hazard exists. Go through the steps of critical thinking: Is this correlation or causation? Are people being labeled villains and victims? Are the "experts" speaking outside their discipline? Do they have evidence or just opinions? Based on the answers you get to these questions, join or take a pass on the campaign. There are many deserving organizations and good causes that need your support; don't waste it spreading unnecessary fear and panic.

5. Support environmental organizations that exercise eco-sanity. You might have gathered from the tone of our discussion so far that there are very few environmental organizations that exercise eco-sanity. Not true. We know of nearly twenty organizations that are reliable and generally level-headed on the issues of human health and the environment, and there are probably scores more that we don't know about. The number of such organizations is growing as new groups are started by environmentalists who are tired of the tactics of the corporate giants in the environmental field. None of these groups engages in the "crisis-of-the-month" fundraising tactics we have been discussing. On the following page is a list of our favorite groups; we recommend that you contact several of them and join the ones that come closest to sharing your perspective on environmentalism.

American Council on Science and Health
1995 Broadway, 16th Floor
New York, NY 10023-5860
212/362-7044

Cascade Holistic Economic Consultants
14417 Southeast Laurie
Oak Grove, OR 97267
503/652-7049

Committee for a Constructive Tomorrow
P.O. Box 65722
Washington, DC 20035
202/429-2737

Conservation International
1015 18th Street NW
Washington, DC 20036
202/429-5660

Defenders of Wildlife
1101 14th Street #1400
Washington, DC 20005
202/682-9400

Ducks Unlimited, Inc.
One Waterfowl Way
Memphis, TN 38120
901/758-3825

EcoTrust
1200 N.W. Front Avenue #470
Portland, OR 97209
503/227-6225

Evergreen Foundation
300 Medford Heights Lane
Medford, OR 97504
503/733-1931

Forest Trust
P.O. Box 519
Santa Fe, NM 87504
505/983-8992

Foundation for Research on Economics and the Environment
4900 25th Street NE #201
Seattle, WA 98105
206/548-1776

Great Lakes Water Quality Coalition
200 E. Randolph Street #5223
Chicago, IL 60601
312/819-1111

National Wilderness Institute
25766 Georgetown Station
Washington, DC 20007
703/836-7404

The Nature Conservancy
1815 N. Lynn Street
Arlington, VA 22209
703/841-5300

Political Economy Research Center
502 S. 19th Avenue #211
Bozeman, MT 59715
406/587-9591

Resources for the Future
1616 P Street NW
Washington, DC 20036
202/328-5000

Sand County Foundation
P.O. Box 3037
Madison, WI 53704
608/244-3511

Science & Environmental Policy Project
2101 Wilson Boulevard #1003
Arlington, VA 22201
703/527-0130

Trout Unlimited
1500 Wilson Boulevard #310
Arlington, VA 22209
703/522-0200

9. The end of the road

"WE STAND NOW where two roads diverge," wrote Rachel Carson at the start of *Silent Spring*'s final chapter. She could not have known that her book, and similar works by authors soon to follow, would send the environmental movement down the road to chemophobia, panicky predictions of the end of the world, and one embarrassing false alarm after another. Today, 32 years later, it is time to ask whether we have taken this road far enough. It is time, as Carson also wrote, to "look about and see what other course is open to us."

Staying on the present path means relying on fear to get people to help us protect the environment. Fear of pesticides, or toxic chemicals, or ozone depletion, or nuclear power, or electromagnetic fields . . . take your pick. This is how environmental organizations mobilize supporters, attract media attention, and raise money in the 1990s. As we have demonstrated repeatedly in past chapters, there is little evidence to support any of these fears. Yet, one can hardly pick up a newsletter from a major environmental organization without seeing at least one of these "crises."

To paraphrase George Washington, the scare tactic is a powerful servant, but a fearful master. Somewhere along the line, fear stopped being a servant of many environmental organizations and became instead their master. Far from being just one of many weapons in an arsenal, the scare tactic literally controls the largest and most powerful environmental organizations in the U.S. today. It controls their agendas, their funding, their legislative strategies, and even their *thinking* about environmental issues.

The eco-sanity exit

Eco-sanity means applying reason, sound science, and a respect for the rights of others to environmental issues. A commitment to eco-sanity necessarily means abandoning scare tactics and relying instead on the good judgment of individual environmentalists and the general public.

The Common-Sense Agenda presented in Chapter 8 is anything but moderate. It involves sweeping changes in how we go about identifying environmental problems and then solving them. It doesn't tinker around the edges of current government programs or merely call for doing more of the same. Instead, it changes the way tens of billions of dollars are spent each year. It *changes the incentives* of a hundred million people who commute to work every day, prompting them to tune their cars or drive on routes where, or at times of day when, congestion is less likely. It makes factory managers, ranchers, farmers, and foresters focus on how to protect the environment instead of how to dodge a regulation, get a subsidy, or boost a budget.

It is difficult even to imagine how immensely better off the environment would be if the Common-Sense Agenda were in place. Here are some examples of the kinds of changes that could be expected:

- The air in our cities would be cleaner because the one car in ten that pollutes will be tuned, and fewer cars will be caught in traffic.

- The cost per unit of pollution abatement by factories would fall by 75 percent or more. The result: billions of dollars of savings each year *and* cleaner air and water.

- Holding polluters accountable to the victims of pollution would compel each of us to become alert to the need to find ways to reduce the pollution we are responsible for creating.

- Ending water subsidies would save taxpayers over $1 billion a year and, in a few years, would lead many farmers to change wasteful irrigation practices or give up on irrigation entirely. Depleted aquifers and dry rivers would finally see relief.

- Ending grazing subsidies, price supports, and acreage retirement programs would allow hundreds of thousands of acres of land to return to natural conditions. Many agricultural practices that today destroy wildlife habitat would be replaced by wildlife-enhancing activities.

- The billions of dollars now being wasted by Superfund would finally go toward cleaning up the most dangerous toxic waste sites in the country, and not simply into the pockets of trial lawyers.

- Forest rangers would likely work for people who owned the land they worked on, not just used it for short-term political goals. No more below-cost lumber sales, and no more road-building sprees.

- Our mailboxes wouldn't be filled with dire warnings of the coming global environmental crisis. Instead, we will get honest and accurate reports on the progress made and the work that still needs to be done.

Exciting as all of this seems, it is only the beginning of what the Common-Sense Agenda would deliver. The biggest pay-off would come when millions of thoughtful and devoted environmentalists, like you, turn their attention from the "crisis of the month" and concentrate instead on solving real environmental problems.

Imagine how much good we could do if the time and money now spent battling nonexistent crises were used instead to solve real problems. Imagine billions of dollars a year spent buying wilderness areas, paying ranchers and other landowners to protect rather than injure wildlife, and defending in court the rights of actual victims of pollution. Now *that's* an exciting vision!

Notes

Preface

Two recent histories of the environmental movement are Robert Gottlieb, *Forcing the Spring*, and Martin W. Lewis, *Green Delusions: An Environmentalist Critique of Radical Environmentalism*.

For a sample of how economists view environmental regulations, see Paul R. Portney, *Public Policies for Environmental Protection*.

Re "anti-environment backlash," see Stephen Budiansky, "The Doomsday Myths," *U.S. News & World Report*, December 13, 1993, p. 81.

Re public support for environmentalism, see "Environmental Concern Remains High," *The Wirthlin Report* 2 (7) (July 1992), p. 1. The article describes a poll that found that "80 percent of Americans agree that 'protecting the environment is so important that requirements and standards cannot be too high, and continuing environmental improvements must be made regardless of cost.'"

Chapter One

Regli quote is from Stig Regli, "Risk vs. Risk: Proposed Decision Tree for Drinking Water Management," *Health & Environment Digest* 7 (3) (June 1993), p. 5.

Re "most scientists agree," see Bruce N. Ames, Renae Magaw, and Lois Swirsky Gold, "Ranking Possible Carcinogenic Hazards," *Science* 236 (April 17, 1987), pp. 271-277.

Re Food and Drug Administration, see Michael Fumento, *Science Under Siege*, p. 69.

Re CFCs and plastic, see discussions in Chapter 4. The figure for polystyrene plastic in landfills is from William Rathje and Cullen Murphy, *Rubbish! The Archeology of Garbage*, p. 98.

EPA cost estimates for air pollution control are from Paul R. Portney, *Public Policies for Environmental Protection*, p. 66.

Re "many independent scholars," see T.H. Tietenberg's review of the literature in *Emissions Trading: An Exercise in Reforming Pollution Policy*.

The communities listed in the first paragraph of "Only a Fable?" were victims of the following scares:

Love Canal, New York	Dioxin from hazardous waste
Times Beach, Missouri	Dioxin in used oil
Harrisburg, Pennsylvania	Radiation
Newark, New Jersey	Dioxin in drinking water
Midland, Michigan	Dioxin in drinking water
Alsea, Oregon	Dioxin in pesticide
Hartford, Tennessee	Dioxin in paper mill effluent
Fountain Valley, California	Electromagnetic fields
Montecito, California	Electromagnetic fields
Guilford, Connecticut	Electromagnetic fields

For accounts of the Alar scare, see Ben Bolch and Harold Lyons, *Apocalypse Not: Science, Economics, and Environmentalism*, pp. 39-43; and Michael Fumento, *Science Under Siege*, pp. 19-44.

Chapter Two

". . . if current trends continue" is from *Global 2000 Report to the President.*

Gore quotes are from Albert Gore, *Earth in the Balance*, pp. 151, 325.

Myers quotes are from Norman Myers, "What Ails the Globe?" *International Wildlife*, February 1994.

Whelan quote is from Elizabeth Whelan, *Toxic Terror*, p. 15.

Simon and Kahn quote is from Julian L. Simon and Herman Kahn, *The Resourceful Earth*, p. 6.

Statement by 425 scientists is reprinted in Global Climate Coalition, *Climate Watch* 1 (7) (June 1993), p. 2.

EPA figures on air quality are from the Council on Environmental Quality, *Environmental Quality 1992*, Table 40, p. 337.

". . . a car built in 1993" is from EPA, *National Air Quality Emissions Trends Report 1992*, October 1993.

Figures on fleet turnover are from Motor Vehicle Manufacturers Association, *Cleaner Motor Vehicles: The Challenge Being Met*, September 1988, p. 10.

Re electrification and pollution, see Edison Electric Institute, *Powering a Cleaner Environment*, 1993.

Re Doll and Peto, see Sir Richard Doll and Richard Peto, *Journal of the National Cancer Institute*, January 1981, p. 1248.

Reference to National Water Quality Inventory, fishable lakes and rivers, and $23 billion a year are from A. Myrick Freeman III, in Paul R. Portney, *Public Policies for Environmental Protection*, pp. 114, 116, 125.

$75 billion is from Paul N. Tramontozzi, *Reforming Water Pollution Regulation*, Center for the Study of American Business, August 1985, p. 10. See also James Lis and Kenneth Chilton, *Clean Water — Murky Policy*, Center for the Study of American Business, January 1992.

"Between 57 and 98 percent" is from A. Myrick Freeman III, in Paul R. Portney, *Public Policies for Environmental Protection*, p. 109.

Freeman quote is from A. Myrick Freeman III, in Paul R. Portney, *Public Policies for Environmental Protection*, p. 120.

Information on Cuyahoga and Androscoggin Rivers is from "Across the U.S., Cleaner Water, but . . .," *U.S. News & World Report*, February 28, 1983, p. 30.

Michigan Department of Natural Resources quote is from "Water Quality and Pollution Control in Michigan: 1992 Report," Vol. 12, p. 84.

Reference to the Council on Environmental Quality is to *Environmental Quality 1992*, pp. 389-391.

International Joint Commission quote is from International Joint Commission, *A Strategy for Virtual Elimination of Persistent Toxic Substances*, Vol. 1, p. 6.

Council on Environmental Quality quote is from *Environmental Quality 1992*, pp. 32-33.

Ames quote is from Bruce N. Ames, Renae Magaw, and Lois Swirsky Gold, "Ranking Possible Carcinogenic Hazards," *Science* 236 (April 17, 1987), p. 272.

Doll and Peto quote is from Sir Richard Doll and Richard Peto, *Journal of the National Cancer Institute*, p. 1249.

Ehrlich quote is from the unnumbered preface of Paul Ehrlich, *The Population Bomb*. The predictions appear in that same book: pp. 36-37, 44-45 (famine) and 62 (death of Lakes Erie and Michigan); and in "Eco-Catastrophe!" *Ramparts*, 1969, p. 28 (food riots and falling life expectancy).

See Chapter 4 for figures on world population growth.

Bailey quote is from Ronald Bailey, *Eco-Scam*, p. 57.

D. Gale Johnson quote is from Ronald Bailey, *Eco-Scam*, p. 54.

Average life expectancy figures are from U.S. Bureau of the Census, *Statistical Abstract of the United States 1992*, Table 103.

Bailey quote is from Ronald Bailey, *Eco-Scam*, p. 42.

Ames quotes are from Bruce N. Ames, Renae Magaw, and Lois Swirsky Gold, "Ranking Possible Carcinogenic Hazards," *Science* 236 (April 17, 1987), pp. 272, 277.

Robert Scheuplein reference appears in Michael Fumento, *Science Under Siege*, p. 69.

The Wilderness Society fundraising letter was not dated, but was received in July 1993.

Hal Salwasser quote is from "Gaining Perspective: Forestry for the Future," *Journal of Forestry*, November 1990, p. 32.

U.S. Forest Service figures are from *Forest Resources of the U.S. 1992*, September

1993, p. 16.

National Forest figures are from the Everegreen Foundation, "The Great Forest Debate," May 1993, p. 12.

Growth in wooded area is from Hal Salwasser, "Gaining Perspective: Forestry for the Future," *Journal of Forestry*, November 1990, p. 32; and the Everegreen Foundation, "The Great Forest Debate," May 1993, p. 12.

Roger Sedjo and Marion Clawson quote is from Julian L. Simon and Herman Kahn, *The Resourceful Earth*, p. 132.

British Columbia Ministry of Forests reference is from Patrick Moore, speech to the Canadian Pulp and Paper Association, January 27, 1993. [Moore is a founding director of Greenpeace.]

The reference to *Last of the Mohicans* is based on John Hood, "Clear-Cut Forestry Lesson on Film," *Wall Street Journal*, March 30, 1993.

Re federal subsidies to logging and 342,000 miles of government-built roads, see Richard Stroup et al., *Progressive Environmentalism: A Pro-Science, Pro-Free Enterprise Agenda for Change*, National Center for Policy Analysis, April 1991, p. 37.

Statistics re landfills, recycling, and incineration are from EPA, *Characterization of Municipal Solid Waste in the U.S.*, 1992 Update, Final Report, July 1992, pp. ES 3-4.

Lehr quote is from Jay H. Lehr, *Rational Readings on Environmental Concerns*, pp. 441-443.

"EPA estimate" is from Jennifer Chilton and Kenneth Chilton, "A Critique of Risk Modeling and Risk Assessment of Municipal Landfills," *Waste Management & Research* 10 (1992), pp. 505-516.

Charles City County example is from Virginia Postrel and Lynn Scarlett, "Talking Trash," *Reason*, August/September 1991, pp. 30-31.

Wiseman quote is from A. Clark Wiseman, "Dumping: Less Wasteful than Recycling," *Wall Street Journal*, July 22, 1991.

"40 percent of PET bottles" and discussion of thermal decomposition is from American Plastics Council, "The Evolution of Plastics Recycling Technology," 1993.

Examples of light-weighting are from Deborah D. Anderson and Laurie Burnham, "Toward Sustainable Waste Management," *Issues in Science and Technology*, Fall 1992, p. 66.

Estimates of oil and natural gas reserves are from *Oil and Gas Journal, Worldwide Production Issue*, 1993. Calculation of number of years supply of natural gas is based on consumption estimate of 69.8 trillion cubic feet annually, per British Petroleum, *Statistical Review of World Energy*, 1993.

Coal estimates are from British Petroleum, *Statistical Review of World Energy*, June 1993.

Re Cairncross estimate of fuel resources, see Frances Cairncross, "Energy and the Environment: A Power for Good, a Power for Ill," *The Economist*, August 31, 1991, p. 5.

Scarlett quote is from Lynn Scarlett, *A Consumers Guide to Environmental Myths and Realities*, National Center for Policy Analysis, September 1991, p. 35.

Whelan quote is from Elizabeth Whelan, *Toxic Terror*, p. 300.

Chapter Three

The words in quotation marks all appear in Rachel Carson, *Silent Spring*. See pp. 6, 12.

The Doll and Peto quote is from Sir Richard Doll and Richard Peto, *Journal of the National Cancer Institute*, p. 1197.

"Man is not the only creature . . . " is based on the "Cancer" entry in *Encyclopaedia Brittanica Macropaedia,* Vol. 3, 1979, p. 763.

Van Nostrand's Scientific Encyclopedia, 5th edition, 1976, p. 413.

Fumento quote is from Michael Fumento, *Science Under Siege*, p. 83.

Doll and Peto quote is from Sir Richard Doll and Richard Peto, *Journal of the National Cancer Institute*, p. 1267.

Doll and Peto quote, "Overall, cancer mortality . . . " is from Sir Richard Doll and Richard Peto, *Journal of the National Cancer Institute*, p. 1210.

American Council on Science and Health quote is from American Council on Science and Health, *Cancer in the U.S.: Is There An Epidemic*? March 1983, p. 27.

Ames quote is from Bruce N. Ames, Renae Magaw, and Lois Swirsky Gold, "Ranking Possible Carcinogenic Hazards," *Science* 236 (April 17, 1987), p. 277.

Doll and Peto quote "For our present limited purpose . . ." is from Sir Richard Doll and Richard Peto, *Journal of the National Cancer Institute*, p. 1250.

American Medical Association statement is from *Journal of American Medical Association*, July 7, 1981. For a more recent statement, see "How Do We Interpret the 'Bad News' About Cancer?" *Journal of American Medical Association* 271 (6) (February 9, 1994), p. 488. This editorial criticizes a study appearing in the same issue (by Devra Lee Davis et al.) that purports to find a rising incidence of cancer. The editorial notes that the researchers failed to adequately control for an aging population or to account for declining rates of cancer among the nonelderly population.

Ames quote is from Bruce N. Ames, Renae Magaw, and Lois Swirsky Gold, "Ranking Possible Carcinogenic Hazards," *Science* 236 (April 17, 1987), p. 276.

Re 427 chemicals tested, see Joel Brinkley, "Animal Tests as Risk Clues: The Best Data May Fall Short," *The New York Times*, March 21, 1993.

Edith Efron quote is from Elizabeth Whelan, *Toxic Terror*, pp. 35-36.

Whelan quote is from Elizabeth Whelan, *Toxic Terror*, p. 78.

Edith Efron quote is from Elizabeth Whelan, *Toxic Terror*, p. 34.

Goodman quote is from Jay I. Goodman, "A Rational Approach to Risk Assessment," *Regulatory Toxicology and Pharmacology* 19 (1994), pp. 51-59.

Ames quote is from Bruce N. Ames, Renae Magaw, and Lois Swirsky Gold, "Ranking Possible Carcinogenic Hazards," *Science* 236 (April 17, 1987), p. 271.

Schneider quote is from Keith Schneider, "Second Chance on Environment," *The New York Times*, March 25, 1993.

Fumento quote is from Michael Fumento, *Science Under Siege*, p. 77.

Chapter Four

Sagan quote is from his January 5, 1993 address to the American Astronomical Society upon receiving the first Annenberg Foundation Award for Leadership. Quoted in *World Climate Review*, Winter 1993, p. 5.

January: Global Warming

Time magazine quote is from "Global Warming: Feeling the Heat," *Time*, January 1989, p. 36.

Re the IPCC report, see Intergovernmental Panel on Climate Change, *Scientific Assessment of Climate Change*.

Balling quote is from Robert C. Balling, Jr., *The Heated Debate*, p. 134.

"Within the constraints" is from Robert Jastrow, William Nierenberg, and Frederick Seitz, *Scientific Perspectives on the Greenhouse Problem*, p. 14.

Plantico quote is from M.S. Plantico, T.R. Karl, G. Kukla, and J. Gavin, "Is Recent Climate Change Across the U.S. Related to Rising Levels of Anthropogenic Greenhouse Gases?" *Journal of Geophysical Research* (D-10) (1990), p. 16,617.

Revelle quote is from Fred Singer, Roger Revelle, and Chauncey Starr, "What To Do About Greenhouse Warming: Look Before you Leap," *Cosmos*, 1991.

Re Singer, see S. Fred Singer, *Global Climate Change*; and "Global Warming: Do We Know Enough to Act?" in Kenneth Chilton and Melinda Warren, *Environmental Protection: Regulating for Results*.

Re Christy, see J.R. Christy, "Update of Microwave Sounding Unit Temperature Data Through March 1993," University of Alabama-Huntsville. Also cited in Global Climate Coalition, "Atmospheric Update: Satellites Show Cooling," *Climate Watch*, June 1993, pp. 2-3.

Re Michaels, see Patrick J. Michaels and D.E. Stooksbury, "Global Warming: A Reduced Threat?" *Bulletin of the American Meteorological Society* 73 (1992), pp. 1563-1577. Also Patrick J. Michaels, "Global Warming: Failed Forecasts and Politicized Science," Center for the Study of American Business, *Policy Study Number 117*, July 1993.

Lindzen quote is from Richard S. Lindzen, "Global Warming: The Origin and Nature of the Alleged Scientific Consensus," *Regulation*, Spring 1992, p. 92. See also Richard S. Lindzen, "Some Coolness Concerning Global Warming," *Bulletin of the American Meteorological Society* 71 (1990), pp. 288-299.

Gallup poll is reported in Patrick Michaels, "Conspiracy, Consensus, or Correlation?" *World Climate Review*, Winter 1993, pp. 8-9; and also in Richard S. Lindzen, "Global Warming: The Origin and Nature of the Alleged Scientific Consensus," *Regulation*, Spring 1992, p. 92.

Singer's survey, the excerpt from the letter from leaders of the American Meteorological Society, and the number of practicing climatologists are from Patrick Michaels, "Conspiracy, Consensus, or Correlation?" *World Climate Review*, Winter 1993, pp. 8-11. He describes an effort in 1988 by the National Oceanic and Atmospheric Administration to create a Climate Trends Panel of all such experts in the U.S. About sixty persons were identified.

Re actual record of temperature changes, see J.R. Christy, "Update of Microwave Sounding Unit Temperature Data Through March 1993," University of Alabama-Huntsville. Also cited in Global Climate Coalition, "Atmospheric Update: Satellites Show Cooling," *Climate Watch*, June 1993, pp. 2-3. See also J.D. Kahl et al., "Absence of Evidence for Greenhouse Warming Over the Arctic Ocean in the Past Forty Years," *Nature* 361 (1993), pp. 335-337; Patrick Michaels, "Global Warming: Failed Forecasts and Politicized Science," Center for the Study of American Business, *Policy Study No. 117*, July 1993, p. 11; and various issues of *World Climate Review*, published by the Department of Environmental Sciences, University of Virginia. The basis for earlier claims that significant global warming had occurred between 1980 and 1990 was ground-based thermometers, which measured a .16 degree Celsius increase during this time. The contradictory satellite data suggest that human measurement errors and the "heat island effect" caused by the presence of human structures made ground-based measurements the less accurate of the two measurement techniques.

Re support for the satellite data among advocates of the popular view, Michaels reported in Summer 1993 that "White House environmental coordinator-designate Robert Watson stated in May on worldwide television that these records are indeed correct." See Patrick J. Michaels, "Wasted Energy," *World Climate Review* 1 (4) (Summer 1993), p. 20.

Re changes in carbon dioxide levels, see Sherwood B. Idso, *Carbon Dioxide and Global Change: Earth in Transition*, p. 67.

Re research on the arctic ice pack, see J.W.C. White, "Don't Touch that Dial," *Nature* 364 (July 15, 1993), p. 186.

Lindzen quote is from Richard S. Lindzen, "Global Warming: The Origin and Nature of the Alleged Scientific Consensus," *Regulation*, Spring 1992, pp. 88-89.

Re cloud cover, see Robert Jastrow, William Nierenberg, and Frederick Seitz, *Scientific Perspectives on the Greenhouse Problem*, p. 17.

The reference to Bonan is from Gordon B. Bonan, "Comparison of Atmospheric Carbon Dioxide Concentration and Metabolic Activity in Boreal Forest Ecosystems," *Tellus* 44B (1992), pp. 173-185.

Weaver quote is from Andrew J. Weaver, "The Oceans and Global Warming," *Nature* 364 (July 15, 1993), p. 193.

Michaels quote is from Patrick J. Michaels, "Global Warming: Failed Forecasts and Politicized Science," Center for the Study of American Business, *Policy Study No. 117*,

July 1993, pp. 11-12. On this subject, see also M.I. Hoffert and C. Covey, "Deriving Global Climate Sensitivity from Paleoclimate Reconstructions," *Nature* 360 (1990), pp. 573-576.

Balling quote is from Robert C. Balling, Jr., *The Heated Debate*, p. 134. For similar assessments by other climatologists, see G. Miller and A. deVernal, "Will Greenhouse Warming Lead to Northern Hemisphere Ice Sheet Growth?" *Nature* 355 (1992), p. 245; and many of the previous citations for this chapter.

Idso quote is from Sherwood B. Idso, *Carbon Dioxide and Global Change: Earth in Transition*, p. 9.

Teeri research was published as Donald R. Zak, Kurt S. Pregitzer, Peter S. Curtis, James A. Teeri, Robert Fogel, and Diana L. Randlett, "Elevated CO_2 and Feedback Between Carbon and Nitrogen Cycles," *Plant and Soil* 151 (1993), pp. 105-117. See also Peter S. Curtis and James A. Teeri, "Seasonal Responses of Leaf Gas Exchange to Elevated Carbon Dioxide in Populus grandidentata," *Canadian Journal of Forest Research* 22 (9) (September 1992), pp. 1320-1325.

U.S. Department of Agriculture study was published as B.A. Kimball et al., "Effects of Elevated CO2 and Climate Variables on Plants," *Journal of Soil and Water Conservation* 48 (1993), pp. 9-14.

Re *Time* retraction of global warming predictions, see "The Ice Age Cometh?" *Time*, January 31, 1994, p. 79.

February: Ozone

Caplan quote is from Ruth Caplan, *Our Earth, Ourselves*, p. 51.

Melvyn Shapiro quote is from Micah Morrison, "Ozone Scare," *Insight*, April 6, 1992, p. 13.

Re the potential danger of substitutes for CFCs, see discussion in Dixy Lee Ray and Lou Guzzo, *Environmental Overkill*, pp. 44-45.

Effect on auto owners is based on Julie Edelson Halpert, "Scarcity of Car Coolant Could Prove Costly," *The New York Times*, December 26, 1993, p. 5.

Food transport cost is from "The Ultraviolet Radiation: Friend or Foe?" Chapter 6 in Roger A. Maduro, *The Holes in the Ozone Scare*, pp. 3-5.

Effect on Third World countries is described in Dixy Lee Ray and Lou Guzzo, *Environmental Overkill*, p. 45.

Liz Cook quote is from Julie Edelson Halpert, "Scarcity of Car Coolant Could Prove Costly," *The New York Times*, December 26, 1993, p. 5.

For a complete statement of the theory of ozone depletion, see F. Sherwood Rowland, "Stratospheric Ozone in the 21st Century: The Chlorofluorocarbon Problem," *Environmental Science and Technology* 25 (4) (1991), pp. 622-628.

EPA estimate is from a statement by William Reilly, administrator of the EPA, on April 4, 1991, quoted in Micah Morrison, "The Ozone Scare," *Insight*, April 6, 1992.

Gore quote is from Albert Gore, *Earth in the Balance*, p. 87.

Increase in global ozone from 1962 to the early 1970s is reported in J.K. Angell and J. Korshover, "Global Analysis of Recent Total Ozone Fluctuations," *Monthly Weather Review* 104 (1976), pp. 63-75; A.D. Christie, "Secular or Cyclic Change in Ozone," *Pure and Applied Geophysics*, 1973, pp. 1000-1009; J.S. Johnston, G. Whitten, and J. Birks, "Effects of Nuclear Explosions on Stratospheric Nitric Oxide and Ozone," *Journal of Geophysical Research* 78 (1973), pp. 6107-6135; and W. D. Komhyr, E.W. Barrett, G. Slocum, and H.K. Weickmann, "Atmospheric Total Ozone Increase During the 1960s," *Nature* 232 (1971), pp. 390-391.

Figures for 1969 to 1986 are from F. Sherwood Rowland, "Stratospheric Ozone in the 21st Century: The Chlorofluorocarbon Problem," *Environmental Science and Technology* 25 (4) (1991), pp. 622-628.

Rate of increase since 1986 is from the George C. Marshall Institute, *Two Environmental Issues: 1. Ozone, 2. The Greenhouse Problem*, pp. 1-7.

Re low temperatures in Antarctica, see Ben Bolch and Harold Lyons, *Apocalypse Not*, p. 87. Re the effects of the solar cycle, see P. Rigaud and B. Leroy, "Presumptive Evidence for a Low Value of the Total Ozone Content Above Antarctica in September 1958," *Annales Geophysicae* 8 (11) (1990), pp. 791-794; also S. Fred Singer, "My Adventures in the Ozone Hole," *National Review*, June 30, 1989.

Re existence of the AOH in the 1950s, see G.M.B. Dobson, *Ozone in the Atmosphere*; also S. Fred Singer, "My Adventures in the Ozone Hole," *National Review*, June 30, 1989; and P. Rigaud and B. Leroy, "Presumptive Evidence for a Low Value of the Total Ozone Content Above Antarctica in September 1958," *Annales Geophysicae* 8 (11) (1990), pp. 791-794.

Both Ellsaesser quotes are from H.W. Ellsaesser, "An Atmosphere of Paradox: From Acid Rain to Ozone," in Jay H. Lehr, *Rational Readings on Environmental Concerns*, p. 550.

Scotto quote is from Joseph Scotto, G. Cotton, F. Urback, et al., "Biologically Effective Ultraviolet Radiation: Surface Measurements in the U.S., 1974-1985," *Science* 293 (February 12, 1988), pp. 762-764. See also Stuart A. Penkett, "Ultraviolet Levels Down Not Up," *Nature* 343 (September 28, 1989), p. 283.

Re NOAA's confirmation of Scotto's measurements, see Ronald Bailey, *Eco-Scam*, p. 133.

Ellsaesser quote is from H.W. Ellsaesser, "An Atmosphere of Paradox: From Acid Rain to Ozone," in Jay H. Lehr, *Rational Readings on Environmental Concerns*, p. 550; John Frederick quote is from Ronald Bailey, *Eco-Scam*, p. 130; *Science News* quote is from "UV Pours Through Ozone Hole," *Science News*, October 5, 1991, p. 214.

Re effect on phytoplankton, see Ronald Bailey, *Eco-Scam*, p. 130. Bailey cites interviews with Osmond Holm-Hansen, a marine ecologist with the Scripps Institute of Oceanography.

Re University of California study, see Patrick Michaels, *World Climate Review* 1 (4) (Summer 1993), p. 4. The following Michaels quote is from the same source.

Singer quote is from S. Fred Singer, "My Adventures in the Ozone Hole," *National Review*, June 30, 1989.

Ellsaesser quote is from H.W. Ellsaesser, "An Atmosphere of Paradox: From Acid Rain to Ozone," in Jay H. Lehr, *Rational Readings on Environmental Concerns*, p. 551. He cites the National Academy of Sciences, *Environmental Impact of Stratospheric Flight.*

Re biodegredation of CFCs, see Aslam Khalil and R.A. Rasmussen, "The Potential of Soils as a Sink of Chlorofluorocarbons and other Man-Made Chlorocarbons," *Geophysical Research Letters* 16 (7) (July 1989), pp. 679-682; and by the same authors, "The Influence of Termites on Atmospheric Trace Gases," *Journal of Geophysical Research* 95 (D-4) (March 20, 1990), pp. 3619-3634. For discussion, see Dixy Lee Ray and Lou Guzzo, *Environmental Overkill*, p. 47.

March: Acid Rain

Re "relatively acidic," the more technical definition is pH levels lower than 5.5 to 5.0.

Capra quote is from Fritjof Capra, *The Turning Point*, pp. 237-238.

Cost of Clean Air Act Amendments is from Frances Cairncross, *Costing the Earth*, pp. 60-61.

All NAPAP quotes are from National Acidic Precipitation Assessment Program, *Acidic Deposition: State of Science and Technology.*

NAPAP quote re forests is from Vol. 3, p. 16-145; re red spruce is from Vol. 3, p. 16-94; and re lack of correlation between pollution and forest conditions is from Vol. 3, p. 16-51.

NAPAP quote re effects of sulfur dioxide is from Vol. 3, p. 22-100; re effects of nitrogen dioxide, from Vol. 3, p. 22-106; re effects of acidic aerosols, from Vol. 3, p. 22-102.

NAPAP quotes re indirect effects on health are from Vol. 3, p. 23-146.

NAPAP quotes re effect on agriculture are from Vol. 3, p. 18-37, and Vol. 4, p. 27-127.

NAPAP quote re soybeans is from Vol. 4, p. 18-121. The 1983 study is cited in Vol. 4, p. 27-131, and is P. Irving, "Acid Precipitation Effects on Crops: A Review and Analysis of Research," *Journal of Environmental Quality* 12 (1983), pp. 442-453.

Re the table, although we use NAPAP's figure of 5.5 pH in the table, some critics use the lower figure of 5.0 pH to designate truly acid lakes. Less than 1 percent of lakes in the eastern U.S. are truly acidic by this alternate definition. See Edward C. Krug, "Fish Story: The Great Acid Rain Flimflam," *Policy Review*, Spring 1990, p. 46.

"Half of the surface area . . . " and "No acidic lakes . . . " are from NAPAP, Vol. 2, p. 9-340.

Re natural and human sources of lake acidity, see NAPAP, Vol. 2, pp. 10-34 to 10-63, 10-133 to 10-135, 11-33 to 11-55, and Appendix 9B.

Re 38 percent of Florida's acid lakes, see NAPAP, Vol. 2, p. 9-343.

Re Krug's views, see Edward Krug, "Assessment of the Theory and Hypotheses of the Acidification of Watershed," *Illinois State Water Survey Contract Report 457*, 1989;

and "Acid Rain on Acid Soil: A New Perspective," *Science* 221 (1983), pp. 520-525.

NAPAP quote re Edward Krug is from Vol. 2, p. 10-134.

Krug quote is from Edward C. Krug, "Fish Story: The Great Acid Rain Flimflam," *Policy Review*, Spring 1990, p. 46.

Re liming, see NAPAP, Vol. 2, Report 15.

The "insider" was David Hawkins, an EPA administrator at the time. The quote appears in William Anderson, "Acid Test," *Reason*, January 1992, p. 25.

Senator Glenn quote is from *Congressional Record* 27, March 1990, S. 3254.

April: Deforestation

"Little net change" is based on Roger A. Sedjo and Marion Clawson, "Global Forests," in Julian L. Simon and Herman Kahn, *The Resourceful Earth*, pp. 146-147. Sedjo and Clawson report a 2 percent increase in total land area of temperate forests from 1949 to 1980.

Moore quote is from Patrick Moore, speech to the Canadian Pulp and Paper Association, January 27, 1993.

Miller quote is from "Glitz Is the Winner In Logging Wars," *Report on Business*, August 7, 1993, p. B-1.

British Columbia Ministry of Forests research is cited by Patrick Moore, speech to the Canadian Pulp and Paper Association, January 27, 1993.

Roger Sedjo and Marion Clawson reference is based on Julian L. Simon and Herman Kahn, *The Resourceful Earth*, pp. 158-159; the subsequent quote is from *The Resourceful Earth*, p. 159.

U.N. figure is from an interview with Mr. Rene de Montalembert, Director of Forestry Policies and Planning Division, U.N. Food and Agriculture Organization, which appeared in *Papercast*, Communication Consil International, Paris, December 1992, p. 10.

Re Myers' prediction on deforestation, see Norman Myers, "Conversion of Tropical Moist Forests," a report prepared for the Committee on Research Priorities on Tropical Biology of the National Research Council (Washington, DC: National Academy of Sciences, 1980).

NRDC quote is from Scott Lewis, *The Rainforest Book: How You Can Save the World's Rainforests*, p. 10.

The Skole and Tucker findings are described by Stephen Budiansky in "The Doomsday Myths," *U.S. News & World Report*, December 13, 1993, p. 87.

For a description of the ecology of logging in the tropics, see Albert Gore, *Earth in the Balance*, pp. 115-117.

Re Myers' prediction on species extinction, see Norman Myers, *The Sinking Ark*.

Re Wilson's predictions on species extinction, see E.O. Wilson and Frances M. Peter,

Biodiversity; E.O. Wilson, *The Diversity of Life*; and E.O. Wilson, "Is Humanity Suicidal?" *The New York Times Magazine*, May 30, 1993, pp. 24-29.

Simon and Wildavsky quote is from Julian L. Simon and Aaron Wildavsky, "On Species Loss, the Absence of Data, and Risks to Humanity," in Julian L. Simon and Herman Kahn, *The Resourceful Earth*, p. 175.

Re the relationship between forest area and species, see Charles C. Mann, "Extinction: Are Ecologists Crying Wolf?" *Science* 253 (August 16, 1991), pp. 736-738. Also see the discussion in Stephen Budiansky, "The Doomsday Myths," *U.S. News & World Report*, December 13, 1993, p. 87. The Vernon Haywood quote is also from Budiansky.

For a chilling description of West Africa's cultural and economic collapse, see Robert D. Kaplan, "The Coming Anarchy," *The Atlantic Monthly*, February 1994, pp. 44-76.

For a discussion of policies in Brazil and their reversal, see Frances Cairncross, *Costing the Earth*, pp. 84ff; and "How Brazil Subsidises the Destruction of the Amazon," *The Economist*, March 18, 1989, p. 69.

Worldwatch Institute quote is from John C. Ryan, "Conserving Biological Diversity," in Lester R. Brown, *State of the World 1992*, p. 10.

Sedjo and Clawson quote is from Roger A. Sedjo and Marion Clawson, "Global Forests," in Julian L. Simon and Herman Kahn, *The Resourceful Earth*, p. 166.

May: Pesticides

Carson quote is from Rachel Carson, *Silent Spring*, p. 12.

Regenstein quote is from Lewis Regenstein, *America the Poisoned*, p. 342.

Brown's prediction appears in Lester R. Brown et al., *State of the World 1992*, p. 177.

For a good review of reseach on the effects of DDT and other pesticides on birds, see Robert W. Risebrough and David B. Peakall, "An Assessment of the Relative Importance of the Several Organochlorines in the Decline of Peregrine Falcon Populations," in T.J. Cade et al., *Peregrine Falcon Populations: Their Management and Recovery*. For a vigorous rebuttal of this literature, see J. Gordon Edwards, "DDT Effects on Bird Abundance and Reproduction," in Jay H. Lehr, *Rational Readings on Environmental Concerns*, pp. 195-215.

Re recovering eagle populations, see Lora J. Finnegan, "The Bald is Back," *Sunset* 188 (2) (February 1992), p. 30.

Quote regarding peregrine falcons and the reference to 200 tons of DDT are from Robert W. Risebrough and David B. Peakall, "An Assessment of the Relative Importance of the Several Organochlorines in the Decline of Peregrine Falcon Populations," in T.J. Cade et al., *Peregrine Falcon Populations: Their Management and Recovery*.

Price of DDT in 1969 is from a U.N. Food and Agriculture Organization report cited in Elizabeth Whelan, *Toxic Terror*, p. 80.

Werezak quote is from George Werezak, "A Report on Chlorine to the Virtual Elimination Task Force," Appendix B of International Joint Commission, *A Strategy for Virtual Elimination of Persistent Toxic Substances*, pp. 35-36. See also Anne Simon

Moffat, "New Chemicals Seek to Outwit Insect Pests," *Science* 261 (July 30, 1993), pp. 550-551.

Comparison of pesticide use in U.S. versus the E.C. is from OECD data reported in the Global Climate Coalition, *The U.S. Versus European Community: Environmental Performance*, p. 11.

Comparison of pesticide use in U.S. versus Japan is from Jerry Taylor, "Pesticides and Food Safety: Separating Fact from Fiction," *The State Factor*, American Legislative Exchange Council, July 1992, p. 4.

Description of the FDA standard appears in Jerry Taylor, "Pesticides and Food Safety: Separating Fact from Fiction," *The State Factor*, American Legislative Exchange Council, July 1992, p. 5.

Archibald and Winter finding appears in Sandra Archibald and Carl Winter, "Pesticides in Our Food Chain: Assessing the Risks," *Chemicals in the Human Food Chain*, University of California Agricultural Issues Center, 1990.

EPA estimate of cancer risk is from "EPA Proposes Cancellation of Most Uses of EBDC Fungicides, Citing Cancer Risk," *Chemical Regulation Reporter*, Bureau of National Affairs, December 8, 1989.

Richard Hill estimate is from "Exposure Data Can Lower Risk Number by as Much as 100,000, EPA Scientist Says," *Chemical Regulation Reporter*, Bureau of National Affairs, May 12, 1989.

James Wells quote is from Jerry Taylor, "Pesticides and Food Safety: Separating Fact from Fiction," *The State Factor*, American Legislative Exchange Council, July 1992, p. 6.

C. Everett Koop quote is from his testimony before the House Committee on Energy and Commerce, Subcommittee on Health and the Environment, June 19, 1991.

Sanford Miller quote appears in Warren T. Brookes, "EPA's Misguided Hysteria Over Pesticide Risks," *Human Events*, April 21, 1990, p. 9.

Robert Hollingsworth quote is from Jerry Taylor, "Pesticides and Food Safety: Separating Fact from Fiction," *The State Factor*, American Legislative Exchange Council, July 1992, p. 4.

Study on the offspring of fish-eating mothers is J.J. Jacobson et al, "Effects of In Utero Exposure to Polychlorinated Biphenyls and Related Contaminants on Cognitive Functioning in Young Children," *Journal of Pediatrics* 116 (1990), pp. 34-38; see also J.J. Jacobson et al., "Effects of Exposure to PCBs and Related Compounds on Growth and Activity in Children," *Neurotoxicology and Teratology* 12 (1990), pp. 319-326.

Norman Borlaug quote is from his preface to Elizabeth Whelan, *Toxic Terror*, p. xiv. The next reference to Borlaug is also from *Toxic Terror*, p. xv.

Alvin Young quote and reference to National Academy of Sciences study are from Jerry Taylor, "Pesticides and Food Safety: Separating Fact from Fiction," *The State Factor*, American Legislative Exchange Council, July 1992, pp. 20-21.

The GRC study is *The Value of Crop Protection Chemicals and Fertilizers to American Agriculture and the Consumer*, February 1990.

Figures on malaria and Robert Turner quote are from Barry Shlachter, "Malaria on Rise in Many Third World Areas," Associated Press wire story, May 6, 1985.

Kaplan quote is from Robert D. Kaplan, "The Coming Anarchy," *The Atlantic Monthly*, February 1994, pp. 48, 54.

June: Nuclear Power

Bernard Cohen quote is from Karl Cohen, "Nuclear Power," in Julian L. Simon and Herman Kahn, *The Resourceful Earth*, p. 547.

Whelan quote is from Elizabeth Whelan, *Toxic Terror*, p. 233.

NCI quote is from "Highlights of NCI's Carcinogenesis Studies," *Cancer Facts*, National Cancer Institute, June 23, 1993, p. 7.

Bernard Cohen quote is from Karl Cohen, "Nuclear Power," in Julian L. Simon and Herman Kahn, *The Resourceful Earth*, p. 547.

Survey of clinical studies was reported in T.D. Luckey, *Hormesis and Ionizing Radiation*. See also L.A. Sagan, "On Radiation, Paradigms, and Hormesis," *Science*, August 11, 1989, pp. 574ff; J. Fremlin, "Radiation Hormesis," *Atom*, April 1989; and B.L. Cohen, "Tests of the Linear No Threshold Dose Response Relationship for High LET Radiation," *Health Physics* 52 (5) (May 1987), pp. 629-636.

Re cancer rates in western states, see C.M. Fleck, H. Oberhummer and W. Hofmann, *Inference of Chemically and Radiologically Induced Cancer at Environmental Doses, Fourth International Symposium on the Natural Radiation Environment*, December 1987. According to Table No. 118 of the *Statistical Abstract of the United States 1992*, the death rate by cancer for Mountain States in 1989 was 158.0 per 100,000 resident population, versus the national average rate of 199.9.

China study was conducted by the High Background Radiation Research Group and was published as "Health Survey in High Background Radiation Areas in China," *Science*, August 22, 1980, pp. 877-880.

Bolch and Lyons quotes are from Ben Bolch and Harold Lyons, *Apocalypse Not*, pp. 65-66, 106.

Description of Three Mile Island accident is from J.B. Kemeny (Chairman), *Report of the President's Commission on the Accident at Three Mile Island*. Description of Chernobyl accident is from Ben Bolch and Harold Lyons, *Apocalypse Not*, pp. 107-111; and Elizabeth Whelan, *Toxic Terror*, pp. 238ff.

NRC report is the above-cited J.B. Kemeny, *Report of the President's Commission on the Accident at Three Mile Island*. See also J.L. Kraushaar and R.A. Ristinen, *Energy and Problems of a Technical Society*, pp. 135-137; and H. Inhaber, "Risk with Energy from Conventional and Nonconventional Sources," *Science*, February 23, 1979, p. 718.

Discussion of the volume of nuclear waste is based on J.L. Kraushaar and R.A. Ristinen, *Energy and Problems of a Technical Society*, p. 146.

Disposal process is described in B.L. Cohen, "Long Term Waste Problems from Electricity Production," *Nuclear and Chemical Waste Management* 4 (1984). Further discussion and references to the extensive literature on the subject are contained in Karl

Cohen, "Nuclear Power," in Julian L. Simon and Herbert Kahn, *The Resourceful Earth*, pp. 387-414.

Re long-range detection of nuclear waste, see "It's Like a Geiger Counter for Toxins," *Business Week*, February 21, 1994, p. 58.

July: Automobiles

Gore quote is from Albert Gore, *Earth in the Balance*, p. 325.

Figures on transportation-related emissions are from U.S. Bureau of the Census, *Statistical Abstract of the U.S. 1992*, Table 354.

New car emissions are based on 1994 federal Tier 1 Standards.

Lifetime emissions estimates are from Jonathan H. Adler, "Clean Fuels, Dirty Air," in Michael S. Greve and Fred L. Smith, Jr., *Environmental Politics: Public Costs, Private Rewards*, p. 20.

Figures for 1991 versus 1970 are from EPA, *National Air Quality Emissions Trends Report 1992*, October 1993.

GM vs. Japanese models is from General Motors, *General Motors and the Environment*, October 1991, p. 14.

Comparisons to the European Community are from Global Climate Coalition, *The U.S. versus European Community: Environmental Performance.*

Figures on fleet turnover are from Motor Vehicle Manufacturers Association, *Cleaner Motor Vehicles: The Challenge Being Met*, September 1988, p. 10.

Figures regarding reformulated gasoline are from American Petroleum Institute, "New Transportation Fuels," January 7, 1993, p. 1.

Smith quote is from Fred L. Smith, "Auto-nomy: The Liberating Benefits of a Safer, Cleaner, and More Mobile Society," *Reason*, August/September 1990, p. 25.

Ford estimate of the cost of the Clean Air Act is from Timothy Noah, "Clear Benefits of Clean Air Act Come at a Cost," *Wall Street Journal*, November 15, 1993.

Clean fuels cost is from the National Petroleum Council, *U.S. Petroleum Refining, A Report of the National Petroleum Council*, August 30, 1993, p. 1.

Nine out of ten cars figure is from Rick Henderson, "Going Mobile," *Reason*, August/ September 1990, p. 29.

Re Stedman's emissions testing device, see Rick Henderson, "Going Mobile," *Reason*, August/September 1990, p. 29; and Jonathan Adler, "A Better Recipe for Clean Air," *Richmond Times-Dispatch*, November 13, 1991.

Re pollution caused by slow-moving vehicles, see Catherine G. Burke, "The Myths of Mass Transit," *USA Today*, July 1982, p. 27.

Re electronic toll collection, see Robert W. Poole, Jr., "Private Tollways: Resolving Gridlock in Southern California," Reason Foundation, *Policy Study No. 111*, May 1988. The Environmental Defense Fund has endorsed congestion fees. See "Strategies for

Unsnarling Traffic in Southern California," *EDF Letter*, March 1994, p. 4.

Re improving fuel efficiency, see Thomas H. Hanna, president, Motor Vehicle Manufacturers Association, "The Myths About CAFE," July 15, 1991.

Re technological changes already made, see Robert C. Stempel, chairman, GM Corporation, "Statement on Fuel Economy," May 13, 1991, p. 8.

Re Crandall and Graham research, see Robert Crandall and John Graham, "The Politics of Energy: New Fuel-Economy Standards?" *The American Enterprise*, March/April 1991, p. 68.

Sykuta and Chilton quote is from Michael Sykuta and Kenneth Chilton, "No Benefits From Toughened Fuel-Economy Standards," *Sacramento Bee*, October 24, 1991.

Oil recycling figures are from the American Petroleum Institute.

Delco battery and electrical energy figures are from General Motors, *General Motors and the Environment*, p. 21.

Sixty pounds of recycled paper figure is from William Rathje and Cullen Murphy, *Rubbish! The Archaeology of Garbage*, p. 196.

Figures for Delco battery recycling are from General Motors, *General Motors and the Environment*, p. 31.

USCAR project description is from *USCAR: Sharing Technology for a Stronger Tomorrow*, n.d.

August: Resource Depletion

Sale quote is from Kirkpatrick Sale, *Human Scale*, 1980, pp. 300-301.

Capra quote is from Fritjof Capra, *The Turning Point*, pp. 215-216.

Re *Limits to Growth*, see Donnella H. and Dennis L. Meadows, *The Limits to Growth.*

For a prominent economist's explanation of how the price system works, see F.A. Hayek, "The Use of Knowledge in Society," in F.A. Hayek, *Individualism and Economic Order*, pp. 77-91.

Singer quote re prices is from Max Singer, *Passage to a Human World*, pp. 87-88.

World Resources Institute estimate is reported by Ronald Bailey in *Eco-Scam*, p. 67.

Moore quote is from Stephen Moore, "Doomsday Delayed: America's Surprisingly Bright Natural Resource Future," Institute for Policy Innovation, *IPI Policy Report No. 118*, August 1992, p. 51.

Ehrlich/Simon bet is described in John Tierney, "Betting the Planet," *The New York Times Magazine*, December 2, 1990, pp. 52ff.

Worldwatch Institute quote is from John E. Young, "Mining the Earth," in Lester R. Brown et al., *State of the World 1992*, p. 104.

Ehrlich prediction appears in Paul Ehrlich, *The Population Bomb*, p. 18.

Population growth rates are from World Bank, *World Population Projections 1992-93*

Edition. The reference to other organizations supporting this forecast is based on Max Singer, *Passage to a Human World*, p. 67.

Jacksonville and Texas examples are based on Ben Bolch and Harold Lyons, *Apocalypse Not*, pp. 26-27. The land area of Jacksonville is 776 square miles, enough to provide just over 4 square feet for each person. Texas occupies 262,017 square miles, or about 1,400 square feet for every person alive in the world in 1990.

Figures on human settlements are from Max Singer, *Passage to a Human World*, p. 105.

Figures on roads are from Max Singer, *Passage to a Human World*, pp. 105-106.

Science Advisory Committee and Buringh studies are described by Max Singer in *Passage to a Human World*, pp. 106-107. The U.S. team's findings were only 6 percent below those of the Buringh group. The Singer quote is from p. 118.

Quote regarding Pakistan is from V.A. Jaffery, "Breaking the Vicious Circle of Poverty and Environmental Degradation: Sustainable Development in Pakistan," *Economic Review (Pakistan)*, June 1993, p. 113ff. Notice that all the resources being "depleted" are actually renewable.

Kaplan quote is from Robert D. Kaplan, "The Coming Anarchy," *The Atlantic Monthly*, February 1994, p. 75.

Figures on the status of women are from Brad Knickerbocker, "Save the Environment: Teach Girls to Read," *Christian Science Monitor*, February 14, 1994.

"Root cause" remark is by Nafis Sadik, executive director of the U.N. Population Fund, quoted in M. Holloway, "A Powerful Voice for Women," *Scientific American*, June 1993, pp. 36, 40.

Re the poor record of government aid to Third World countries, see Peter Bauer, *Dissent on Development*; and Peter Bauer, *Equality, the Third World, and Economic Delusion*.

September: Plastic

Steger and Bowermaster quote is from Will Steger and Jon Bowermaster, "Garbage Must be Reduced at Its Source," in Neal Bernards, *The Environmental Crisis: Opposing Viewpoints*, p. 147.

EPA estimates are from Franklin Associates, Ltd., *Characterization of Municipal Solid Waste in the United States 1992 Update*, July 1992, p. ES-8.

Rathje estimates are from William Rathje and Cullen Murphy, *Rubbish! The Archeology of Garbage*, pp. 97-101.

Oregon statistics are from Oregon Department of Environmental Quality, "Oregon Solid Waste Characterization and Composition 1992-1993," draft, November 1993, p. 28.

Figures for cups and plates, phone books, etc. are from Franklin Associates, Ltd., *Characterization of Municipal Solid Waste in the United States 1992 Update*, July 1992, p. 2-31.

Figures on soft drink bottles etc. are from Franklin Associates, *Characterization of Municipal Solid Waste in the United States 1992 Update*, July 1992, Table 23, p. 2-40.

1992 figure for PET is from correspondence from the American Plastics Society, February 1994. Recovery rates for various materials are from Franklin Associates, Ltd., *Characterization of Municipal Solid Waste in the United States 1992 Update*, July 1992, p. 2-41 and Table 21 on p. 2-38.

Re McDonald's episode, see William Rathje and Cullen Murphy, *Rubbish! The Archeology of Garbage*, pp. 221ff; and Phyllis Berman, "McDonald's Caves In," *Forbes*, February 4, 1991, pp. 73-74.

Re difficulty of recycling plastic, see EPA, Office of Solid Waste and Emergency Response, "Methods to Manage and Control Plastic Wastes (Report to the Congress)," Washington, DC: Environmental Protection Agency, February 1990.

Re thermal decomposition, see American Plastics Council, *The Evolution of Plastics Recycling Technology*, 1993, p. 10.

Re the absence of biodegradation in landfills, see William Rathje and Cullen Murphy, *Rubbish! The Archeology of Garbage*, pp. 110ff.

"Less than 2 percent" is from correspondence with the American Petroleum Institute, March 1994.

Hocking quote is from Martin B. Hocking, "Paper versus Polystyrene: A Complex Choice," *Science* 1991.

Re plastic bags, see Lynn Scarlett, *A Consumers Guide to Environmental Myths and Realities*, National Center for Policy Analysis, September 1991, p. 14.

German study is "Packaging without Plastic: Ecological and Economic Consequences of a Packaging Market Free from Plastic (in FRG)," Gesellschaft fur Verpackungmarkforschung mbH (Frankfurt), December 1987.

Wirka quote is from Jeanne Wirka, "Choking on Disposables," *Environmental Action*, March/April 1989.

Lyman quote is from Francesca Lyman, "Diaper Hype," *Garbage*, January/February 1990.

Re Arthur D. Little study, see "Disposable versus Reusable Diapers: Health, Environmental and Economic Comparisons," Arthur D. Little, March 16, 1990, p. I-1.

Re Franklin Associates study, see "Energy and Environmental Profile Analysis of Children's Single Use and Cloth Diapers," Franklin Associates, Ltd., 1990, revised 1992.

Rathje quote is from William Rathje and Cullen Murphy, "Cotton vs. Disposables: What's the Damage?" *Garbage*, October/November 1992, p. 31.

Re American Academy of Pediatrics and American Public Health Association endorsements, see "Caring for Our Children — National Health and Safety Performance Standards: Guidelines for Out-of-Home Child Care Programs," American Academy of Pediatrics/American Public Health Association, 1992.

Poor quote is from Patricia Poor, "Disposable Diapers are OK," *Garbage*, October/November 1993, p. 31.

October: Electromagnetic Fields

For general discussions of EMFs, see U.S. Congress, Office of Technology Assessment, *Biological Effects of Power Frequency Electric & Magnetic Fields - Background Paper*; and Michael Fumento, *Science Under Siege*, Chapter 7.

Re Wertheimer and Leeper report, see Wendy Wertheimer and Ed Leeper, "Electrical Wiring Configurations and Childhood Cancer," *American Journal of Epidemiology* 109 (1979), pp. 273-284.

Second report by Wertheimer and Leeper was Wendy Wertheimer and Ed Leeper, "Possible Effects of Electric Blankets and Heated Waterbeds on Fetal Developments," *Bioelectromagnetics* 7 (1) (1986), pp. 18-21.

Re Brodeur, see Paul Brodeur, *Currents of Death*; and three issues of *The New Yorker* (June 12, 1989; June 19, 1989; June 26, 1989) for Brodeur's three-part series titled "The Annals of Radiation: The Hazards of Electromagnetic Fields."

First Brodeur quote is from the dust jacket of Paul Brodeur, *Currents of Death*; second is from p. 35.

Fumento quote is from Michael Fumento, *Science Under Siege*, pp. 227-228.

For criticism of Wertheimer and Leeper study, see Taylor Moore, "Pursuing the Science of EMF," *EPRI Journal* 15 (1) (January-February 1990); and Michael Fumento, *Science Under Siege*, pp. 222ff.

Rhode Island study was published as J.P. Fulton, "Electrical Wiring Configurations and Childhood Leukemia in Rhode Island," *American Journal of Epidemiology* 111 (1980), pp. 292-296.

Savitz study was published as David Savitz et al., "Case Control Study of Childhood Cancer and Exposure to 60 Hz Magnetic Fields," *American Journal of Epidemiology* 128 (1988), pp. 21-38.

OTA quote is from U.S. Congress, Office of Technology Assessment, *Biological Effects of Power Frequency Electric & Magnetic Fields - Background Paper*, pp. 3, 63.

Adair quote is from Eleanor Adair, "Nurturing Electrophobia," *IEEE Spectrum* 27 (8) (August 1990), p. 11.

Edwin Carstensen quote appears in Michael Fumento, *Science Under Siege*, p. 222.

The Connecticut Academy of Science and Engineering report is quoted by Michael Fumento, *Science Under Siege*, p. 249.

John Boice quote appears in Michael E. Newman, "The Search for the Missing Link - Electromagnetic Fields and Cancer," *Journal of the National Cancer Institute* 81 (22) (November 15, 1989), p. 1687.

Re universal statements and inductive generalizations, see Karl R. Popper, *The Logic of Scientific Discovery*, Chapter 1; and Henry S. Leonard, *Principles of Reasoning*, pp. 590-607.

For more on understanding risk, see Aaron Wildavsky, *Searching for Safety*.

The panics in Guilford, Montecito, and Fountain Valley were caused by Brodeur's *New Yorker* story titled "Calamity on Meadow Street" alleging that cancer epidemics were occurring in these communities. See Michael Fumento, *Science Under Siege*, pp. 248-249. The panic in Hewlett, New York, was caused by community concern over power lines near a local high school. See Peter Marks, "On Long Island, Fear From Electric Fields," *The New York Times*, January 6, 1994.

November: Oil Spills

Hilton quote is from Jack Hilton, "Valdez: Do-Gooders' Feeding Frenzy," *The New York Times*, May 15, 1989.

Re natural sources of oil in the Sound, see Agis Salpukas, "A New Slant on Exxon Valdez Spill," *The New York Times*, December 1, 1993; and David S. Page, Paul D. Boehm, Gregory S. Douglas, and A. Edward Bence, "Identification of Hydrocarbon Sources in the Benthic Sediments of Prince William Sound and the Gulf of Alaska Following the Exxon Valdez Oil Spill," Third Symposium on Environmental Toxicology and Risk Assessment, American Society for Testing and Materials, 1993.

National Academy of Sciences study was published as *Oil in the Sea: Inputs, Fates, and Effects*.

Re the Texas A&M research, see James M. Brooks et al., "Deep-Sea Hydrocarbon Seep Communities: Evidence for Energy and Nutritional Carbon Sources," *Science* 238 (November 20, 1987), pp. 1138-1141; James J. Childress et al., "A Methanotrophic Marine Molluscan (Bivalvia, Mytilidae) Symbiosis: Mussels Fueled by Gas," *Science* 233 (September 19, 1986), pp. 1306-1308; I. Rosman MacDonald, "Chemosynthetic Mussels at a Brine-Filled Pockmark in the Northern Gulf of Mexico," *Science* 248 (June 1, 1990), pp. 1096-1099; and Richard A. Geyer, "Natural Hydrocarbon Seeps," *Ecolibrium* 8 (4) (Fall 1979).

Re dilution, see Jack Hilton, "Valdez: Do-Gooders' Feeding Frenzy," *The New York Times*, May 15, 1989. Re evaporation and biodegradation, see Bhushan Bahree, "Oil Eating Bacteria Thrive on Inipol, A Tonic That Proved Itself in Valdez," *Wall Street Journal*, September 7, 1993.

Jeffreys quote is from Kent Jeffreys, "Whale of an oil-slick deal," *The Washington Times*, November 4, 1991.

NOAA sources are Jay Field and David Kennedy. They are quoted in Caleb Solomon, "Exxon Attacks Scientific Views of Valdez Spill," *Wall Street Journal*, April 15, 1993.

Re Exxon expenses, see Agis Salpukas, "A New Slant on Exxon Valdez Spill," *The New York Times*, December 1, 1993.

Re closer inspection of tankers and insurance industry reforms, see Ken Wells, Daniel Machalaba, and Caleb Solomon, "Unsafe Oil Tankers and Ill-Trained Crews Threaten Further Spills," *Wall Street Journal*, February 12, 1993.

Re MSRC, see Steve Duca, "Marine Spill Response Corporation, The World's Largest Oil Response Organization," and Steve Duca, "Questions and Answers: Marine Spill Response Corporation," Marine Spill Response Corporation.

Re Inipol, see Bhushan Bahree, "Oil Eating Bacteria Thrive on Inipol, A Tonic That

Proved Itself in Valdez," *Wall Street Journal*, September 7, 1993.

Re Elastol and Heller's Beads, see Adam L. Peneberg, "Slick Solutions to the Environmental Scourge," *The New York Times*, August 15, 1993, p. F-11.

Re requirements of the Oil Pollution Act, see Ken Wells, Daniel Machalaba, and Caleb Solomon, "Unsafe Oil Tankers and Ill-Trained Crews Threaten Further Spills," *Wall Street Journal*, February 12, 1993; and American Petroleum Institute, "The Petroleum Industry Answers Your Questions," January 6, 1993.

Re problem of tankers operating under foreign flags, see Ken Wells, Daniel Machalaba, and Caleb Solomon, "Unsafe Oil Tankers and Ill-Trained Crews Threaten Further Spills," *Wall Street Journal*, February 12, 1993.

December: Toxic Chemicals

Re dose makes the poison, see Robert E. Gosselin, *Clinical Toxicology of Commercial Products*.

Dower quotes and reference to 60,000 chemicals are from Roger C. Dower, in Paul R. Portney, *Public Policies for Environmental Protection*, pp. 159, 219, and 160.

Re "a single person whose cancer . . ." is from Dr. Thomas W. Orme, "Superfund: Is it Bulldozing Our Public Health Dollars?" *Priorities*, Summer 1992, p. 7.

EPA figures re municipal solid waste sites are reported in Jennifer Chilton and Kenneth Chilton, "A Critique of Risk Modeling and Risk Assessment of Municipal Landfills Based on U.S. EPA Techniques," *Waste Management & Research* 10 (1992), pp. 505-516.

Re the "new paradigm," see S. Schmidheiny, *Changing Course: A Global Business Perspective on Development and the Environment*; Brian Wynne and Sue Mayer, "How Science Fails the Environment," *New Scientist*, June 5, 1993; Alex Milne, "The Perils of Green Pessimism," *New Scientist*, June 12, 1993; and David Moberg, "The Perils of Chlorine," *The Reader* (Chicago), February 25, 1994.

Milne quote is from Alex Milne, "The Perils of Green Pessimism," *New Scientist*, June 12, 1993, p. 36.

Wildavsky quote is from Aaron Wildavsky, *Searching for Safety*, p. 20.

Jack Weinberg quote is in David Moberg, "The Perils of Chlorine," *The Reader* (Chicago), February 25, 1994, p. 14.

Re evidence of human injury from current concentrations of toxic chemicals, see discussions of dioxin and chlorine later in this chapter.

Re naturally occurring chlorinated compounds, see Gordon W. Gribble, "Naturally Occurring Organohalogen Compounds - A Survey," *Journal of Natural Products* 55 (10) (October 1992), p. 1353.

". . . an inherent bias" is from the International Joint Commission, *A Strategy for Virtual Elimination of Persistent Toxic Substances*, Appendix C, p. 74.

Milne quote is from Alex Milne, "The Perils of Green Pessimism," *New Scientist*, June

12, 1993, p. 37.

For discussions of Love Canal and Times Beach, see Eric Zuess, "Love Canal: The Truth Seeps Out," *Reason*, February 1981, pp. 17-33; and Michael Fumento, *Science Under Siege*, pp. 116-136.

Thomas panel quote is from Lewis Thomas (Chairman), *Report of the New York Governor's Panel to Review Scientific Studies and the Development of Public Policy on the Problems Resulting from Hazardous Waste*, October 1980.

New York State Department of Health was published as *Adverse Pregnancy Outcomes in the Love Canal Area*, April 1980.

Vernon Houk quote is from Tom Uhlenbrock, "Official: Times Beach Evacuation Order an Overreaction," *St. Louis Post-Dispatch*, May 23, 1991, p. A1.

AMA resolution was reported in Philip J. Hilts, "AMA Votes to Fight Dioxin 'Witch Hunt,'" *The Washington Post*, June 23, 1983.

Bolch and Lyons quote is from Ben Bolch and Harold Lyons, *Apocalypse Not*, p. 60; they are quoting David J. Hanson, "New Reports Find Little Effect by Agent Orange on Veterans," *Chemical and Engineering News*, April 15, 1991, p. 15.

NIOSH study was published as Marilyn A. Fingerhut et al., "Mortality Among U.S. Workers Employed in the Production of Chemicals Contaminated with 2,3,7,8-Tetrachlorodibenzo-p-dioxin (TCDD)," *New England Journal of Medicine* 324 (4) (January 24, 1991), pp. 212-213.

Kimbrough quote is from Renate D. Kimbrough, "Consumption of Fish: Benefits and Perceived Risk," *Journal of Toxicology and Environmental Health* 33 (1991), p. 85.

Houk quote is from Vernon N. Houk, "The Health Effects of Dioxin on Humans," paper submitted at a conference on "Current Views on the Impact of Dioxins and Furans on Human Health and the Environment," held in Berlin, Germany, on November 10, 1992.

Regenstein quote is from Lewis Regenstein, "Across America, Dioxin," *The New York Times*, March 8, 1983, p. A31.

Thomas panel quote is from Lewis Thomas (Chairman), *Report of the New York Governor's Panel to Review Scientific Studies and the Development of Public Policy on the Problems Resulting from Hazardous Waste*, October 1980.

IJC quote re shifting burden is from International Joint Commission, *Seventh Biennial Report on Great Lakes Water Quality*, pp. 1-2.

Re persistence and toxicity of chlorinated compounds, George Werezak writes: "[V]irtually all the chlorinated alkanes and alkenes, and most of the lower chlorinated monoaromatics, in present use have relatively short half-lives in water, air, sediment and biological tissues and therefore do not accumulate in these media. . . . Body burdens of such chlorinated organic chemicals do not accumulate to toxic concentrations because they are rapidly metabolized and excreted by organisms in the environment." International Joint Commission, *A Strategy for Virtual Elimination of Persistent Toxic Substances*, Appendix B, "A Report on Chlorine to the Virtual Elimination Task Force," p. 35.

Figure of 1 percent of chlorinated compounds is from International Joint Commission, *A Strategy for Virtual Elimination of Persistent Toxic Substances*, Appendix B, D.K. Phenicie, "Virtual Elimination in the Pulp and Paper Industry," p. 43.

Re Gribble, see Gordon W. Gribble, "Naturally Occurring Organohalogen Compounds - A Survey," *Journal of Natural Products* 55 (10) (October 1992), pp. 1353-1395.

IJC quote re precautionary principle is from International Joint Commission, *Seventh Biennial Report on Great Lakes Water Quality*, p. 7.

Jacobson study was published as J.L. Jacobson et al., "Effects of In Utero Exposure to Polychlorinated Biphenyls and Related Contaminants on Cognitive Functioning in Young Children," *Journal of Pediatrics* 116 (1990), pp. 38-40; and J.L. Jacobson et al., "Effects of Exposure to PCBs and Related Compounds on Growth and Activity in Children," *Neurotoxicology and Teratology* 12 (1990), pp. 319-326.

Re critiques of Jacobson, see Nigel Paneth, director, program in epidemiology, Michigan State University, "Human Reproduction After Eating PCB-contaminated Fish," *Health & Environment Digest* 5 (October 1991), pp. 4ff.; Renate D. Kimbrough, "Consumption of Fish: Benefits and Perceived Risk," *Journal of Toxicology and Environmental Health* 33 (1991), p. 85; Renate D. Kimbrough, "How Toxic is 2,3,7,8-tetrachlorodibenzodioxin to Humans?" *Journal of Toxicology and Environmental Health* 30 (1990), pp. 261-273; and G. M. Matanoski, "Review of Michigan Studies of Children with PCB Exposure and Comparison with Similar North Carolina Studies," n.d., typed manuscript. [Matanoski is professor of epidemiology at the Johns Hopkins School of Hygiene and Public Health.]

IJC quotes re its lack of proof are from International Joint Commission, *A Strategy for Virtual Elimination of Persistent Toxic Substances*, Appendix D, "The Injury," pp. 96-97, 90.

IJC quote re zero discharge is from International Joint Commission, *Seventh Biennial Report on Great Lakes Water Quality*, p. 7.

Re falling levels of persistent substances, see Council on Environmental Quality, *Environmental Quality 1992*, pp. 377, 378, 383, 388-391, 396; EPA, *National Water Quality Inventory: 1990 Report to Congress*, 1992; and International Joint Commission, *A Strategy for Virtual Elimination of Persistent Toxic Substances*, Appendix E, "Progress to Date."

Three-quarters of paper mills statistic is from International Joint Commission, *A Strategy for Virtual Elimination of Persistent Toxic Substances*, Appendix B, D.K. Phenicie, "Virtual Elimination in the Pulp and Paper Industry," p. 42.

Re evidence of paper mill effluent and wildlife, see S. Swanson et al., "Fish Populations and Biomarker Responses at a Canadian Bleached Kraft Mill Site," *Tappi Journal*, December 1992, pp. 139-149; and Pamela J. Kloepper-Sams and J. William Owens, "Environmental Biomarkers as Indicators of Chemical Exposure," *Journal of Hazardous Materials*, 1993, pp. 1-12.

Ten percent figure is from Great Lakes Water Quality Coalition, *Factbook*, p. 11.

Re requiring that discharges be cleaner than intake water, see Great Lakes Water Quality Coalition, "Comments of the Great Lakes Water Quality Coalition on the Proposed

Water Quality Guidance for the Great Lakes System," September 13, 1993, pp. 15ff.

IJC quote regarding "ethically and morally unacceptable" is from International Joint Commission, *Seventh Biennial Report on Great Lakes Water Quality*, p. 8.

IJC quote re cost-benefit analysis is from International Joint Commission, *Seventh Biennial Report on Great Lakes Water Quality*, p. 5.

Second IJC quote re cost-benefit analysis is from International Joint Commission, *A Strategy for Virtual Elimination of Persistent Toxic Substances*, Appendix C, p. 74.

IJC estimate of medical costs appears in International Joint Commission, *A Strategy for Virtual Elimination of Persistent Toxic Substances*, Appendix D, "The Injury," p. 95.

Re benefits of chlorine in drinking water, see Stig Regli, "Risk vs. Risk: Proposed Decision Tree for Drinking Water Management," *Health & Environment Digest* 7 (3) (June 1993), p. 5; International Agency for Research on Cancer, *IARC Monographs on the Evaluation of Carcinogenic Risks to Humans; Chlorinated Drinking-water, Chlorination Byproducts; Some other Halogenated Compounds; Cobalt and Cobalt Compounds*, World Health Organization, 1991; and G.F. Craun, *Safety of Water Disinfection: Balancing Chemical and Microbial Risks*.

Nine million deaths figure is from EPA, Office of Drinking Water, *Comparative Health Effects Assessment of Drinking Water Treatment Technologies*, Report to Congress, November 4, 1988.

Cost of chlorine phase-out is from Charles River Associates, *Assessment of the Economic Benefits of Chlor-Alkali Chemicals to the United States and Canadian Economies*, April 1993, prepared for The Chlorine Institute, Inc.

Chapter 5

Worldwatch quote is from Sandra Postel, "Denial in the Decisive Decade," in Lester R. Brown et al., *State of the World 1992*, pp. 3-4.

The $1 trillion since 1970 estimate is based on Table 8 of Council on Environmental Quality, *Environmental Quality 1992*, p. 281. That table shows total spending in current dollars from 1972 to 1990 of $1.009 trillion.

$150 billion per year figure is based on Keith Schneider, "New View Calls Environmental Policy Misguided," *New York Times*, March 21, 1993. Schneider writes: "The result was a tangle of regulations that the Environmental Protection Agency estimates cost more than $140 billion a year, roughly $100 billion spent by industry and $40 billion by government."

EOP Group, Inc., report is Global Climate Coalition, *The U.S. versus European Community, Environmental Performance*, August 11, 1993, p. 1.

Cairncross quote is from Frances Cairncross, *Costing the Earth*, p. 22.

Chemical industry emissions are reported in Chemical Manufacturers Association, *U.S. Chemical Industry Statistical Handbook 1992*, p. 135.

Re the fiber optics story, see George Gilder, "Into the Fibersphere," *Forbes ASAP*, pp. 111-120.

A company actually exists that specializes in recycling copper wire and its plastic coating; it is Waxman Inc. based in Hamilton, Ontario.

Bulleted items are from Council on Environmental Quality, *Environmental Quality 1992*, p. 185.

Chris Hampson quote is from Frances Cairncross, *Costing the Earth*, pp. 261-262.

Singer quotes are from Max Singer, *Passage to a Human World*, pp. 27-28.

Scully quotes are from Gerald W. Scully, "The Institutional Framework and Economic Development," *Journal of Political Economy* 96 (3) (1988), pp. 652-662.

Bulleted items are from Peter J. Hill, "Environmental Problems Under Socialism," *Cato Journal* 12 (2) (Fall 1992), pp. 321-335.

Re the history of capitalism, see Friedrich A. Hayek, *Capitalism and the Historians*.

Cairncross quote is from Frances Cairncross, *Costing the Earth*, p. 22.

Re privately owned elephants, see Urs P. Kreuter, "Politics and African Elephant Conservation," *NWI Resource*, Spring 1993, pp. 22-25; Stephen M. Weaver, "The Elephant's Best Friend," *National Review*, August 12, 1991, pp. 42-43; and Randy Simmons and Urs Kreuter, "Save an Elephant - Buy Ivory," *The Washington Post*, October 1, 1989.

Re the workings of price systems, see Friedrich A. Hayek, "The Use of Knowledge in Society," in *Individualism and Economic Order*, pp. 77-91.

Chapter 6

Stroup quote is from Richard Stroup et al., *Progressive Environmentalism: A Pro-Human, Pro-Science, Pro-Free Enterprise Agenda for Change*, National Center for Policy Analysis, April 1991, p. 37.

$3 billion figure is from Robert N. Stavins, "Clean Profits: Using Economic Incentives to Protect the Environment," *Policy Review*, Spring 1989, p. 62.

Re Yellowstone, see Alston Chase, *Playing God in Yellowstone*; Tom Blood, "Wolf Reintroductions Producing Howls," *Albuquerque Journal*, February 25, 1988; and Terry L. Anderson, "Wolves in the Marketplace," *Wall Street Journal*, August 12, 1992.

Cairncross quote is from Frances Cairncross, *Costing the Earth*, p. 75.

Singer quote is from Max Singer, *Passage to a Human World*, p. 137.

O'Toole quote is from Randal O'Toole, *Reforming the Forest Service*, pp. 196-197.

". . . the Forest Service gets to keep 25 percent" is from Terry L. Anderson, "The Forests and the Fees," *The New York Times*, June 28, 1993.

Tietenberg findings are from T.H. Tietenberg, *Emissions Trading: An Exercise in Reforming Pollution Policy*.

Amoco Oil Company project is described in Bradley I. Raffle and Debra F. Mitchell, *Effective Environmental Strategies: Opportunities for Innovation and Flexibility*

Under Federal Environmental Laws, Amoco Corp., June 1993.

Michael Levin and Daniel Dudek quotes are from Carolyn Lochhead, "Pollutants Reined by Market Rules," *Insight*, July 3, 1989, pp. 10-13.

Science quote is from Philip H. Abelson, "Pathological Growth of Regulations," *Science* 260 (June 25, 1993), p. 1859.

Sid Marder quotes are from an interview with Joseph Bast in July 1993.

Mathews quote is from Jessica Mathews, "Ecology in the Marketplace," *The Washington Post*, November 9, 1992, p. A21.

Estimate of Clean Air Act costs is from Robert W. Hahn, "No More Blank Checks for Regulators," *The New York Times*, August 12, 1992.

Resources for the Future estimate is reported in Frances Cairncross, *Costing the Earth*, pp. 60-61.

EPA spending on hazardous waste cleanup is reported in Chemical Manufacturers Association, *Superfund is Broken! Time to Fix it!* June 1993.

Cost of industry compliance is from John Shanahan, "How to Help the Environment Without Destroying Jobs," The Heritage Foundation, January 19, 1993, p. 5.

Clinton statement was reported in the *Los Angeles Times*, May 10, 1993.

Cairncross quote is from Frances Cairncross, *Costing the Earth*, p. 222.

Landy and Hague quote is from Marc Landy and Mary Hague, "The Coalition for Waste: Private Interests and Superfund," in Michael S. Greve and Fred L. Smith, *Environmental Politics: Public Costs, Private Rewards*, p. 67.

Dower quote is from Roger C. Dower, "Hazardous Wastes," in Paul R. Portney, *Public Policies for Environmental Protection*, p. 181.

Re "edible dirt" and "drinkable leachate," see Keith Schneider, "Rules Easing for Urban Toxic Cleanups," *The New York Times*, September 20, 1993, p. A-8; and William Tucker, "Superfund Sparks Industrial Flight," *Insight*, November 29, 1993, p. 9.

Litigation and cleanup estimates are from John Shanahan, "How to Help the Environment Without Destroying Jobs," The Heritage Foundation, January 19, 1993, p. 5; and Keith Schneider, "Rules Easing for Urban Toxic Cleanups," *The New York Times*, September 20, 1993, p. A-8.

Re businesses moving out of cities because of Superfund, see Keith Schneider, "Rules Easing for Urban Toxic Cleanups," *The New York Times*, September 20, 1993, p. A-8; and William Tucker, "Superfund Sparks Industrial Flight," *Insight*, November 29, 1993, p. 9.

Numbers of endangered and threatened species are from Suzanne Winckler, "Stopgap Measures," *The Atlantic Monthly*, January 1992.

Stroup quote is from Richard L. Stroup, "The Endangered Species Act: A Perverse Way to Protect Biodiversity," *PERC Viewpoints*, April 1992, p. 1. See also Jim Huffman and John Baden, "The Endangered Endangered Species Act," *FREE Perspectives*, August 1992, p. 8.

For contact information on many of the organizations mentioned, see Chapter Eight.

Fischer quote is from Hank Fischer, "Paying for Wolves," *FREE Perspectives*, August 1991, p. 9.

Weaver quote is from Stephen Weaver, "The Elephant's Best Friend," *National Review*, August 12, 1991, p. 42. For more on elephants, see Urs P. Kreuter, "Politics and African Elephant Conservation," *NWI Resource*, Spring 1993, pp. 22-25.

Re Exotic Game Association, see Ike C. Sugg, "To Save an Endangered Species, Own One," *Wall Street Journal*, August 31, 1992.

Chapter Seven

Simon reference is to Julian L. Simon, *The Ultimate Resource*, pp. 345-348.

Bailey quote is from Ronald Bailey, *Eco-Scam*, p. 49.

Whelan quote is from Elizabeth Whelan, *Toxic Terror*, p. 44.

$638 million figure is from Tim Brown, "Environmental Groups Turn into Fat Cats," *Insight*, October 11, 1993, p. 33.

43 million figure is from Leslie Spencer et al., "The Not So Peaceful World of Greenpeace," *Forbes*, November 11, 1991, p. 179.

Bailey quote is from Ronald Bailey, *Eco-Scam*, pp. 21-22.

Whelan quote is from Elizabeth Whelan, *Toxic Terror*, p. 57.

Chapter Eight

Gore quote is from Albert Gore, *Earth in the Balance*, p. 274.

Hahn quote is from Robert W. Hahn, "Toward a New Environmental Paradigm," *The Yale Law Journal*, May 1993, p. 1740.

Re offsets, see Carolyn Lochhead, "Pollutants Reined by Market Rules," *Insight*, July 3, 1989; and Paul R. Portney, "The Evolution of Federal Regulation," in Paul R. Portney, *Public Policies for Environmental Protection*, pp. 7-25.

Re tradeable permits, see James L. Johnston, "A Market without Rights: Sulfur Dioxide Emissions Trading," *Regulation*, Fall 1991, pages 24-29; and James L. Johnston, "How Market Oriented is the RECLAIM system?" presentation at the WEA International Pacific Rim Conference, Hong Kong, January 11, 1994.

Re nuclear power plant certification and policies in France, see Ben Bolch and Harold Lyons, *Apocalypse Not*, pp. 113-114.

Re carbon taxes, see W. David Montgomery et al., *No Free Lunch: A Review of Technology-Based Studies on Costs of Controlling Carbon Emissions*; Ronald L. McMahan et al., *The Costs and Implications of Controlling CO2 Emissions in the U.S.*; and Congressional Budget Office, *Carbon Charges as a Response to Global Warming: The Effects of Taxing Fossil Fuels*.

Re the U.N. global warming treaty, see John Shlaes, "Outlook on U.N. Climate Treaty,"

Climate Watch 2 (2) (February 1994), pp. 2-3.

Re San Francisco Bay, see "It's the Ecosystem, Stupid!" *National Wildlife*, February/ March 1994, p. 41.

Re Los Angeles water market, see Robert N. Stavins, "Clean Profits: Using Economic Incentives to Protect the Environment," *Policy Review*, Spring 1989, pp. 61-62.

Re inefficient use of federal waste water treatment subsidies, see Paul N. Tramontozzi, *Reforming Water Pollution Regulation*, Center for the Study of American Business, August 1985, p. 13.

Re paper mill effluent, see S. Swanson et al., "Fish Populations and Biomarker Responses at a Canadian Bleached Kraft Mill Site," *Tappi Journal*, December 1992, pp. 139-149; Pamela J. Kloepper-Sams and J. William Owens, "Environmental Biomarkers as Indicators of Chemical Exposure," *Journal of Hazardous Materials* 34 (1993), pp. 1-12; and D.K. Phenicie, "Virtual Elimination in the Pulp and Paper Industry," Appendix B of *A Strategy for Virtual Elimination of Persistent Toxic Substances*, International Joint Commission, 1993, pp. 41-46.

The first four bullets on this page are based on the discussion in John Shanahan, *How to Help the Environment Without Destroying Jobs*, The Heritage Foundation, January 19, 1993.

Re state activities, see Keith Schneider, "Rules Easing for Urban Toxic Cleanups," *The New York Times*, September 20, 1993, p. A8.; and William Tucker, "Superfund Sparks Industrial Flight," *Insight*, November 29, 1993.

Re auctioning orphan Superfund sites, see Richard Stroup, "Privatize Superfund Waste Sites," *PERC Reports*, December 1991, p. 8.

Re mandatory use reduction, see *U.S. Chemical Industry Statistical Handbook 1992*, Chemical Manufacturers Association, pp. 3, 135. For an example of how mandated source reduction would affect a wide range of consumer goods, see *Assessment of the Economic Benefits of Chlor-Alkali Chemicals to the U.S. and Canadian Economies*, a study conducted by Charles River Associates (Boston, Massachusetts) for The Chlorine Institute, Inc., April 1993.

Re management for multiple benefits, see two Forest Service publications, *Strategy for the 90s* (1990), and *Forestry Research: A Mandate for Change* (1990). An overview appears in Hal Salwasser, "Gaining Perspective: Forestry for the Future," *Journal of Forestry*, November 1990.

Stroup and Baden quotation is from Richard L. Stroup and John A. Baden, *Natural Resources: Bureaucratic Myths and Environmental Management*, p. 118.

Re increasing fees for recreational users, see Randal O'Toole, *Reforming the Forest Service*, chapters 14 and 15.

Re the Endangered Species Act and private initiatives, see Richard Stroup, "The Endangered Species Act: A Perverse Way to Protect Biodiversity," *PERC Viewpoints*, April 1992.

Cairncross quote is from Frances Cairncross, *Costing the Earth*, page 269.

"25 to 45 percent reduction . . . " is from Lisa A. Skumatz, *Variable Rates for Municipal Solid Waste: Implementation Experience, Economics, and Legislation*, Reason Foundation, June 1993, p. 1. See also Susan Taras, "Pay-per-bag Garbage Adds a New Twist to Recycling," *City & State*, July 31, 1989, p. 25.

Re the economics of recycling, see Christopher Boerner, "Recycling Myths and Unfashionable Truths," Center for the Study of American Business, *Occasional Paper 132*, October 1993; Kenneth Chilton, "Solid Waste Policy Should Be Directed By Fundamental Principles, Not Ill-Founded Feelings," *Resources, Conservation and Recycling* 8 (1993), pp 1-20 Harvey Alter, "The Future Course of Solid Waste Management in the U.S.," *Waste Management & Research* 9 (1991); and the exchange of views in Letters to the Editor, *Wall Street Journal*, September 7, 1993, page A14.

Re product bans, see Kenneth Chilton, "Solid Waste Policy Should Be Directed By Fundamental Principles, Not Ill-Founded Feelings," *Resources, Conservation and Recycling* 8 (1993), pp. 1-20; William Rathje and Cullen Murphy, *Rubbish! The Archaeology of Garbage*, pp. 220ff; and Lynn Scarlett, *A Consumers Guide to Environmental Myths and Realities*, National Center for Policy Analysis, September 1991, p. 36.

Re German Green Dot system, see Christopher Boerner and Kenneth Chilton, "Demand-Side Recycling: Lessons from the German Green Dot Program," Center for the Study of American Business, *Occasional Paper 126*, July 1993; Virginia Postrel and Lynn Scarlett, "Talking Trash," *Reason*, August/September 1991, pp. 29-30; and "Recycling is Not Always Right," *Papercast*, Communication Consil International, Paris, December 1992, p. 22.

Schneider quotation is from Keith Schneider, "New View Calls Environmental Policy Misguided," *The New York Times*, March 21, 1993.

Bibliography

Anderson, Terry L. and Donald R. Leal. *Free Market Environmentalism.* San Francisco, CA: Pacific Research Institute for Public Policy, 1991.

Bailey, Ronald. *Eco-Scam.* New York, NY: St. Martin's Press, 1993.

Balling Jr., Robert C. *The Heated Debate: Greenhouse Predictions Versus Climate Reality.* San Francisco, CA: Pacific Research Institute for Public Policy, 1992.

Bauer, Peter. *Dissent on Development.* London: Weidenfeld & Nicholson, 1976.

———. *Equality, the Third World, and Economic Delusion.* Cambridge, MA: Harvard University Press, 1981.

Bernards, Neal (Ed.). *The Environmental Crisis: Opposing Viewpoints.* San Diego, CA: Greenhaven Press, Inc., 1991.

Bernstam, Mikhail S. *The Wealth of Nations and the Environment.* London: Institute of Economic Affairs, 1991.

Bolch, Ben and Harold Lyons. *Apocalypse Not: Science, Economics, and Environmentalism.* Washington, DC: Cato Institute, 1993.

Brodeur, Paul. *Currents of Death.* New York, NY: Simon and Schuster, 1989.

Brown, Lester R., et al. *State of the World 1992.* New York, NY: W.W. Norton and Company, 1992.

Cade, T.J., et al. (Eds.). *Peregrine Falcon Populations: Their Management and Recovery.* Santa Cruz, CA: The Peregrine Fund, Inc., 1988.

Cairncross, Frances. *Costing the Earth: The Challenge for Governments, the Opportunities for Business.* Boston, MA: Harvard Business School Press, 1992.

Caplan, Ruth. *Our Earth, Ourselves.* New York, NY: Bantam Books, 1990.

Capra, Fritjof. *The Turning Point.* New York, NY: Bantam Books, 1982.

Carson, Rachel. *Silent Spring*. Boston, MA: Houghton Mifflin Company, 1962.

Chase, Alston. *Playing God in Yellowstone*. Boston, MA: The Atlantic Monthly Press, 1986.

Chilton, Kenneth and Melinda Warren. *Environmental Protection: Regulating for Results*. Boulder, CO: Westview Press, 1991.

Commoner, Barry. *Science and Survival*. New York, NY: The Viking Press, 1966.

Congressional Budget Office. *Carbon Charges as a Response to Global Warming: The Effects of Taxing Fossil Fuels*. Washington, DC: U.S. Government Printing Office, August 1990.

Council on Environmental Quality. *Environmental Quality: The Twenty-Third Annual Report of the Council on Environmental Quality together with the President's Message to Congress 1992*. Washington, DC: Council on Environmental Quality, January 1993.

Cowen, Tyler (Ed.). *The Theory of Market Failure*. Fairfax, VA: George Mason University Press, 1988.

Craun, G.F. *Safety of Water Disinfection: Balancing Chemical and Microbial Risks*. Washington, DC: ILSI Press, 1993.

Dobson, G.M.B. *Ozone in the Atmosphere*. London: Oxford University Press, 1968.

Doll, Sir Richard and Richard Peto. "The Causes of Cancer: Quantitative Estimates of Avoidable Risks of Cancer in the United States Today." *Journal of the National Cancer Institute* 66 (6) (June 1981).

Ehrlich, Paul R. *The Population Bomb*. New York, NY: Ballantine Books, Inc., 1968.

Fumento, Michael. *Science Under Siege*. New York, NY: William Morrow and Company, Inc., 1993.

George C. Marshall Institute. *Two Environmental Issues: 1. Ozone, 2. The Greenhouse Problem*. Pittsburgh, PA: World Affairs Council, December 1991.

Global 2000 Report to the President. Washington, DC: Government Printing Office, 1980.

Global Climate Coaltion. *The U.S. versus European Community: Environmental Performance*. Washington, DC: Global Climate Coaltion, August 1993.

Gore, Albert. *Earth in the Balance*. New York, NY: Plume, 1993.

Gosselin, Robert E. *Clinical Toxicology of Commercial Products*. 5th edition. Williams & Wilkins, 1984.

Gottlieb, Robert. *Forcing the Spring: The Transformation of the American Environmental Movement*. Washington, DC: Island Press, 1993.

Greve, Michael S. and Fred L. Smith, Jr. (Eds.). *Environmental Politics: Public Costs, Private Rewards*. New York, NY: Praeger Publishers, 1992.

Hayek, F.A. *Capitalism and the Historians*. Chicago, IL: University of Chicago Press, 1954 (Phoenix edition, 1968).

———. *Individualism and Economic Order*. Chicago, IL: Henry Regnery Co., 1972.

Idso, Sherwood B. *Carbon Dioxide and Global Change: Earth in Transition*. Tempe, AZ: IBR Press, 1989.

International Joint Commission. *A Strategy for Virtual Elimination of Persistent Toxic Substances*. Windsor, Ontario: International Joint Commission, August 1993.

———. *Seventh Biennial Report on Great Lakes Water Quality*. Windsor, Ontario: International Joint Commission, 1993.

International Panel on Climate Change. *Scientific Assessment of Climate Change*. June 1990.

Jastrow, Robert, William Nierenberg, and Frederick Seitz. *Scientific Perspectives on the Greenhouse Problem*. Ottawa, IL: The Marshall Press, 1990.

Kemeny, J.B. (Chairman). *Report of the President's Commission on the Accident at Three Mile Island*. Washington, DC: U.S. Government Printing Office, 1979.

Kraushaar, J.L. and R.A. Ristinen. *Energy and Problems of a Technical Society*. New York, NY: John Wiley and Sons, 1988.

Lehr, Jay H. (Ed.). *Rational Readings on Environmental Concerns*. New York, NY: Van Nostrand Reinhold, 1992.

Leonard, Henry S. *Principles of Reasoning: An Introduction to Logic, Methodology, and the Theory of Signs*. New York, NY: Dover Publications, Inc., 1967.

Lewis, Martin W. *Green Delusions: An Environmentalist Critique of Radical Environmentalism*. Durham, NC: Duke University Press, 1992.

Lewis, Scott. *The Rainforest Book: How You Can Save the World's Rainforests*. Los Angeles, CA: Living Planet Press, 1990.

Luckey, T.D. *Hormesis and Ionizing Radiation*. Boca Raton, FL: CRC Press, Inc., 1980.

Maduro, Roger A. *The Holes in the Ozone Scare*. Washington, DC: 21st Century Science Associates, 1992.

McMahan, Ronald L., et al. *The Costs and Implications of Controlling CO2 Emissions in the U.S.* Boulder, CO: DRI, January 1993.

Meadows, Donnella H. and Dennis L. *The Limits to Growth: A Report to The Club of Rome's Project on the Predicament of Mankind*. New York, NY: Universe Books, 1972.

Montgomery, W. David, et al. *No Free Lunch: A Review of Technology-Based Studies on Costs of Controlling Carbon Emissions*. Lexington, MA: DRI/McGraw-Hill, June 9, 1993.

Myers, Norman. *The Sinking Ark*. New York, NY: Pergamon, 1979.

National Academy of Sciences. *Environmental Impact of Stratospheric Flight*. Washington, DC: National Academy Press, 1975.

———. *Oil in the Sea: Inputs, Fates, and Effects*. Washington, DC: National Academy Press, 1985.

National Acidic Precipitation Assessment Program. *Acidic Deposition: State of Science and Technology*. 4 vols. Washington, DC: U.S. Government Printing Office, July 1990.

Osborn, Fairfield. *Our Plundered Planet*. Boston, MA: Little, Brown and Company, 1948.

O'Toole, Randal. *Reforming the Forest Service*. Washington, DC: Island Press, 1988.

Popper, Karl R. *The Logic of Scientific Discovery*. New York, NY: Harper & Row, 1968.

Portney, Paul R. (Ed.). *Public Policies for Environmental Protection*. Washington, DC: Resources for the Future, 1990.

Rathje, William and Cullen Murphy. *Rubbish! The Archaeology of Garbage*. New York, NY: Harper Collins Publishers, 1992.

Ray, Dixie Lee with Lou Guzzo. *Environmental Overkill*. Washington, DC: Regnery Gateway, 1993.

———. *Trashing the Planet*. Washington, DC: Regnery Gateway, 1990.

Regenstein, Lewis. *America the Poisoned*. Washington, DC: Acropolis Books, 1982.

Sale, Kirkpatrick. *Dwellers in the Land: The Bioregional Vision*. San Francisco, CA: Sierra Club Books, 1985.

———. *Human Scale*. New York, NY: Coward, McCann, and Geoghegan, 1980.

Schmidheiny, S. *Changing Course: A Global Business Perspective on Development and the Environment*. Cambridge, MA: The MIT Press, 1992.

Simon, Julian L. *The Ultimate Resource*. Princeton, MA: Princeton University Press, 1981.

Simon, Julian L. and Herman Kahn (Eds.). *The Resourceful Earth*. New York, NY: Basil Blackwell Inc., 1984.

Singer, Max. *Passage to a Human World*. Indianapolis, IN: Hudson Institute, Inc., 1987.

Singer, S. Fred (Ed.). *Global Climate Change*. New York, NY: Paragon House, 1989.

Stroup, Richard L. and John A. Baden. *Natural Resources: Bureaucratic Myths and Environmental Management.* San Francisco, CA: Pacific Institute for Public Policy Research, 1983.

Tietenberg, T.H. *Emissions Trading: An Exercise in Reforming Pollution Policy.* Washington, DC: Resources for the Future, 1985.

U.S. Bureau of the Census. *Statistical Abstract of the United States 1992.* Washington, DC: Government Printing Office, 1992.

U.S. Congress, Office of Technology Assessment. *Biological Effects of Power Frequency Electric & Magnetic Fields - Background Paper.* Washington, DC: U.S. Government Printing Office, May 1989.

Weiner, Jonathan. *The Next One Hundred Years.* New York, NY: Bantam Books, 1990.

Whelan, Elizabeth M. *Toxic Terror.* Ottawa, IL: Jameson Books, 1985.

Wildavsky, Aaron. *Searching for Safety.* New Brunswick, NJ: Transaction Books, 1988.

Wilson, E.O. *The Diversity of Life.* New York, NY: W.W. Norton & Co., 1993.

Wilson, E.O. and Frances M. Peter (Eds.). *Biodiversity.* Washington, DC: National Academy Press, 1988.

World Bank, *World Population Projections 1992-93 Edition.* Baltimore, MD: The Johns Hopkins University Press, 1992.

Index

Acid rain 74–81
Acidic aerosols 76
Adair, Eleanor R. 143
Adirondacks 80
Agent Orange 164, 167
Air quality 11–15
  and automobiles 110–116, 247, 251
  and cancer 14
  and health 14, 40, 40–41
  global 13
  point vs. nonpoint pollution 33, 208
  reasons for improvement 12–14
  recommended policies 247-252
Alar 5, 98
Alsea 5
Amazon rainforest. *See* Forests: deforestation
Ames, Bruce N. 17, 20–21, 40, 44, 46, 97, 103, 158
Ammonium 17, 18
Animal tests 21, 43–47, 168, 235, 236, 255
  weaknesses of 44–47, 168–170
Antarctic ozone hole 66–69
Aracruz Celulose 88
Archibald, Sandra 96
Asbestos 40, 154
Automobiles 110–121, 230, 247, 251

Baden, John 258
Bailey, Ronald 19, 233, 241
Balling, Robert C. 53–54, 60
Bioaccumulation 91
Biological oxygen demand 17, 18
Boice, John 144
Bolch, Ben 105, 106, 167
Borlaug, Norman E. 99
Bowermaster, Jon 132
Brazil. *See also* Forests: deforestation
  government policies in 89
  sustainable forestry in 88
Brodeur, Paul 7, 36, 142, 144–145, 147
Brown, Lester 36, 90, 181, 233
Brownstein, Ronald 164
Buringh, P. 128–129

CAFE standards 116–118
Cairncross, Frances 183–184, 193, 205, 210–211
Caldicott, Helen 237
Cancer 35–49
  and air quality 14
  and animal tests 21
  and dioxin 166–170
  and drinking water 3
  and elderly 37, 38–40
  and EMFs 144–145
  and food supply 20–22, 41–42, 96, 98
  and genetics 41, 43
  and ozone depletion 65
  and pesticides 3, 20–22, 41–43, 96–98
  and pollution 40–42
  and radiation 104–105
  and toxic chemicals 20–22, 157–158, 176
  and ultraviolet radiation 65, 71
  and water quality 17
  definition 36–37
  incidence 37–40, 49, 97, 229

mortality 37–40, 49, 229
Capitalism
and the environment 188–192
Capra, Fritjof 74, 121
Carbon monoxide 11, 12, 110–113
Carson, Rachel vii, 5, 35–36, 90, 91, 267
Carstensen, Edwin L. 143
Cascade Holistic Economic Consultants 217, 259, 266
Causation
vs. correlation 144–145, 168–169, 231
CFCs
and ozone depletion 3, 63–68, 71–73
concentration in atmosphere 71–73
Chemicals. *See* Toxic chemicals
Chernobyl 106–108
Chilton, Kenneth 118
Chlordane. *See* Pesticides
Chlorine 170–176, 255
and ozone depletion 64
in drinking water 3
naturally occurring 170
Chloroflourocarbons. *See* CFCs
Christy, John 54
Clawson, Marion 23, 83, 84, 90
Clean Air Act 11, 12, 75, 81, 112, 114, 183, 209, 250
Clinton administration 210, 225, 257, 258
The Club of Rome 121
Cohen, Bernard L. 103, 104
Common law
and pollution 219–222, 220–221, 249, 254
evolution of property rights 198
Common-sense agenda 243–266, 268, 269
Commoner, Barry 91, 102
Communism
and the environment 188–192
Correlation
vs. causation 144–145, 168–169, 231
Cost-benefit analysis 159, 161–163, 175–176, 212, 256
Council on Environmental Quality 17, 94
Crandall, Robert 117
Critical thinking 231–234
Cuyahoga River 15, 16

DDE. *See* Pesticides
DDT. *See* Pesticides
Defenders of Wildlife 218, 238, 259, 266
Deforestation. *See* Forests: deforestation
Denver 141–142, 143
Diapers 139–140
Dieldrin. *See* Pesticides
Diminishing returns
and air pollution 114, 209–210
and fuel economy 118
and need to make choices 233–234
Dioxin 154, 163–170, 176, 255
Dobson, G.M.B. 68
Doctors 4, 231
Doll, Richard 14, 17, 36, 39, 40, 41–43, 47, 48–49, 97, 104
Dose-response curve 46–47, 155, 235, 255
Dower, Roger 155, 157, 211
Drinking water 3, 17, 161, 163, 174, 175
Ducks Unlimited 217, 219, 238, 259, 266
Dudek, Daniel 208

Earth Summit 9, 55, 85
Eco Spheres 152
Eco-sanity x, 225–242, 268
EcoTrust 259, 266
Efficiency
and air quality 14
and the environment 184–187, 240
Efron, Edith 44–45
Ehrlich, Paul 7, 19, 20, 36, 102, 124, 125, 233, 237
Elastol 152
Electricity
and air quality 13
increasing use of 13–14
Electromagnetic fields. *See* EMFs
ELF. *See* EMFs
Ellsaesser, Hough W. 68–69
EMFs 141–148, 177–178
Endangered species
and property rights 216–219
recommended policies 259
Endangered Species Act 201, 212–

215, 217, 257, 259
Energy
and GNP 31
and per-capita income 191
conservation of 30
consumption
and automobiles 116–118
and plastics 137–138
demand for 30–31
supplies 28–32
reserves vs. resources 28–30
Environmental movement
history vii–x, 5
importance of 10, 52, 87–89, 90–91, 120, 154
"new paradigm" 154, 158–163, 170–176, 211–212
tactics vii–x, 5, 10, 52, 56, 73–74, 81, 86, 102, 109–110, 120–121, 132, 134, 140, 148, 154, 177–179, 201, 210, 222, 226, 243, 247, 264–265, 267–268
Environmental quality 7–34, 229
and population growth 129–131
defined 10
Epidemiology 47–49, 168–170, 235–236
weaknesses of 47–49
Epstein, Samuel 164
Exotic Wildlife Association 218
Exxon Valdez 148–151, 219. *See also* Oil spills

Fear 1–5, 35–36, 107–108, 109–110, 141, 148, 242, 267–268. *See also* Scare tactics
Fischer, Hank 218
Florida 79–80
Food supply 19–22
abundance of 19–20, 128–129
and cancer 20–21, 41–43, 98
and pesticides 99
safety of 20–22
Forest Trust 217, 266
Forests 22–24
deforestation 82–90, 230
growth vs. harvest 22–23
plantation 82, 88
recommended policies 257–260
second growth 24
subsidized logging 24, 34, 203, 204
subsidized roads 24, 203
sustainable yield 23, 82, 88
Fossil fuels. *See* Energy supplies
Fountain Valley 5
Franklin Associates 133–134, 135, 139
Free enterprise
and the environment 188–192, 215–216
Freeman, A. Myrick 15
Fuel economy 116–118
Fumento, Michael 39, 47, 142, 169

Gasoline 111–113
Gibbs, Lois 164
Global 2000 7, 8
Global warming 53–62, 230, 241, 249–252
Goodman, Jay I. 46
Gore, Al 8, 85, 110, 243, 247
Government
and information 239–240
and over-grazing 204
as landowner 202–206
as regulator 206–210, 210–212
failure to protect endangered species 212–215
failure to protect environment 201
farm programs 204
incentive structures 239
subsidies and waste 240
subsidized irrigation 205
vs. property rights 221–223
Graham, John 117
Great Lakes 15, 16
Greenpeace 83, 154, 160, 163, 169, 170, 174, 175, 178, 234, 241
Gribble, Gordon W. 171
Guilford 5, 143

Hague, Mary 210–211
Hahn, Robert W. 209–210, 243
Harrisburg 4
Hartford 5
Haywood, Vernon 86–87
Heller's beads 152
Hill, Richard 96
Hocking, Martin B. 138
Hollingsworth, Robert 98
Houk, Vernon N. 166–168

Hydrocarbons 110–113

Idso, Sherwood B. 61
Imagination
  and the environment 187–188, 230
Incentives
  and government 239
  and the environment 193–195, 238–239, 247–249
Information
  and government 239–240
  and the environment 195–196, 231–233, 247, 252
Inipol 152
Innovation
  and environmental regulation 209–210
  and pollution 186–188, 199, 230
International Joint Commission 170–176
International Panel on Climate Change 53, 55

Jacobson, J.L. 172–173
Jastrow, Robert 54

Kahn, Herman 8
Kaplan, Robert D. 100–101, 130
Koop, C. Everett 97
Krug, Edward 80

Lake Erie 15, 19, 20
Lake Michigan 15, 19, 20
Landfills. *See also* Solid waste: landfills
  and cancer risk 157
  plastics in 132–134
Landy, Marc K. 210–211
Lead 154
  in air 11, 12
  in water 18
Leeper, Ed 141–143
Lehr, Jay H. 25
Levin, Michael 208
Life expectancy 20, 229
Light-weighting 27, 117, 177
Lindzen, Richard S. 54–55
Love Canal 4, 163–164, 165, 166
Lyman, Francesca 139
Lyons, Harold 105, 106, 167

Malaria
  and pesticides 100–101
Marder, Sid 209
Marine Spill Response Corporation 152, 154
"Market failure" 215–216
Markets
  and the environment 188–192, 215–216, 221–222, 238–239
Mathews, Jessica 209
Media 4, 5, 7, 22, 48, 49, 53, 56, 62, 107-108, 141, 149, 151, 231, 241, 264
Mercury 154
Michaels, Patrick 54, 60
Midland 5
Miller, Sanford 98
Milne, Alex 159, 163
Miscarriages 4, 231
Mississippi River 17, 18
Montecito 5
Moore, Stephen 124
Muller, Paul 100
Murphy, Cullen 120, 139–140
Myers, Norman 8, 85, 86

Nader, Ralph 7, 36, 164, 237
National Acid Precipitation Assessment Program (NAPAP) 75–81, 230
Natural Resources Defense Council (NRDC) 84, 178
The Nature Conservancy 217, 219, 238, 259, 266
Newark 5
Nierenberg, William 54
Nitrates 17, 18, 74
Nitrogen dioxide 11, 12, 74, 76, 110–113
Nuclear power 102–110
  and radiation 103–104
  recommended policies 249
  safety of 106–108
  unlike bombs 106
  waste disposal 108–109

Oceans 17
Oil spills 148–154, 230
Oil supply. *See* Energy supplies
Osborn, Fairfield 102
O'Toole, Randal 206, 225
Ozone 4
  and automobiles 110, 113

creation of 66
depletion of 62–74, 241
and cancer 65
emissions of 11
Ozone hole. *See* Antarctic ozone hole

The Phoenix Group 55
Paigen, Beverly 168–169
Paper 87, 119, 133, 134, 135, 137, 138, 139–140
and energy consumption 138
Particulates 11, 12, 110–113
PCBs 16, 95, 98, 154, 167, 170, 171, 172, 173, 175
Pesticides 35–36, 90–102, 154, 220, 252
and cancer 3, 20, 41–43, 96–98
and other illnesses 98–99
and wildlife 5, 91–93, 94–96
chemical composition of 94–96
DDE 93
DDT 91, 93, 94, 95, 100, 101, 102, 161, 163, 170, 171, 175
dieldrin 91, 93, 170, 171
importance of 99–101
for malaria prevention 100–101
to food supply 99–100
patterns of use of 94–96
unique among chemicals 158
PET 135, 261. *See also* Plastic
Peto, Richard 14, 17, 36, 39, 40, 41–43, 47, 48–49, 97, 104
Phosphates 18
Plantico, Marc S. 54
Plastic 3, 27, 132–140, 261–264
Polystyrene. *See also* Plastic
and energy consumption 138
recycling of 135–136
Poore, Patricia 140
Population growth 19, 125–132
Poverty
and population growth 126–127
and the environment 182–184
Precautionary principle 158, 160–161, 171–174, 211, 242
Prices
and the environment 195–196
impact on energy demand 116–117
impact on resource scarcity 122–124
Prince William Sound 148–151. *See also* Oil spills
Privatization
of wildlife 216–219, 259–260
Property rights
and deforestation 89–90
and exchange solutions 196, 197, 239
and pollution 219–221, 238
and population growth 130
and the environment 193–194, 196, 197, 215–216, 238
and wildlife 216–219, 238
evolution of 198, 238
vs. government 221–223
Prosperity
and environment 87–89, 181–199, 230
and population growth 126–127

Radiation
and cancer 104–105
and nuclear power 103–104
natural vs. man-made 103–104
Rainforests. *See* Forests: deforestation
Rathje, William 120, 133–134, 139–140
Recycling. *See* Solid waste: recycling
Regenstein, Lewis 90, 164, 168
Regli, Stig 3
Regulation 206–210, 210–212
and innovation 209–210
costs of 4, 5, 16, 52, 63–64, 74–75, 81, 114, 120, 162, 162–163, 175, 177–178, 209–210, 212
recommended reforms 247–264
vs. incentives 238–239
vs. least-cost 207, 215
Resource depletion 121–132, 230
and prices 122–124
predictions of 121–122
Resources for the Future 15, 23, 83, 208, 211
Revelle, Roger 54
Reverse onus principle 158, 159–160, 170–171, 211, 234, 242
Richard, John 164
Rio de Janeiro 9, 55
Risk
and need to make choices 145–148, 162, 236–237
comparison among sources 147–148
potential vs. actual 147–

148, 155, 234–235, 236–237
unavoidability of 145–148, 159, 233

Sagan, Carl 52
Sale, Kirkpatrick 121
Salwasser, Hal 22
Sand County Foundation 217
Savits, David 143
Scare tactics ix, 10–11, 19, 22, 35–36, 51–52, 73–74, 141, 148, 229–230, 233, 240–242, 267–268. *See also* Fear
Scheuplein, Robert J. 21
Schneider, Keith 46
Schneider, Stephen 231
Schwarzenegger, Arnold 232
Science
and politics 237
importance of ix, 52, 81
lessons from 234–237
misuse of 9, 85, 160–161, 168–170, 176
Scientific community
opinion of acid rain 81
opinion of dioxin 166–168
opinion of EMFs 142–144
opinion of Exxon Valdez 149–151
opinion of global warming 53–55, 62
Scotto, Joseph 69
Scully, Gerald W. 189
Sedjo, Roger A. 23, 83, 84, 90
Seitz, Frederick 54
Sierra Club 178
Simon, Julian 8, 86, 124, 230
Singer, Max 123, 127–128, 129, 187, 205
Singer, S. Fred 54–55
Skole, David 84
Smith, Fred L. 113
Smith, Robert J. 92
Socialism
and the environment 188–192, 199, 240
Solid waste 24–27
amount of 24–25, 260–261
and plastic 4, 132–134
content of 25
disposal of 25
incineration
amount of 25
safety of 26
landfills
amount of garbage in 25
safety of 26
shortage of 26–27, 260–261
siting of 27
technology 25–26; 34, 230, 261
recommended policies 260–264
recycling
amount of 25
automobiles 119, 120
evaluation of 34, 260–262
growth of 27
plastic 27, 135–137, 260–262
Species extinction
and deforestation 85–87
and private property 92
Starvation 19, 19–20
Stedman, Donald 115–116
Steger, Will 132
Stroup, Richard 203, 213–214, 236, 258
Sulfates 74
Sulfur dioxide 11, 12, 74, 76, 110–113
Superfund 207, 210–212, 256–257, 269
Sustainable yield. *See* Forests
Sykuta, Michael 118

Teeri, James 61
Thermal decomposition
and plastics recycling 136–137
Thomas, Lewis 166, 168–169
Three Mile Island 106–108
Tietenberg, T.H. 207
Times Beach 4, 164, 166–167
Toxic chemicals 154–176
and cancer 20–22, 157–158
and hazardous waste 155–158
chlorine 170–176
dioxin 163–172
fear of 2, 5
importance of dose 234–235
recommended policies 255–257
threat to health 155–158
Trends 231
Trout Unlimited 217, 266
Tucker, Compton 84
Turner, Robert L. 100

Ultraviolet (UV) radiation

and cancer 65, 71
and ozone depletion 64–65
dangers of 70–71
reaching Earth's surface 69–70

Victims and villains 165, 241–242
VOCs 12, 110–113
Volatile organic compounds. *See* VOCs

Waste disposal. *See* Solid waste. *See also* Nuclear power; Toxic chemicals
Wastewater treatment 16, 253, 254
Water. *See* Drinking water
Water quality 15–18, 51, 129, 139, 161, 170
and cancer 17
and chlorine 170–176
and toxic chemicals 170–176, 173, 175
lakes 16
oceans 17
point vs nonpoint pollution 16, 17–18, 33, 118–119, 174, 208, 252
recommended policies 252–255
rivers 17, 18
Wealth. *See* Prosperity
Weaver, Stephen M. 218, 218–219
Weinberg, Jack 160–161
Wells, James 97, 104
Werezak, George 94–95
Wertheimer, Wendy 141–143
Whelan, Elizabeth 8, 34, 234, 242
Wildavsky, Aaron 86, 159–160
Wilderness Society 22
Wildlife
and oil spills 148, 154
and pesticides 91–93, 94–96
and property rights 216–219
recommended policies 259–260
Wilson, Edward O. 86
Winter, Carl 96
Wirka, Jeanne 139
Wiseman, A. Clark 27
Women 126, 130–131
World Resources Institute 85, 124, 209
Worldwatch Institute 90, 124, 132, 181, 187

Young, Alvin 99

Zero discharge principle 159, 161, 174, 211–212, 234
Zuesse, Eric 165

Authors

Joseph L. Bast is president of The Heartland Institute, a nonprofit research organization established in 1984 to study and propose solutions to state and local public policy problems. Born on a farm in rural Wisconsin, Bast grew up camping and backpacking in Wisconsin and Michigan. A committed environmentalist, he has planted trees, rebuilt river banks, helped to restore a prairie, and backpacked alone deep into some of America's wildest areas. He and his wife, Diane, built their own geodesic dome home in northern Wisconsin (they learned about domes by reading *The Last Whole Earth Catalogue*, of course), and after seven years they still haven't gotten around to installing electricity or running water. Joe and Diane were copy editors for *Lake and Prairie*, the newsletter of the Chicago Sierra Club, for a while during the 1980s, but resigned to protest the organization's increasing involvement in politics. Bast remains a member of many environmental organizations.

Peter J. Hill is a senior associate with the Political Economy Research Center (PERC) of Bozeman, Montana, and the George F. Bennett Professor of Economics at Wheaton College, Wheaton, Illinois. PERC is a leading nonprofit think tank that concentrates on environmental and resource issues. Hill grew up on a cattle ranch in eastern Montana and managed the family operation after he finished his Ph.D. program at the University of Chicago, combining ranching with his academic career. In 1992 he sold the land, which had been in his family since 1894. Suffering from profound anomie with separation from the land and the outdoors, he purchased a ranch in the Madison Valley in western Montana, where he plans to spend his summers. Hill has published numerous articles on environmental issues, property rights theory, and economic history in such respected publications as the *American Journal of Agricultural Economics* and the *Southern Economic Journal*.

Richard C. Rue is a senior policy analyst and vice president of The Heartland Institute. He has nearly twenty years' experience with public policy organizations, including the Wisconsin Legislative Reference Bureau, Public Expenditure Survey, and Wisconsin Policy Research Institute. He holds a Masters Degree in Public Administration from the University of Texas. While in graduate school in Austin, he spent weekends and vacations wandering the Gulf Coast and the west Texas desert areas. Rue returned to Wisconsin and for many years spent summer weekends commuting to a cabin in Northern Wisconsin, where his wife and children spent the summer. He and his children still spend a good deal of their free time hiking in Door County, Parfies Glen, and the Baraboo Hills of Wisconsin.

The Heartland Institute

The Heartland Institute is a nonprofit research and education organization focusing on state and local public policy issues. Since 1984 its research has been used by concerned citizens across the country to cut taxes and reduce government spending.

Heartland is a genuinely independent source of research and commentary: It is not affiliated with any political party, business, or foundation. It does not accept government funds and does not conduct "contract" research for special interest groups. Its activities are tax-exempt under Section 501(c)(3) of the Internal Revenue Code.

Heartland publications have been called "among the premier economic documents being produced anywhere today." In addition to occasional books, The Heartland Institute publishes *Heartland Policy Studies*, in-depth studies 28 to 40 pages in length; *Heartland Perspectives*, opinion essays three to four pages in length; and *Intellectual Ammunition*, a magazine sent to every governor, state legislator, and state constitutional officer in the U.S. In November 1993, The Heartland Institute launched ***PolicyFax***, a new fax-on-demand information source.

Offices of The Heartland Institute are located in Palatine, Illinois, and Detroit, Michigan. Each office is locally supported and produces publications and educational programs that respond to specific state and local needs.

Further information about The Heartland Institute is available for free through the ***PolicyFax*** system; have a fax machine number ready, call 510/208-8000, and follow the voice prompts. Alternatively, call 708/202-3060 or write to The Heartland Institute, 800 East Northwest Highway, Suite 1080, Palatine, Illinois 60067.

The opinions expressed in this book are those of the authors alone. Nothing here should be construed as reflecting the views of The Heartland Institute or as an attempt to aid or hinder the passage of any legislation.